Words *about* Words *about* Words

Murray Krieger

Words *about* Words *about* Words: *Theory, Criticism, and the Literary Text*

The Johns Hopkins University Press
Baltimore / London

© 1988 The Johns Hopkins University Press
All rights reserved
Printed in the United States of America

The Johns Hopkins University Press
701 West 40th Street
Baltimore, Maryland 21211
The Johns Hopkins Press Ltd., London

The paper used in this publication meets the minimum
requirements of American National Standard for
Information Sciences—Permanence of Paper for Printed
Library Materials, ANSI Z39.48-1984. ∞

Library of Congress Cataloging-in-Publication Data

Krieger, Murray, 1923–
    Words *about* words *about* words.

    Includes index.
    1. Criticism.   2. Canon (Literature)   3. Progress in
literature.   I. Title.
PN85.K67   1988   801'.95   87-45482
ISBN 0-8018-3534-8 (alk. paper)

Once again for Joan
these words . . . and more than words

Contents

Preface

The earliest of the essays in this volume was published in 1981 and the latest only recently completed, so that the collection represents a compact period of barely half a dozen years. I mention this chronology because, in a career like mine, which has been marked by shifts in theoretical emphasis if not in theoretical allegiance, it seems useful to delineate the extended moment in which the ideas in these essays have their sway. Not only do these essays, with their several interests, reflect upon one another, but the three groups into which I have arbitrarily placed them overlap sufficiently for me to move some of them from one to the other with almost as much justification as I can provide for having arranged them as they are. I have reserved for the final group ("Reconsiderations of Special Texts for Special Reasons") essays whose arguments largely depend on my responses to individual literary works, even if in some cases those arguments might be appropriate to one of the other two groups of essays. That each of the works I have chosen is hardly a casual example but rather has been most pointedly selected for the argument I can get out of it I would not pretend to dispute. I have divided the remaining essays into two other groups: those that emphasize the implications for social or intellectual or academic institutions yielded by recent movements in criticism and theory and those that emphasize the nature of these movements themselves, or of individual critics, especially as these reflect upon my own theoretical development.

I am not being altogether accurate when I speak of this as a collection of previously written essays. In order to come closer to reflecting my current thinking and to help relate them to one another, I have added new essays and have revised almost all the others, some of them substantially. Indeed, faced with the opportunity of this publication, I rewrote and enlarged a number of them so that they have not before appeared in anything like the form they take here. But in these revisions, some of them extensive, I have tried not to alter either the position or the spirit I intended them to display in their original form, so that some potential collisions between the earlier and later essays have been permitted to stand.

I do not want here to summarize the arguments that follow by making an extended theoretical statement; I prefer to let the essays, with their different shadings, speak for themselves. But I would like briefly to justify my title as a serious one by saying a word on behalf of the prepositions, the *abouts*, that hold it together. Recent theory has made the status of the *about*-ness of discourse thoroughly problematic, and I find myself trying to rescue some sense of that *about*-ness without blinding myself (as some others have done) to all that my theorist colleagues have written to make us question our previous certainties. Yet, though I now add qualifications that reflect my epistemological skepticism, I still urge that the capacity of a discourse to stand in a secondary and descriptive relationship to another discourse—if not to the world—is one that no serious writer about writings can altogether give up for the chaos of words upon words, texts upon texts, that threatens if the *about* is withdrawn. It is out of this lingering stubbornness that I have italicized the *abouts* I use in my title.

In my continuing dialogue with poststructuralists, I must acknowledge—for all that I give way to in their arguments—that in the end I remain, with respect to literary studies, a *sauve qui peut* theorist, in retreat but still anxious to take with me what I can of the critical tradition, even while I join in undermining its grounds. For I agree with them that the traditional place of the poem as art object, in effect a spatial entity, requires ontological assumptions that have been undone by what we have learned about the nature of human experience as well as about the workings of language and of its texts. Yet I insist that the critical tradition held its long sway because it confirmed the ways in which our culture had apprehended and valued its literary works; and it collaborated in creating that culture's literary canon that in turn validated the literary criticism produced to sustain it. That canon and those works, however institutionally ordained, achieved and held their status under the aegis of a theory of the aesthetic, both as a mode of experiencing and as a kind of object, that licensed them. It has all been a circular procedure, but it has worked for us: it has had a salutary function in producing the richness and the depth of the vision our culture has handed to us, whatever else it has, unfortunately, given us with it that might make us suspect darker motives. It is this claim for an aesthetic domain, traced back to Kant at least—if not to Aristotle—that has been most under seige, most subject to suspicion, perhaps even totally obliterated, by recent theory in its more extreme versions. Such versions of late have come to include historical and social-political critics, against whom I also must defend a qualified version of this claim.

I continue to allow for some residue of the aesthetic dispensation, though only as circumscribed by an acceptance of how certain kinds of verbal sequences have functioned for us in our culture, at least until the explosions of postmodernism in the arts and in theory. So, in seeking to keep this cultural awareness with us, despite our underminings, I do hang back from reducing away the aesthetic: what I have given away in ontology I try to get back via anthropology. But of course what I then have is far different—and less—than what I used to have. Still, I remain convinced that our culture cannot, even now, do without a concept of the aesthetic, even in this hedged-in and reduced form, and for more than reasons of nostalgia—indeed, for reasons deeply rooted in our most civilized sensibilities that want to flourish still, even in the face of so shattering a challenge. But all this is for the pages that follow to establish.

Parts of this book have appeared earlier, mainly in other forms, in journals and in essay collections. I wish to thank the following editors of journals and publishers of books for granting permission to use these materials here: the editors of *Academe: Bulletin of the American Association of University Professors, Critical Inquiry, New Literary History, New Orleans Review,* and *Theatre Journal,* as well as the University of California Press, Columbia University Press, Harvard University Press, the University of Michigan, and the University Press of New England (Dartmouth College).

In the development of these essays I am grateful to greatly varied university audiences in the United States, in Germany, East and West, in Hungary, and in Asia—India, the Peoples Republic of China, and Hong Kong—who responded with sympathy and suggestions to many of these essays. Above all I am grateful to the responsiveness of my wife, Joan Krieger, who continually insisted on nothing less than clarity, no matter how strongly I complained, in my defense, about the unavoidable complexities of the theoretical problems I was addressing. To her persistence I owe considerable improvements throughout my manuscript, although I am, doubtless, still some way from satisfying her high standards.

I   *Theory and Institutions:*
   Critical Movements and
   Academic Structures

Words *about* Words *about* Words: Theory, Criticism, and the Literary Text

I thought it might be useful to survey some basic questions about literary theory, addressing problems the answers to which we may take for granted—though we may not actually have such answers—and looking at its recent history to discover where we have been and where we are going. This will mean going over some old ground, but I seek—from a bird's-eye view—to consider at one time a variety of concerns that usually cannot be addressed in the space of one essay. I hope to find some advantages in trying, for once, to see everything in a single survey. Perhaps such a procedure may clear the ground on which I have been building for some thirty years of books and essays. I find this procedure especially necessary at a moment when a chaos of conflicting movements is all we can see as the field—or rather the arena—of current theory, and as I work to find my own place within these newer confusions. So I seek here to pause and to look again, as if for the first time, in hopes that we all can return to more advanced questions in possession of some helpful, even if elementary, notions we have not seen assembled in this way before.

This is a revised version of the Distinguished Faculty Lecture delivered at the University of California, Irvine, on February 24, 1983. Copyright of the original version is held by the University of California Regents. A shortened adaptation of the lecture appeared in *Academe: Bulletin of the American Association of University Professors* 70 (March–April 1984): 17–24.

I recognize that special difficulties arise when scholars, each in a separate discipline, address a general literary audience. At one time, not long ago, only those in the sciences faced the problem of using technical language while seeking to reach those beyond their immediate field of study. Humanists, many of them perhaps as far removed from my subject as I am from the scientist's, have had the right to feel less alien and more assured, confident that any literary person on a literary subject should present less of challenge to the common understanding, should—that is—be more immediately accessible. It is true that we all read and talk about literature, so we may expect the literary scholar, for all the intensity of his study, to be only a little ahead of the rest of us and, however far ahead, at least to use language and methods familiar to all literate members of his audience. But I assure you that, however much this may once have been the case, my subject, in comparison with the scientist's, may these days be only a little less technical, and nearly as filled with its local jargon, so that you may begin to have a preliminary sense of the direction in which literary theory has been moving in recent years: namely, it has become more difficult. Without much effort, I could slip into the current habit of making a presumably simple literary subject almost impossible for the nonliterary person (and some literary ones) to understand. Consequently, the difference between a professional and a popular paper these days may be only slightly smaller in the field of literary theory than it is in the sciences. All of which is my way of warning that the difficulty of making oneself understood without oversimplifying complex matters is not substantially less troublesome for me today than it would be for scholars in more obviously rarefied fields.

It seems to me important for the theoretical humanist to justify to his community why he must these days claim the right, or indeed the need, to be as obscure as his scientific colleagues; why, that is, his subject has changed so profoundly during these last decades; what, indeed, that subject has become that makes it now so difficult for anyone who is not a professional in theory to follow the debates, or even to understand what is at stake in them. There used to be an unquestioned acceptance of our immediate aesthetic responses to what was called belles lettres—emotional and not intellectual responses, warmly delicate and of the heart rather than coldly rigorous and of the mind—so that we can understand the discomfort that has attended the recent introduction into criticism of the language and problems of philosophy as theory interjects itself into the supposedly sacred moment that unites a reader to his literary text. Consequently, in recent years we continually read, in the weekly book-review sections and elsewhere, impatient charges

Theory and Institutions

against academic critics because of the self-complicating jargon they employ nowadays in order—so the charges go—to obscure the age-old simplicities that should be used to describe our appreciation of literary works—still a worthy objective for the critic, but no longer the only one. So, despite such charges, I want to argue that criticism has done well to probe its own theoretical groundwork and that it can, in the end, provide a greater service to literature by doing so. I would further argue that, in growing theoretical, criticism, in its role as a discipline, has had to develop self-complications that encourage the more cryptic and even self-indulgent character it has recently taken on, although I grant that these difficult habits of expression may well annoy the common reader, and that in the hands of some critics it has been carried to self-defeating excess.

A generation ago, students engaged in literary study at the university level never heard of literary theory, indeed, were never exposed to the notion that theory was worth hearing about. Until recent decades, the study of literary history and biography, together with the amateur appreciation of "great works," was all there was. When a concern with theory began to enter a very few literature departments, it was treated as a dangerous infection and was carefully quarantined within those departments in which it had begun to appear and was systematically excluded, as long as that was possible, from the rest. If, as the old popular slander maintains, those who can't write become critics, what incapacity was to be attributed to the theorist? Theory was perceived as an overintellectual threat to the preservation of a delicate literary sensibility that was to be devoted to emotional response and hence was sublimely *un*cerebral. This warm, belletristic devotion considered all philosophical concerns as cold-bloodedly antagonistic and became increasingly defensive as it saw itself threatened with intellectual contamination by the new awareness that theory brought.

But the carriers of literary theory, perhaps encouraged by the increasing theoretical self-consciousness of the sciences and social sciences, rather saw themselves as a healthier infusion into the body of critical activity. They saw the advantages to the advancement of learning in their attempt to question what had not been questioned but should have been, and, consequently, in their attempt to bring into the domain of systematic investigation those confusing activities that—under the protection of the realm of emotion—had been too blithely exempted from the operations of reason. In other words, they saw that criticism, as a form of knowledge and not just a play-by-play description of our emotional encounter with literature, must turn theoretical. Under the rising influence of such scholars, the role of theory has deepened and spread—and, I like to think, more as an antidote than as the infection its enemies might have thought of it as being. I must acknowledge myself to be one of theory's more aggressive proponents, more, I hope, than a deadly carrier undermining the previous subjectivities of poetic experience, though I have spent a career encouraging a dissemination of theory that has helped alter the constitution of literary study in the United States and abroad.

Today it is not possible to escape from theory anywhere within the provinces of academic literary study. Its effect upon what we are now able to say about literature and our reception of it is far-reaching, and goes a long way toward clarifying (through whatever verbal mists) the nature of those complex activities that accompany the creation and the confrontation by a culture of its imaginative verbal expressions. So if these days literary scholars say things that seem abstruse, it is—we like to think—because what they say is more and more deeply penetrating, moving beyond immediate poetic responses and toward the philosophical questions they may pose for their culture and its products.

Words about words about words: theoretical statements about critical statements about the verbal sequences we call literary works, whether poems, plays, or prose fictions, long or short. This process, and its sequence of dependencies, has been assumed in the development of literary studies in the West for over two centuries. The temporal process occurs in the reverse order: It begins with the reader's experience of the literary work and his response to it; obviously these experiences will tend to be as varied as are the readers. The critic, as the more self-conscious and practiced reader, takes on the task of producing the rationalization of a single preferred reading—his own. And the literary theorist attempts to establish a system of principles that authorizes one consistent style of preferred readings (what we call critical interpretations) of a variety of texts—the wider the variety in these texts of languages, periods, and genres, the more ambitiously far-reaching the theory. In this framework in which he plays his role, the theorist uses his words to help us understand the methodological and philosophical implications of the critic's words, as the critic helps the reader respond to the poet's words, which are the original source of this succession that leads to words about words about words. The poet, luckily, should be affected by the words of neither theorist nor critic, for his work presumably originates the sequence rather than receives its products. But theorist, critic, and—I hope—reader are involved in these several levels of language which might produce a mutual enlightenment, thanks to the increasing awareness of theory.

Certainly, literary scholars have become more and more aware of their theoretical responsibility: they increasingly acknowledge the claim that every critic, however systematic or however casual in his procedures, has his commentary grounded in theoretical principles. So theory may be self-consciously explicit, or quite subliminal, or something between these, in the critic's work; but the assumptions are there for the critic of the critic (that is, the theorist) to find and set forth. Theory, then, as a systematic set of assumptions about the production and reception of literary works, is always there, whether or not the practicing critic recognizes it beneath his own writing as that which propels it. It has always been there, beckoning, although until recent years, when reading criticism, we preferred not to look for it, or to see it, out of what used to be our defensive posture on behalf of the intuitive, emotional, other-than-rational realm of belles lettres. Still conducting the old war between poets and philosophers begun by pre-Socratic Greeks, and conducting that war on the poet's side and against the philosopher, we wanted to keep the literary experience pure, to keep it free of any intellectual intrusion.

It has become clear, however, that the critic's choice is not whether he will have an underlying theory or not, but whether he (or we) will recognize and take account of the theory—or, in worse cases, the conflicting theories—which he inevitably has and, consciously or unconsciously, displays. The experienced reader of literature, as critic, comes to each next piece of literature armed with expectations and with unspoken operational definitions gleaned from his earlier literary experiences, and these expectations and definitions will shape what he sees and how he judges it. They serve, in effect, as his theoretical subtext. And a major task of theoretical scholarship has been to bring such submerged elements of control to the surface so that they can be examined and subjected to philosophical scrutiny. In the usual scholarly habit of overkill, of course, the study of theory now begins to proceed out of an infinitely regressive self-consciousness that may, alas, purge all spontaneity from literary response. But we must not leap ahead of our story.

In what follows I mean, first, to set forth the criteria for a literary theory—any literary theory—then, to examine the dominant theory of the past two hundred years as an example that satisfies these criteria, and finally, to put next to it the revolutionary thinking of recent years that would explode not just that dominant theory, but the very system of theorizing that permits it or its competitors to be thought.

What are the elements that constitute a theory of literature? (Or should I, following the lead of my regressive title, "Words *about* Words *about* Words," call it a theory of criticism, since it is the perceptions and judgments of literary works, rather than the literary works themselves, for which a theoretical basis is being sought? This is a question—whether it is a literary theory or a critical theory we are talking about—which I intend to confront directly before I close. But not yet.) So, back to my attempt to identify the constitutive elements of a theory. They are the answers, implicit or explicit, that form the set of assumptions behind any critical act. The questions they respond to are those that surround the aesthetic transaction in its several moments from the creation through the reception of the literary works.

I suggest four groups of questions. First, what is the nature of the author's creative act, its relation—whether mimetic or transformative—to his prior experience with his world, its relation to his verbal medium, its similarity to or difference from our other verbal acts of expression? The second: What is the nature of the reader's or audience's response to the created object? How special (i.e., specially aesthetic) is this response as compared to our experience of other verbal objects? And—perhaps most important—can we speak prescriptively about the response or must we speak only descriptively, categorizing all possible responses without privileging any of them as the proper response?

The third group of questions: Can we isolate a literary object between author and reader, independent of them both, or must we, more skeptically, reduce it to a mere projection of author or reader, so that our sense of it as a separate entity is seen as a mystification from which psychological considerations can free us? And what are the consequences of this answer upon the possibility of evaluating that object and seeking some consensus for that claim to value? We may ask this third group of questions another way: Does that object or does it not (or, ought it or ought it not) display features that distinguish it from other verbal constructs, features that control our experience of it and give that experience *its* appropriate character? And how do we define and recognize those features? Or, on the other—more skeptical—side, does the object blend into other verbal objects, so that only our self-deceived commitment to the aesthetic mysteries leads us to bestow special properties upon it?

Our fourth and final group of questions asks how we relate the elements of the aesthetic transaction to the surrounding cultural realities—social, moral, political, psychological, linguistic, or any others—realities that come before and after; it asks what we shall say of its extra-aesthetic function, that is, its function in the world beyond the aesthetic transaction. A theoretical perspective shows us how our answers to one of the groups of questions implies and is implied by our answers to the others. To the extent that we find a critic's assumptions ranging their answers to all these groups of questions within a set of model interrelationships, to that extent we can claim to find a systematic literary theory.

A major thrust of the traditional Western poetic, in the dominant form it has taken in the last couple of centuries, has been propelled by the notion that the aesthetic constitutes a separate realm, a central notion since the revolutionary work of Immanuel Kant in the late eighteenth century. As a result of our myopic commitment to modernity, we may neglect to remember that the notion of the aesthetic, as a separate mode of activity and as a separate kind of object which sponsors it—indeed the very word *aesthetic* itself as we know it—is an invention that goes back only to the mid-eighteenth century. With the word *aesthetic* came a newly defined discipline, and by the time Kant was through with it in his third Critique (*The Critique of Aesthetic Judgment*, to be sharply distinguished from the earlier two *Critiques, of Pure Reason* and *of Practical Reason*), this activity and the objects associated with it came to be seen as a special kind indeed. What was to be special about them was their freedom from the objectives imposed by the scientific pursuit of knowledge (governed by pure reason) or by the moral pursuit of the good (governed by practical reason). Both these latter two, the cognitive and the practical, served and were controlled by interests stemming from outside those activities and directing them, while the aesthetic—free from any outside interest or purpose—could be directed only by its own internally generated purposes that thus seem to trap and hold our *disinterested* contemplation. So an object is aesthetic only to the extent that it avoids leading us toward our worldly concerns and, instead, exploits its own system of internal relations.

Clearly, any object created under the aesthetic dispensation would find its definition as aesthetic guided by its capacity to elude what were conceived to be our "normal" worldly interests by creating its own self-sufficiency. This theory privileges the literary text over others, sets it up as an idol to be adored and endlessly interpreted, pursuing the interactions its language generates among its elements. The theory's emphasis on disinterestedness requires that we set the text apart from the world and from the rest of the world of language, just as we frame a painting to cut it off from the surrounding wall and then place it in the separate sanctity of the museum. In the case of a verbal artifact worthy of being called "aesthetic," it begins to define its system as its words deviate from the ways we commonly tend to use language. The domain of the aesthetic would require that the medium of normal communication be manipulated into functioning in ways consistent with disinterested contemplation—in ways that may well distort, subvert, or even violate its usual procedures as they occur outside the aesthetic.

If I may put the matter more specifically as regards poems, the forms of language as we employ them every day—what the poet Stéphane Mallarmé contemptuously referred to as newspaper language—must be worked with and worked against, and in such a way that in each poem we are forced to contemplate this aesthetically remade language as a complexly woven web of interrelationships functioning in a manner that seems self-justifying. We are to look at words and verbal sequences so as to permit them to disrupt our normal reading habits and to force us to play with them as they appear to play with us. In many cases (most notably in metered and rhymed poems), the phonetic character of words is also exploited to help force us to disrupt the automatic attachment of a word's sound to its meaning. A word's meaning usually runs us through the transparent word as if it weren't there, but the poem disrupts that passage in order to fix us momentarily on the verbal surfaces so that we can apprehend words as entities themselves instead of mere pointers to a world elsewhere. The pun that holds opposed meanings within a coincidental phonetic identity is perhaps the most obvious—though hardly the only—example of ways in which this effect can be produced. Such poetic devices of reader entrapment are ever being invented by poets who want their work read as other than newspapers.

It is for this reason that the teacher of literature has the harder task (harder than that of the teacher of the other arts) because his elementary students come to him assuming they already know how to read, and they *can* read—at least the morning newspaper. But they do not comprehend their need to *un*learn their usual reading habits if they are to read works as poetic entities in accordance with the Kantian habit of our aesthetic tradition, which I am assuming for now is the proper habit. I say that the teacher of literature has the harder task because in the other arts—the plastic arts, for example—there is little else we can do with the object except contemplate it. (Even in the trompe l'oeil painting—which seems to want to trick the eye into believing it is a part of the real world and not just a representation of it—we aren't really supposed to walk through that shrewdly pictured door, nor in the still life are we to eat the fruit off the canvas.) But all we have to do is to watch young students—or sometimes, not so young students, or faculty, too, for that matter—read a poem as if it *were* a newspaper to see how many other things, usually dreadful ones, we can do to the words of a poem—just words after all—besides reading them as a poem.

This, then, is the dual character of words in poems: they are like all our words in all our discourse and yet we must be attentive to a power they generate among each other which seems to make them responsible to the form they create together. Since they function both as intelligible, transparent carriers of meaning, like other words, and, simultaneously, as dense, sensible entities on their own, they demonstrate the special nature of poetry's verbal medium in a conception of poetry that finds it different from other modes of discourse: its verbal manipulations force upon it and upon us deviations from the way words are normally supposed to behave. What seems wayward and subversive in this language-play simply (or not so simply) reinforces the poem's claim to be performing successfully something quite different from the normal discourse that its devices would otherwise seem to be obstructing.

Now, all this is a good deal to require of literary language, this uncommon function of the common currency of words. T. S. Eliot, one of our poets who in his work most fully realizes what this tradition promises, calls for just such a dual function within poetic language, "that perpetual slight alteration of language, words perpetually juxtaposed in new and sudden combinations." And in his *Four Quartets* Eliot sets his poetic seal upon these juxtapositions and combinations:

Words move, music moves
Only in time; but that which is only living
Can only die. Words, after speech, reach
Into the silence. Only by the form, the pattern
Can words or music reach
The stillness, as a Chinese jar still
Moves perpetually in its stillness.

Here, in the still-moving stillness, is just the operation of pun that I commented upon earlier. What it captures and holds at one instance for us is the tempo of normal living and speaking and dying joined by its opposite, the freezing of that tempo into a poetic form, the poem, that in its fixity never stops moving, is *still moving*.

To turn such verbal manipulation into the aesthetic medium is especially characteristic of lyric poetry. But of course there are forms of literature other than poems which satisfy those who read in accordance with the demands of this aesthetic tradition, and—consequently—there are other literary media besides words which the author may exploit. Anything may serve the author as a medium so long as he can force a similar duality into it, thus leading it to serve an other-than-normal form of discourse.

Take the stage itself in the drama. On the one hand, the action that occurs on stage and the characters who walk and talk on it remind us enough of real-life experience for us to respond appropriately to what is going on; but, on the other hand, that stage keeps those characters (or rather those actors who we know are only impersonating the characters) from being real people, keeps their actions from being real actions. We accept their fictional, make-believe status and do not leap onstage to interfere with what is about to happen. For part of us knows it *has* to happen—and just that way—and with consequences that we believe in and yet do not quite believe really: though these happenings deeply affect our response, in another sense they don't actually affect us, nor can anything we do affect them. They do not literally share our reality, however much they in some sense represent reality. There is good reason, then, for theaters to have introduced the proscenium arch as a frame to cut off those players—and the moving pictures they create within that frame—from the surrounding reality we all inhabit. And it is the stage which creates that strange middle and double realm in which the playwright can intermingle reflections of our world with that world onstage: the two worlds relate to one another ambiguously in that the two are at once mutually dependent and mutually exclusive.

The same double effect that we have noted in the language of poems and in the stage-space of plays can in prose fiction be attributed to yet other manipulations, this time of narrative elements. The novel, as a mock history or mock biography (or, in the case of first-person fiction, a mock autobiography or mock journal or mock confession), is again a self-consciously deceptive (and so not actually deceptive) "imitation" of nonfictional discourses—what we may think of as shadow genres—that are presumably devoted to "real" persons and experiences. It is an imitation of these and yet also a parody of them for the special purposes of the fiction. The author, as fiction-maker, can make our sense of historical-biographical time into his medium to be played with, or he can make into his medium our expectations about a narrator's (storyteller's) relation to the "facts" of the story he is telling. These, and others, are elements the author can manipulate as he forces upon us the dual realities and the ambiguous awareness of his independent, self-sufficient fictional world as well as that world's relations—at once representational and illusory—to what we think of as our own world. Again, as in the other literary genres I have discussed, aesthetically directed discourse sets itself apart from the more usual, less-self-enclosed kind of discourse we normally direct to other purposes.

These, then, are the expectations with which criticism, under the aegis of such a theory as the one I have been assuming, would arm itself as it came to confront a work that pretended to be literary. Given sufficient time, we could now return to measure this dominant aesthetic of the past two hundred years against those four groups of questions I proposed earlier as ways to discover the several cooperating elements that constitute a model theory. Its answers suggest the consistent pattern that a theory would require. Let me here only briefly outline what they would be like and how they would be theoretically intertwined. First, in his act of creation, the author is seen as distorting— "defamiliarizing," as the Russian Formalist would put it—the elements of his medium so that they swerve aside from the paths they normally pursue in everyday discourse toward a system of internal relations whose parts would be sustained by mutual justification instead of by reference to outside realities. Second, for us as readers to respond appropriately to such an object, we would try to suspend our normal habits of dealing with language in order to pursue the swervings and allow the disinterested response to a closed system which the work, licensed by our aesthetic habit of response, would seem to call for. Third, we then could talk about the object as displaying features that solicit such a response and, to the extent that we find that it does, we would see it as quite unique, utterly marked off from all other texts, and consequently, would claim a high degree of aesthetic value for it. Finally, the work would be seen as a special way of ordering the confusing materials of ordinary experience into a satisfyingly complete system of vision that should illuminate what otherwise remains inchoate in its culture at a given moment in its development.

This has been an exemplary excursion through a single dominant pattern of criticism and theory. It has also shown a consistency with my theme, words about words about words: one text (theoretical) devoted to a prior text (critical) which had earlier come into being in answer to a yet prior—and presumably original—literary text, the first of the series of successively dependent texts. For my discussion has assumed without question our capacity to formulate a theory which sought to account for a style of criticism which in turn was to account for the specially literary character of literary words. This is to testify to the successive dependence of one level of discourse on the one preceding, with a faith that one can account for the other and that a first, in its self-sufficiency, can be the source of this succession of accountings. The critical text wants to mediate between its theoretical obligations on the one side and the almost unapproachable language of the literary text on the other; in its turn the theoretical text wants to mediate between the rigors of philosophical discourse on the one side and the practical work of the critical text on the other.

These attempts at mediation reveal the struggle in critical and theoretical discourse between the drive toward coherence (the consistency of relations among the propositions in the discourse) and the desire for correspondence (the adequacy of reference between the statements in a text and their would-be objects outside language). Each of these objectives seems to counteract the other, so that the stronger our inevitable drive toward consistency in our discourse, toward theoretical system, the more likely it is that our theoretical assumptions intrude themselves upon the critical act and obstruct, if they do not altogether obliterate, our hopes to speak with adequacy about the literary text for whose sake we are presumably undertaking the critical text. As a teacher of mine used to remind me, the critic can always manage to find what he is looking for. Yet it is the literary text that the critical text is presumably *about*, and it apparently seeks to speak truly about it. This problem must lead us to question the relation between one discourse as a secondary discourse to the primary discourse that it seeks to serve. It is just this *about*-ness and this relation which have been *un*questioned in my earlier discussion and in the theory that was its subject. But what can we say with confidence concerning the power of the critic's language to refer to the poem if each text is trimmed in advance to what its own nature as a text permits it to claim to see?

I presented earlier but one among many possible theories, one that, like its fellow competing theories, is based not on universal truths but on its own series of assumptions. It is the job of the scholar of theory to search out such assumptions beneath a critical text, despite the apparent intention of that text to be devoted to a literary text. We must be concerned about the source of these assumptions and about the extent to which they circumscribe and even predict the would-be truths that the critical text claims to "find," so that those truths shrink into being no more than self-reinforcing claims responsible to those original assumptions rather than to the outside realities (i.e., the literary text) they supposedly are *about*. The language of an argument thus seems circularly to confirm only itself. Can it ever be about something other than what already has been preinscribed within its own terms?

In these questionings I am anticipating the questions asked by revolutionary theories being developed in recent years (and I am speaking here of general movements rather than of theorists in order to avoid my being diverted to detailed discussion of individual positions). These theories have taken upon themselves the role of questioning the capacity of words, as they operate in what we used to think of as ordinary discourse, to reach outside themselves to refer to the world when that world has already been prearranged by them. This radical skepticism

Theory and Institutions

threatens to have profoundly unsettling consequences for the development of theory—and for the development of the humanities themselves as a collection of various kinds of texts—presumably both primary and secondary texts—from the several disciplines.

Like these theorists I have been raising the *about*-ness of words to a fourth level (words about words-about-words-about-words) by putting into question the set of assumptions, previously unquestioned, which permitted the Western tradition confidently to put forth its several literary theories. As I have put it forward, the upward dependence of reading upon criticism, and criticism in turn upon theory, out of which criticism in the West has developed since at least the late eighteenth century, rests upon an internally directed set of separatist notions, with literary theory (or aesthetics of literature) in control. But, from outside, several and various claims of external pressures can be urged that have loaded and predirected the entire structure of argument, reducing apparent logic to rhetorical manipulation. Consequently, the theorizing about criticism about literature, like the criticism itself, begins to be delegitimated. Through the undercutting of claims by means of Nietzschean or Marxian or Freudian subversions, *literary* theory is made to give way to what the Frankfurt School termed *critical* theory. This is theory that is critical of theory and that, in many of its forms, seeks to do away with literary theory—and the literary itself—altogether. Instead of pursuing what a text appears to be claiming about a prior text, we are to explore the hidden *sub*text that reveals the pressures—institutional, ideological, or personal—that undermine the integrity of the text and point us elsewhere, toward its unseen motives as well as toward other texts: traditional hermeneutics, permitting the interpretation of what a text appears to be saying, is to be replaced by a hermeneutics of suspicion.

If the about-ness of a critical or a theoretical text—its very capacity to refer to another text—comes to be seen as a self-deceiving myth, as it is by recent critical theorists, then all texts must consist of self-authorizing fictions and should be treated as such, even though some may be more self-deceived about their intention and others—those we used to call literary—may be more self-conscious about theirs. But this notion would deprive the literary text of its primacy: it is no longer privileged in its freedom from reference, a freedom that we saw permits it to develop its fiction. For if all texts consist of self-authorizing fictions, then we no longer have a receding sequence of successively dependent texts, each responsible to the preceding and all descending from the one kind of text—the uniquely literary fiction—that is the presumed origin of commentary, though it is not, of course, itself a commentary. Instead, we now are to treat all texts as equally primary and susceptible to the kind of treatment formerly reserved for "literary" ones. And that treatment itself becomes yet another equal text, its claim to commentary but another fiction. For there no longer is any merely "normal" discourse any more than there is a special literary discourse for the normal to bow down before and seek to comment upon. There are no longer first texts in the endless series of texts that comprise a culture, no longer any elite texts from which commentary, first critical and then theoretical, could ensue. Once *about*-ness is denied, words *about* words *about* words are reduced to Hamlet's nihilistic reply to Polonius when asked what he was reading: only "Words, words, words." It is a mere torrent of words, a jumbled confusion with no priority, no reference, no meaning. As if to emphasize the other side, this present text of mine, yet another level of commentary, would—as I have said—raise the *about*-ness of words to the fourth power, by turning on the other three. Yet, once the search for *about*-ness is viewed skeptically, this—even more than the others—becomes a self-deceiving exercise in futility.

Thus, to say that all texts are equally primary is really to say that none of them are. But neither can they be considered secondary since there is no longer a primary text for them to serve. This new equivalence among texts makes the terminology of "primary" and "secondary," or "privileged" and "dependent" texts—like the notion of commentary itself—obsolete. All texts, trapped within the verbal systems created out of their own assumptions, are really about themselves, despite their self-deceived claims to refer, to tell the truth *about* another text. Threatened also with obsolescence are privileged categories like "aesthetic" and "literary," now consigned to history's dustheap of nostalgic mystifications. And the previously thriving discipline of literary theory, which occupied our attention earlier in this essay (as has occupied my attention throughout my career), is to be expanded into the broader interdisciplinary studies now called *critical theory* and intended to encompass the many varieties of theoretical texts in what we used to think of as the humanities and some of the social sciences, what—after the French—we now call the "human sciences." It is the equalizing power of recent language theory—beginning with the revolution associated with the names "structuralism" and "semiotics"—that, having leveled literature into the general domain of all writing, raises the individual texts in that domain until they all are similar candidates for commentary, except that we no longer have a language empowered to comment. Such a leveling, were we to take it literally, would radically alter our academic organizations and our

Theory and Institutions

course syllabi, all of which have long rested on disciplinary distinctions and privileges—on the myth of *about*-ness—that recent theory refuses to sustain.

There is yet another, at least as revolutionary, variety of recent theory which would also reduce the aesthetic to a self-deceptive mystification, except that here the aesthetic delusion is seen as serving a surreptitious purpose, whether psychological or political. The aesthetic is seen as a conspiratorial disguise for the author's rhetorical quest for control. Accordingly, it is claimed that what lies under the text (the literary or any other text) is the pursuit of power—ego-driven and private or politically driven and social—which the false, deceiving objective of the aesthetic is forced to serve. Thus the very basis of Kantian theory—the hope for a *dis*interested contemplation of an object made to be viewed that way—is undercut. Once we substitute Nietzsche—or, for that matter, Marx or Freud—for Kant, all textuality is seen as most forcefully *interested*, ruthlessly so. And nothing serves the repressions produced by power more ruthlessly, if subtly, than the distractions of the aesthetic myth; or so we are asked to conclude.

In spite of the recent strength and spread of such theories in their revolutionary daring, I am moved to resist the attack brought by them upon the theoretical tradition that has created the most successful procedures by which criticism has accounted for our highly valued literary works. I still am excited by the prospect of more words *about* words *about* words, and still believe they can be instructive words, despite what these words of mine about them in these last paragraphs have begun to indicate. For me, the manipulations worked upon ordinary language to make it function as extraordinarily as it does in our best literature must continue to defy these attempts to deny the differentness of literature in contrast to the rest of discourse. So I find literature's privilege to be secure, thanks to powers that criticism previously was licensed to demonstrate. And I remain content with the modesty of that function for criticism, without arrogating to it the claim of being equal to and in competition with works to whose privilege I am still ready to testify. Neither theory—nor even criticism—should seek to replace the experience of the literary work with itself, of course. Luckily, as the succession of ultimately unsuccessful theories through history should assure us, there is no danger of theory or criticism explaining away literature or eliminating our need to experience it. The critic should accept his humility as being only too well deserved. All that we saw earlier about the unlooked-for deviations in the manipulations of the literary medium should remind us now that there are surprising turns in every new work the critic confronts that may well baffle the theory on which he is operating. He should feel like the forthright but simple and unimaginative Horatio when he is advised—in well-known words—by the brooding Hamlet, so sensitive to the perplexities of life and death and pondering the appearance of his father's ghost, which disrupts all surface realities: "There are more things in heaven and earth, Horatio, / Than are dreamt of in your philosophy." Thus the potential inadequacy of theory and its logic before the manifold complexity of the individual work, which is full of more things than the critic's philosophy can dream of—especially since, like Horatio, theory lacks the dreaming power. Thus also my commitment to preserve literary experience, for all its dreaminess, and to value that theory which would not exclude it and would, instead, authorize a criticism that enhanced it.

Nevertheless, my resistance to our most recent theories may well seem to some to be only a retreat before strenuous arguments that threaten to carry the day—a retreat justified only by my defensive desire to turn aside from the more extreme and destructive consequences to literary institutions that those theories would entail. I prefer to think that is not the case, though I confess my pragmatic interest in allowing literary criticism to proceed with its exhilarating probings of the special texts that are its objects. And I look forward to the debates that will continue, and look forward to my continued participating in them.

These, then, are the lively quarrels pursued these days among literary people and humanists at large in the academy in the face of profoundly revolutionary possibilities that would question the previously unquestionable. And these quarrels are severely consequential: they affect what we read and how we read, and—from the standpoint of the university—what we call our departments in the humanities and what we think we ought to be teaching in each of them, if they continue to be distinguished from one another as they presently are. Indeed, the quarrels affect our decision about whether there *is* literature, and under what conditions we may call it by that honorific name. As for the combatants, it is their recently attained sophistication and self-consciousness in matters theoretical that enable our most aware younger scholars to make these quarrels so risky. (And we must acknowledge the extent to which the humanities *are* today at risk—a state that is probably good for them.) The conclusions of these younger scholars may not always please us, and surely their obsession with theory may not always lead to greater literary appreciation; but we are free to carry the argument back to them, though only if we, too, are prepared to question all our assumptions and if our own theoretical armor is carefully fashioned and up-to-date. The future of the humanities, as well as of the study of our literary heritage, may be at stake. Yet wherever theory goes—both critical theory at large and, more narrowly, literary theory—it appears fated to move with a self-questioning modesty that will allow it to serve that future faithfully, even if its fidelity requires that service to be unheroic.

The Arts and the Idea of Progress

In my undertaking here I feel something of a lonely outsider to these proceedings, or at least I feel that way on behalf of my subject. As we treat the various humanistic, scientific, or near-scientific disciplines in order to explore the idea of progress reflected in them, it is clear that the arts must be singled out from the rest as an exceptional case, indeed must be singled out for exemption. Historians and theorists have customarily treated the arts, in their relation to progress, as radically different from the other disciplines. So much is this the case that, in response to the question, "Can we apply the idea of progress to the arts?" most of our colleagues, thinking the question naïve, would at once reply in the negative. And, given their grounds for this answer, it is difficult to disagree. So long as by "the arts" one means only the individually created artifacts, and so long as by the history of the arts one means only the sequence throughout history in which such artifacts have been produced, critics and historians have properly resisted applying the idea of progress to them.

Art, at least in the Western tradition, is a special subject for us

This essay is an extended version of remarks delivered at the Western Center of the American Academy of Arts and Sciences in Palo Alto at a conference devoted to the "Transformation of the Idea of Progress." The Academy published the essays in a volume intended to coincide with the bicentennial of the founding of the Academy by John Adams: *Progress and Its Discontents,* ed. G. A. Almond, M. Chodorow, and R. H. Pearce (Berkeley and Los Angeles: University of California Press, 1982).

because, as a collection of artifacts ordered chronologically but held as a single group in our minds, it constitutes a canon of fixed works (however shifting its members and whatever the disagreements among us about them in individual cases) that are, in a simple sense, always and identically present for us. These works, individually valued and judged as we seek to make an elite selection among them, are taken by us to be fictions, illusionary "realities" that themselves do not change, though our perceptions of them surely do as we move through time with them as our companions. But, in this limited conception of the arts with which I have begun, my concern is with progress in *them*, as individually ordered works of art viewed as a historical collective, and not with progress in our commentary or conception of them. The latter may well have to be taken up later in these remarks since, before I finish, I want to suggest all the problems attendant upon putting the two terms—progress and the arts—together, and even to suggest how the idea of progress might be transformed so that it and the arts might coexist, indeed how their special place in relation to progress might make them uniquely helpful to our considerations of progress in other areas.

The Neoclassical Problem: The Ancients versus the Moderns

But in this first, commonsense notion of the arts as a collection of completed, illusionary works in a variety of media, we can understand why the consideration of progress in the arts has always stood apart from our considerations of progress in other fields of human endeavor. I am accepting a nonproblematic definition of progress—any of those with which Nannerl Keohane began, all of them characterized by Charles Van Doren's notion of "irreversible meliorative change."[1] The question, then, presents itself quite simply: can it be maintained that later works are (in some as yet unspecified sense) better than earlier ones, and that—therefore—works being produced today are the best of all? To argue for progress from this perspective, we must argue that works of more recent periods represent an improvement over those of earlier periods, since obviously the individual work does not itself improve: the text of *King Lear* does not get better, or alter at all, with the years, however we may improve our capacity to appreciate it.

Even in the early and least self-critical enunciations of the idea of progress during the eighteenth century, there was usually some reluctance, in the field of the arts, to deflate the ancients in order to inflate the

---

1. In another essay in *Progress and Its Discontents*: Nannerl O. Keohane, "The Enlightenment Idea of Progress Revisited," p. 22. She is referring to Charles van Doren, *The Idea of Progress* (New York: Praeger, 1967), p. 3.

moderns. The authority of the classics was too central to the self-definition of neoclassicism to suggest so one-sided a victory in the competition moderns may have felt with them. For the competition was held on the ancients' ground, with the modern gesture of imitation sufficient to guarantee the authority of the original, however improved in refinements the current version may have appeared. Even those on the progressive side in the battle between ancients and moderns rarely hid altogether their sometimes grudging acknowledgment of the excellence and priority of original authority in the arts.

Thus we have the propagation of two myths, the myth of origins, which leads to the idolatry of the ancients by attributing "original genius" uniquely to them, as if they were the absolute beginning, and the myth of the "advancement of learning," which was to account for the superiority of the moderns in those areas in which—since they came along too late in history to be "original"—learning would have to be enough. In the arts the division of labor sponsored by the two myths allowed the moderns to excel in technical refinements ever more impressive without threatening the profundity of the genius that was there, however primitively, at the start. So it was the lasting power of the extant art object of the distant past thrusting itself, always anew, upon the present which set the arts apart from those disciplines of science and philosophic thought which could more single-mindedly turn against the past since these latter were, without qualification, to be responsive to the advancement of learning. The work of art was thus divided in two: the greatness of vision which was there in the earliest works and is always with us in them, beyond competition, and the elegance of refinement which is increasingly ours since, thanks to the advancement of learning, we know so much more than our unhappily ignorant precursors.

In pointing to this distinction between progress in science and progress in art, I cannot do better than quote from David Hume, clearly a liberal who sides with the moderns in their battle with the ancients because he is committed to the belief in intellectual progress. In "Of the Standard of Taste" (1757), he rescues art unambiguously from the framework imposed by the idea of progress, even though he grants that "modern authors" have "an advantage" over the ancients because of "the want of humanity and of decency" in the "rough heroes" of the ancients, which the moderns, no longer barbarous, have in their civilized manner refined.

Theories of abstract philosophy, systems of profound theology, have prevailed during one age: in a successive period, these have been universally exploded: their absurdity has been detected: other theories and systems have supplied their place, which again gave place to their successors: and nothing has been experienced more liable to the revolutions of chance and fashion than these pretended decisions of science. The case is not the same with beauties of eloquence and poetry. Just expressions of passion and nature are sure, after a little time, to gain public applause, which they maintain forever. Aristotle, and Plato, and Epicurus, and Descartes, may successively yield to each other: but Terence and Virgil maintain a universal, undisputed empire over the minds of men. The abstract philosophy of Cicero has lost its credit: the vehemence of his oratory is still the object of our admiration.[2]

In Hume we see the advantage to fiction in its evasion of any criterion of falsifiability. There is no empirical truth or falsity in art, and hence no obsolescence: we need not pull down Virgil to set up Shakespeare. A great work remains always present, commandingly there, undiminished, however much we may learn or read. Unlike the history of other disciplines, the history of an art throws up a series of discrete, value-laden objects as its "facts," and, as repositories of value responsible finally to themselves, they do not lend themselves to being treated in comparison to other similar, though utterly different, entities that constitute the historical sequence of which they may be seen to be a part.

Recent semiology has alerted us anew to the "intertextual" character of literary works and their meanings, so that what may seem to be a discrete work, with its own closure, actually has all sorts of prior works flowing into it as it in turn flows into others. Thus all are to be seen as elements in a single historically developing semiotic code, all of whose members are mutually cooperative—and hence comparable. Nevertheless, I would claim, in the aesthetic experience bounded by one work, what we are caught by is the development of a system of internal manipulations which argues for a momentary integrity that transcends history and disdains comparison, shunning any terms more general than itself. And even if, in spite of such experiences, we should try to treat our masterworks comparatively, the history of their succession hardly suggests a consistently upward movement among them as we move forward through time.

Now, it is certainly true that Hume has left room for the refinements of more civilized modern authors, and, as I have suggested, it has become commonplace to provide for progress in all those aspects of the

---

2. "Of the Standard of Taste," in *The Philosophy of David Hume*, ed. V. C. Chappell (New York: Random House, 1963), p. 495.

arts in which learning and sophistication can pave the way for advancement—for example, in styles and techniques. Here we can find problems to be solved and the elements of a given medium, within an accepted genre, to be manipulated more and more successfully. The solutions and manipulations can be compared and placed within a progressive pattern. But, as Hume suggests, these descriptive judgments, as they relate to sensible and teachable matters, probably do not determine our ultimate aesthetic judgments of candidates for the canon.[3]

Indeed, on this question Hume sounds all too much like his conservative antagonist, Dr. Johnson, who also wanted to free his contemporaries to go beyond their classical forebears where they could, although they still would not match that originality of perception which is the special attribute of antique crudeness. In his dissertation upon poetry in *Rasselas* (1759), Imlac sets forth this limited doctrine of progress, which allows the moderns to be superior in everything that is of secondary importance in aesthetic creativity:

> And yet it fills me with wonder, that, in almost all countries, the most ancient poets are considered as the best; whether it be that every other kind of knowledge is an acquisition gradually attained, and poetry is a gift conferred at once; or that the first poetry of every nation surprised them as a novelty, and retained the credit by consent which it received by accident at first: or whether, as the province of poetry is to describe nature and passion, which are always the same, the first writers took possession of the most striking objects for description, and the most probable occurrences for fiction, and left nothing to those that followed them, but transcription of the same events, and new combinations of the same images. Whatever be the reason, it is commonly observed that the early writers are in possession of nature, and their followers of art: that the first excel in strength and invention, and the latter in elegance and refinement.[3]

When Johnson comments on Pope's translation of the *Iliad* of Homer in his "Life of Pope" (1779–81), he seems, like a proper neoclassicist, to be leaning more heavily toward the advantages of the progress which has led to the civilized moderns:

> There is a time when nations emerging from barbarity, and falling into regular subordination, gain leisure to grow wise, and feel the shame of ignorance and the craving pain of unsatisfied curiosity. To this hunger of the mind plain sense is grateful; that which fills the void removes uneasiness, and to be free from pain for a while is pleasure; but repletion generates fastidiousness, a saturated intellect

---

3. Samuel Johnson, *The History of Rasselas, Prince of Abyssinia*, in *Rasselas, Poems, and Selected Prose*, ed. Bertrand H. Bronson (New York: Holt, Rinehart & Winston, 1958), p. 627.

soon becomes luxurious, and knowledge finds no willing reception till it is recommended by artificial diction. Thus it will be found in the progress of learning that in all nations the first writers are simple, and that every age improves in elegance. One refinement always makes way for another, and what was expedient to Virgil was necessary to Pope.[4]

From Homer to Virgil to Pope. Johnson is apologizing for the loss of Homeric qualities by praising those which Pope has substituted from his later vantage point. In what may seem to be an enormous concession to the progressive advantages enjoyed by Pope, Johnson has subtly displayed his remarkable balance in judgment. Terms like *elegance* and *refinement* carry their negative underside along with the praise they intend. And however splendid Pope's accomplishment, however unequaled anywhere before (as Johnson announces), its greatness is tied to the fact that it is an imitative achievement, an achievement in translation, the carrying over into these times and this language of the original vision of another.

In Johnson's distinction between original, barbaric ancients and imitative, elegant moderns, as in Hume's distinction between the history of the arts and the history of thought, we can find the implicit opposition between the intuitive and the rational, the instinctual and the learned. From the earliest days of aesthetics in the West, theorists had distinguished between the endowments of nature and the enhancements of art. Always it was the first that was the source of genius and absolute artistic vision, beyond all rules and instruction, and it was the second which—though only a subsidiary advantage to be pursued in conjunction with the first—frequently had to be substituted by derivative poets in derivative periods for what history or the genes had denied them. And, in a Hume or in a Johnson, it was only the second sort which was susceptible to rules and hence could be taught and learned; the first remained, in its untouchable mystery, a *je ne sais quoi*. Hence progress could be predicated only in the limited area of the arts (style, devices, general questions of craft) to which reason and learning had access. Progress was denied to the artist's original genius which was built into his nature. Paradoxically, then, the original creative center of art was proclaimed to be *nature*, whereas what was termed the *art* in art was really the science of art. It was only this technical element in the arts, only this scientific element, which turned natural art into artifice with its refinements; it was only this element which, like all science, could be

4. Samuel Johnson, "Pope," in *Lives of the English Poets* (London: Oxford University Press, 1952), 2:320.

seen as subject to the law of progress—whereas the essence of art, and its greatness, its very nature, presumably escaped this as it escaped all laws.

We can now review the standard arguments that we have seen urging the nonprogressive character of the arts. First, there is the most obvious argument: "there were giants in those days," and, by contrast, almost exclusively pygmies in our own time. This is an appeal to the greater number of masterpieces in all the arts of older periods. It is a claim that is widely unchallenged. If it is a just claim, these masterpieces would seem to represent prima facie empirical evidence against progress in the arts. The second argument rests on the opposition between instinct or intuition on one side and reason on the other; and, since art is seen as the product of the first and science as the product of the second, it leads to the claim that art is independent of rational knowledge and its advancement. As another way of putting the first argument, it asks, in effect, how it is that we can be so much more knowledgeable than, say, Homer, and yet cannot boast of nearly so great a poet. The conclusion must be that knowledge is not sufficient to the achievement of greatness in art. A corollary would be that craft or technique—know-how that is of course subject to knowledge—is not the same as art and can progress without art itself progressing: "*poeta nascitur*," and no amount of technical education can produce him. A third argument also follows: the great artwork never becomes obsolete, as scientific formulas can. The artwork cannot be falsified since our appreciation of it should not be dependent on our agreement with the set of beliefs on which it rests. Therefore the work is not exposed to the aging process, which wears out all doctrines, and it cannot be superseded by its successors.

Based on these arguments, the exemption of the arts from the idea of progress was common among progressives and conservatives alike in those early ideological debates about progress in the eighteenth century. The progress in refinement in the arts, then, would seem to come only at the cost of original genius, to which it moves in an inverse relation. From this perspective, the arts—insofar as they are characterized by the masterworks of genius—achieved their highest moment at the beginning. And, ever since, despite the compensatory progress in elegance, they have been in an apparent decline that can produce only the refinements of imitation. This "primitivistic" notion (to borrow a term used by Roy Harvey Pearce to characterize this line of thought)[5]

---

5. Pearce adapts the notion of the "primitivistic" to his own purposes in an unpublished essay, "Poetry and Progress," which he wrote for the meeting of the American Academy of Arts and Sciences devoted to "The Transformation of the Idea of Progress."

Theory and Institutions

conceives of an artless art which had its fullest realization in an antique moment before developments in learning and in scientific and material progress led it on its downward path. (How strange it is that such primitivistic idolatry should accompany the celebration of refinement which constituted the neoclassical aesthetic, a guide for artists to do the best with what history left to them—namely, an imitative task.)

Here indeed is what I earlier referred to as the myth of origins, a narrative structure plotted on the analogy to the Fall of man. Artistic genius is born in innocence and, as a simple tragic hero, falls victim to rational progress and sophistication in other realms. The "noble savage" of late-eighteenth-century thought is created for us by the retrogressive myth of origins and then is destroyed as that myth is forced to coexist with, and give way before, the progressive myth of the advancement of learning. As in the original myth of the Fall, it is reason—together with reason's knowledge—that is the enemy to genial instinct and brings it down. Whatever takes the place of genius is a talent of another sort, one more akin to the scientist's and more at home in the scientist's world of progress.

So to the progressive's belief that "later is better" was opposed the equally reductive belief that, so far as art was concerned, "later is worse" (though with compensations that neoclassical artifice could provide). Except for matters of technique, the doctrine of decline often replaced the doctrine of progress in discussions of artistic genius. Obviously, later critics had less unbalanced or unqualified views: they would no longer be simply content with an upward or downward movement. Instead, some might argue that the individual great work was somehow outside the historical continuum, an unpredictable sport that occurs when it will, early or late. Or some might argue for an historical relativism which saw only a sequence of sealed historical periods, answerable only to themselves, so that they cannot be compared with one another. Consequently, one cannot judge across periods to establish a general movement upward or downward. In both these variations of the arguments about progress in the arts, however, the case against applying a progressive model to the arts is consistently supported.

There have of course been exceptions, especially among poets interested in keeping up their own hopes for a greatness to surpass that of the past. For example, to return to the late-eighteenth and early-

---

A summary of this essay appears in the *Bulletin of the American Academy of Arts and Sciences* 31 (October 1977): 26–27.

nineteenth centuries, we observe, in early preromantic or romantic writers like Schiller or Wordsworth, a desperate attempt to find progress after all in the substitution of the new "sentimental" poet (Schiller's term for the modern poet of a dissociated culture) for the old "naïve" poet (Schiller's term for the original, unselfconscious, instinctual poet). Of course, Schiller finds a high place for the contemporary poet in the name of his contemporary, Goethe, as Wordsworth does on behalf of himself and his fellows. These poets, fighting what Walter Jackson Bate has called "the burden of the past,"[6] would reinvent the hope of progress for the sake of their own role in creating out of themselves a new poetry that could more than compensate for what had been lost, converting poetry's Fall into a fortunate one.[7] But the nonpoets who look beyond them may be less convinced. Thus Schiller tries to find a unique, if utterly different, kind of genius in the "sentimental" poet, which in its own way might match or even surpass the accepted genius of the "naïve" poet, although Schiller seems to concede that an objective greatness seems to have vanished, not to be replaced. His humanism thus creates a consoling alternative, if not a wholly competitive one. But for those who had less of a personal commitment to authorize their contemporary arts, there may have been a more willing acceptance of what was acknowledged to be the unprogressive character of these arts, especially in contrast to the rational disciplines. A belated neoclassicist like Thomas Love Peacock was just such a skeptic about the powers of poetry in the modern world.

It is useful for us to watch as Peacock extends the arguments against progress in the arts to their logical extreme, though with a positivistic antagonism to the role of poetry, in contrast to the protective sympathy we have observed in Hume and Johnson. Peacock turns against poetry precisely because of its resistance to the idea of progress, which blesses all other disciplines, bringing them out of primeval darkness with the light of reason that is denied to poetry. With an attitude toward science that is uncritically progressive, he exemplifies the positivist's exclusive valorization of that which is capable of progress. Here is a composite of condescending quotations from Peacock's *The Four Ages of Poetry* (1820):

> While the historian and the philosopher are advancing in, and accelerating, the progress of knowledge, the poet is wallowing in the rubbish of departed ignorance, and raking up the ashes of dead savages to find gewgaws and rattles for the grown babies of the age.

---

6.   W. Jackson Bate, *The Burden of the Past and the English Poet* (Cambridge, Mass.: Harvard University Press, 1970).

7.   See "William Wordsworth and the Felix Culpa," in my *The Classic Vision: The Retreat from Extremity in Modern Literature* (Baltimore: Johns Hopkins Press, 1971), pp. 149–95. In this chapter, I relate Wordsworth to Schiller and others.

Theory and Institutions

A poet in our times is a semibarbarian in a civilized community. He lives in days that are past. His ideas, thoughts, feelings, associations, are all with barbarous manners, obsolete customs, and exploded superstitions. The march of his intellect is like that of a crab, backward. The brighter the light diffused around him by the progress of reason, the thicker is the darkness of antiquated barbarism, in which he buries himself like a mole, to throw up the barren hillocks of his Cimmerian labors.

Poetry [originally] was the mental rattle that awakened the attention of intellect in the infancy of civil society: but for the maturity of mind to make a serious business of the playthings of its childhood, is as absurd as for a full-grown man to rub his gums with coral, and cry to be charmed to sleep by the jingle of silver bells.[8]

So poets, useful "while society was savage, grow rabid, and out of their element, as [society] becomes polished and enlightened." I thought it worth quoting these excesses at some length so that we could savor the full rhetorical impatience with which the unbridled idolatry of scientific progress has to view the one area of human activity which is apparently excluded from it and even prides itself on its exclusion. In other words, Peacock accepts the division between instinct and reason, but only to celebrate the expulsion of instinct from a mature and civilized culture. He is forecasting that this is the destiny of the one previously valued area of human creation (the arts) which—by both admirers and detractors of the idea of progress—has been singled out as being unaffected by that idea, if not operating historically as an inversion of it.

(Actually, of course, there were many in the nineteenth century who—unlike Peacock—insisted that the arts, no less than anything else, moved only in an upward direction until reaching the summit of the present day. But I shall here skip over these apostles of universal progress who uncritically used the evolutionary metaphor to construct their models of history. Because their too easily optimistic doctrines were so obviously out of accord with what was revealed by a less doctrinaire look at the shape of history's narrative of the arts, they were not long credited. So these doctrines need not distract us now from our concern with more skeptical observations about progress in the arts. Peacock's faith in scientific progress—indeed his faith in progress in everything except the arts—was no less naïve, but the immunity from general progress, which it inflicts upon the arts—even when put in so extreme a form as Peacock's—is part of an intellectual tradition which, because of its later positivistic affiliations, is not without influence even today.)

---

8. Thomas Love Peacock, "The Four Ages of Poetry," in *The Works of Thomas Love Peacock*, ed. Henry Cole (London: Richard Bentley & Sons, 1975), 3:334–36.

Peacock's quasi-positivistic optimism on behalf of progress and reason points toward a scientific utopism, though one that protects its progressive character by leaving the retrograde, even childish, arts far behind. The hope apparently is that they will wither away, like the vestigial state in the Communist dream. Strangely, both protectors and disparagers of the place of art in the modern world can share this utopism on behalf of rational progress. The question that divides them asks whether the arts are to be taken along with science or left behind. And if, unlike Peacock, they want art taken along into the modern, rational utopia, they must decide what sort of art they are speaking for: is it the old masterworks—the unchallenged elite of earlier and less advanced cultural moments—which are seen as our permanent companions, or is it the more progressive, up-to-date companions, which an advancing culture produces to symbolize its own moment of greatest enlightenment? Is a utopia a cultural condition in which everybody will be able to enjoy Bach or Rembrandt or Shakespeare, or is it one in which Bach will be rejected for current inventions that reflect, as they are a match for, the state of our advancement? What is at stake is whether we wish theoretically to justify our feelings concerning the absolute superiority of a Bach or a Rembrandt or a Shakespeare over the moderns who have pretensions of being their successors, or whether the arts themselves progress as reflections of the progress in the other disciplines (for example, music that reflects recent experiments in electronic sound, or paintings that reflect what we now know about optics, or narrative structures that reflect what psychology tells us about the motives behind actions).

The Modern Problem: Progress in Society versus Progress in the Arts

To move to our own times, many modern theorists of the avant-garde argue that recent artists should not try to do better than older masters in performing the same function, but should recognize instead that a different function is now called for. There is in such theorists an outright rejection of elitism in the arts, an insistence on the egalitarian alternative that welcomes all symbolic expressions without discrimination. They would tear down the walls of our museums and turn the world itself into a "museum without walls." Their democratic receptivity claims to represent an advance over the outmoded class consciousness which finds its aesthetic analogue in our setting apart a few select masterworks into a canon (a term whose unfortunate theological implications are now exploited). The avant-garde critics see political

Theory and Institutions

(and theological) metaphors as implicit everywhere in older and traditional criticism, and they press such metaphors to their literal consequences since they wish to condemn the aesthetic convention, out of which older cultural moments produced their masterworks, for its aristocratic exclusiveness. And those works most admired in the past are considered to be as obsolete as the discarded social and political institutions that are reflected by their elitist pretensions as high art.

This rejection of the entire concept of an elite corps of artworks, now treated as if we were dealing with class distinctions among citizens within a social structure, is really a rejection of the political institutions at work in the cultures that produced these works. It is as if, by turning against an aesthetic monument, which history has carefully segregated—and lifted above its fellows—we somehow can wish out of existence the reactionary political context that was thriving when the work was created. Better yet, we are implicitly acknowledging that the special endowments of the elite work somehow require, and grow out of, the undemocratic characteristics of its social-political context. Hardly a sample of "people's art," the great work seems to demand the metaphors of an aristocratic body politic even to find the audacity to ask for the privileged treatment, the idolatry, the claim to special "value," which has been accorded it.

For some anti-elitist moderns, the most objectionable character of the great work of art is its assumption of the absolute value of man-created *order*, its order. Instead of authorizing the human creator to seek a triumph with his order over ordinary life, the anti-elitist asks for the embrace of the ordinary and the condemnation of any order that would disdain it. As an anti-elitist, he distrusts as politically suspect our every impulse to refine the ordinary into a transcendent order that would improve aesthetically upon it. As he relates art to society, he relates aesthetic order to social-political order, believing that a high degree of the first usually has been found only where there is a high degree of the second. And he is aware that a highly ordered society has hardly been the most progressive; indeed, the unprogressive nature of societies in which our greatest art has been produced is hardly an encouragement to his hopes. He fears that, to the extent that art reflects its culture, the art most conducive to order (our high art) is reflective of a most regressive social order since it emerged out of such an order. Conversely, the progress of society, with its breakdown of accepted orders in the name of freedom and equality, may well carry with it the subversion of the potential greatness of elite objects of art. And the continuing insistence on producing such objects poses a threat to the progress of the culture it is to reflect because, if it does indeed reflect its culture, it would still have to work toward a society within which its own penchant for order felt comfortable.

If, then, society dedicates itself to preserve cultural conditions under which such elite objects can still be produced, must it not put a priority on a social order that may well play against the egalitarian impulse usually associated with social progress? So either we try to restrict progress in the arts to progress in their capacity to serve—at whatever cost to themselves—progress in a society moving forward toward liberation, or we accept retrograde notions of social order so that we may encourage a still revered aristocratic art. To insist on such an either/or may seem to represent a strangely unfortunate surrender of art to society, a surrender based on a simplistic and fearful equation made between aesthetic and social orders, as if "order" were the same thing in both realms. Nevertheless, inimical to order as necessarily hierarchical and idolatrous, and in love with indiscriminate, pedestrian experience at large, the anti-elitist rejects elite art along with the obsolete society that cherished its elites. He has come to accept a newer and literally revolutionary notion of (what, for lack of another term, I shall still call) art, and he sees it as more progressive (and hence, in his special sense, better) than the rejected notion of art. He can even claim to find progress in art through the ages, although he is speaking of its function, the immediacy of its relations with an entire society, rather than of its rarefied value as a thing in itself, which he gladly has given up.

So in the avant-garde (and we must note the progressive implications of this metaphorical epithet itself) there must be an implied assertion of progress in the arts quite apart from any claim to an increasing value for the individual work that has been more recently produced. I started this essay by explicitly defining progress in the arts only as the improvement in quality in individual works as we move from earlier to later ones. But the attitude I have been considering deliberately disdains such discriminating individual judgments of aesthetic quality, seeing them as irrelevant, if not reactionary, because the anti-elitist wishes to affirm progress in the arts as a whole as reflections of the progress in institutionalized relations among persons in society. The interest is in historical continuity among equals and not in the ahistorical discontinuity of a transcendent single work. Progress in the arts can be affirmed, then, only because it is now related to their role in fostering an open, egalitarian society.

But does this attitude not shortchange the aesthetic qualities that have undermined the argument for progress by their assuring us our permanent experience of the unsurpassable greatness of early masterpieces? And do we not take such aesthetic judgments and such masterworks for granted even as we try to be receptive to the social and anti-elitist arguments that justify an often anti-aesthetic avant-garde? In our self-prompted postmodernist enthusiasm, we may reluctantly accept many of the most anti-aesthetic experiments as peculiarly representative of our culture. But we can afford to do so, perhaps, because we feel secretly assured that our antique gems of art have already been made and are still with us to be valued in their rarefied separateness. I wonder whether, when we try to respond to electronic music, for example, we do so knowing we can count on Mozart to be there to go back to. In other words, for all our attempts to cooperate with the revolutionary art (or anti-art) that may reflect our moment at this end of the progressive continuum, we quietly rely upon our antiprogressive commitment to works of art with which the modern world does not seek to compete, and very likely could not if it tried.

But now we have moved beyond the single definition of artistic progress with which I began, as we have moved from individual elite works to the historical continuum made up of all our symbolic expressions. And we have seen how some kind of progress could be predicated of the second, but not of the first, provided we were speaking of progress in society (rather than in the arts themselves as isolated entities), or rather—to be more precise—provided we were speaking only of progress in the conception of how the arts were to function in a progressive society as they moved toward the sacrificial end of self-obliteration in the service of the equality of all things. So, besides the obvious notion that would have progress in the arts depend on a simple comparison between the aesthetic qualities of earlier and later works (in which notion progress in the arts is usually denied), we have this second notion, in which the argument for progress depends on a comparison between earlier and later assumptions about how art functions in society. And this turns out to depend on how we judge the respective societies, since we see that progress in society leads it to reshape its role for art in a progressive direction (irrespective of our judgment, on "merely" aesthetic criteria, of the individual works).

Problems of Technique and Critical Response

There is a third notion of what progress in the arts might mean, one that I referred to earlier: it is the matter of craft, the changing and teachable methods of manipulating the expressive medium of the particular art. As readily discernible techniques, these *can* be put into the context of historical progress. Now, it is not that we can claim a long-term upward movement so much as we can claim refinements in the solutions being offered within defined areas of problems concerned with craft. Thus we find a limited degree of what might be called technical progress within various genres in the arts as these develop their traditions. (We must understand the claim that Milton knew more than Virgil to mean, among other things, that this "more" which Milton knew was Virgil himself.) We find such progress also within and between artistic movements, usually within genres: initial breakthroughs in craft, in response to a given problem, give way to the consolidation of gains, perhaps only then revealing dead ends—end-of-the-line problems that suggest nowhere left to go with this peculiar manipulation of the medium—until someone breaks through to a new lode to be explored and exploited, so that the process begins again. This sequence—the exhaustion of once vital movements, then experimentation and successful invention that get it all going again—accounts for the cry, heard in experimental moments in the history of the arts, to "make it new." In this repeated process there may be some significant gains, some technical problems which are taken care of so successfully that they will not present themselves again as problems—at least not in the same form.

Yet it may be too optimistic to claim a single line of improvement, even in small matters of craft, since one can demonstrate progressive development more easily within movements than between them. It may be misleading to apply the organic metaphor too literally to artistic movements or genres, projecting a birth, development, maturity, decay, and death to each movement as if it were a separate life, with each successive one having to start all over again. But it is equally misleading to expect that each movement necessarily stands on the shoulders of its predecessor, each an improvement over what has come before. Further, it must be repeated, critics in our history have generally avoided confounding technical judgments with aesthetic judgments. An aesthetician like R. G. Collingwood, in the post-Crocean tradition, distinguished the technical and external aspects of art as mere matters of "craft" from the internal intuition that for him is the essence of the work of art.[9] It is only the first of these, technique or craft, which is subject to the sequence of learning experiences, to the successive improvements, which constitute progress. But rather than defining art, this discernible element of craftsmanship functions largely to keep us critics in business by giving us something firm to talk about. So

9. R. G. Collingwood, *The Principles of Art* (Oxford: Clarendon Press, 1938), pp. 15–41.

observations about craft may indicate more about changes in criticism than about changes in the arts themselves.

As a fourth way to make a connection between progress and the arts (and the last I shall consider here), we can shift the attempt to find progress from comparing works of several periods to comparing the responses of audiences (and their most specialized representatives, the critics) of several periods. In other words, in speaking about progress in the arts, we may really mean to speak only about progress in criticism—that is, about the increasing self-consciousness with which a culture can account for the power of its arts, past or present. The concern with progress in the arts becomes the concern with progress in the criticism of the arts, and this in turn becomes the concern with progress in criticism as an art, perhaps in the end *the* art. For criticism is seen as a rational (and, for some hermeneuticians among us, as a quasi-scientific) discipline capable of continuous development and thus able to think of itself as progressing. Indeed, it is common, in recent days, for some literary critics, in their arrogance, to argue that what they create is a form of art that has the same status as poetry and is a rival art to it. Thus the usual distinction between the artwork as primary and the criticism of it as subsidiary is put in question.

Though one may well wish to qualify this aggrandizement of criticism, the history of criticism does indeed suggest that there has been progress in the rational manipulations of this discipline. To the extent, then, that criticism is a form of literary art, does not critical progress lead to some degree of progress in the arts? It is at least progress in what we expect or want of art, and in how we interpret and respond to what we get in art. And might not this in turn lead to a hoped-for progress in art itself insofar as it follows criticism (even if such is rarely the case, since—modern self-inflating critics to the contrary notwithstanding—history rather suggests that it is criticism that follows art)? In view of what I have said so far, I would remind the reader that whatever progress art might make in the wake of its criticism is likely to occur only in the conscious manipulation of the medium—that is, in the areas supervised by craft. Further, whatever the artist learns from advances in the critical art over the centuries would not be likely to confer advantages on him which would lead to the creation of works of greater aesthetic power than what was generated by earlier artists unblessed by such articulate companions.

Yet here is another way in which we can speak of progress in the arts of succeeding cultural moments while we evade the obvious fact that the history of our artifacts suggests otherwise. Indeed, each of these ways of construing progress in the arts as something other than the upward march of a culture's monuments is similarly evasive. Whether we find progress in a culture's conception of how arts should function in society (which ends by finding progress in society's own functions), or in the art of criticizing the arts, we have managed to affirm something progressive about our traffic with the arts—but only by turning away from the works themselves which prove so resistant to the idea of progress. And, however persuasive our arguments for these other sorts of progress may be, they should not distract us from this resistance; they should rather remind us of the evasive nature of our efforts to find a way of bringing the arts into the alien realm of discourse about progress.

The Entire Question Questioned

My earlier discussion about relating progress to the changing social function of art leads to a larger questioning of the entire enterprise engaged by this essay. The fact that societies and audiences have through history defined in such different ways the art which reflects and serves them may lead us to ask whether we have been deceived into using the single term *art* to characterize very different entities. Should we, perhaps, turn this essay on itself by asking whether it has not cut its subject out from under itself?

The question to which this essay is devoted, "Can the idea of progress be applied to art?" is itself put in question by the essay, especially if we examine the question from the perspective of recent poststructuralist semiology. The original question assumes a constant entity, "art," that gets better, or gets worse, or stays much the same, as it moves through history. It thus reifies the word *art*. But do we fool ourselves by using the one word as one thing, making "art" a single protagonist, whether in a lengthy history of upward growth, or in an equally lengthy history of decline, or in a sporadic sequence of ups and downs, or—as historical relativists would have it—in an indeterminate succession of enclosed and autonomous periods which cannot withstand mutual comparisons that would produce any larger tendency toward movement one way or the other? In speaking of progress, in whatever way we may relate the entity "art" before change to the entity "art" after change, it is risky to treat the two as one entity. And if they are different things (by which, in a poststructuralist mood, we would have to mean that they have different functions), then they cannot be entered as one item into a simple model of progress. On the contrary, art, as the "thing" that does or does not become better, is not a constant thing or a thing at all, so much as it is a changing function.

The problem is that our linguistic habit of reifying our words leads us to speak of all these functions (which we summarize with the one word *art* as if they were the same entity, first in a more primitive and then in an improved state. It is our anthropomorphism of language that leads us to speak (and to think) this way, as we try to shape the moving world into the stasis of our substantives. This is, in short, a problem in semiology: dare we tie down the "floating signifier," "art," as one "thing" undergoing progress, instead of recognizing its dynamic, unsubstantial character? Each cultural moment, we have observed, seems to require its own "art," which—given its change of function with each successive moment—may hardly deserve to be denominated by a single word. As a changing function (and no longer a thing) within the disposition of the functional forces that constitute culture from moment to moment, we may well question—as poststructuralists—whether art, any more than culture itself, has earned its generic operational name, and whether it would bear it except for the ontologizing habit of our language. If we are dealing with functions so radically different from moment to moment in our cultural history, can our original question—depending as it does on a transhistorical (and transcultural) definition—any longer have any meaning? Or do nominalistic questions about what we call "art" at any given moment swallow it up?

Thus can the poststructuralists, with their "moves" replacing any ontological claims, deconstruct the language in which the myth of progress comes wrapped, thereby undoing that myth, if only—it turns out—to enhance their own. They thus seek to free us from a mystification by language which has caught the rest of us but which they abjure. Earlier, we must remember, the structuralism of Claude Lévi-Strauss sought to undo the notion of historical sequence required for the idea of progress by urging a purely synchronic analysis which revealed similar structures in primitive and in advanced cultures.[10] But of course, in spite of himself, Lévi-Strauss's own perspective on these structures became a privileged position and hence one that—with whatever inconsistency—

10. The final lines of Claude Lévi-Strauss's "The Structural Study of Myth," in *Structural Anthropology*, trans. Claire Jacobson and Brooke Grundfest Schoepf (New York: Basic Books, 1963), give us a pithy summary of the strongly antiprogressive nature of his synchronic appeal:

What makes a steel axe superior to a stone axe is not that the first one is better made than the second. They are equally well made, but steel is quite different from stone. In the same way we may be able to show that the same logical processes operate in myth as in science, and that man has always been thinking equally well; the improvement lies, not in an alleged progress of man's mind, but in the discovery of new areas to which it may apply its unchanged and unchanging powers. (P. 230) represented significant progress over perspectives that had been held before. He was claiming to advance our capacity to understand the fact that there could be no advancement in our capacity to understand.

Now, however, the poststructuralist presses such matters with deconstructive instruments more keenly applied. Through efforts of thinkers like Jacques Derrida and Michel Foucault (though these two proceed in profoundly different ways), the final triumph of discourse, representing the high point in the progress of our reasoning about its capacity to mean, seems to lead to the emptying out of its meaning. An ironic triumph indeed. I have been indulging in a nominalistic deconstruction of the carefully built claims that filled the rational language of progress for two centuries. The ultimate consequence of such semiological self-knowledge is a confidence in methodological linguistic progress that would bring our confidence in substantive progress to naught. But this war on the metaphysical is self-defeating. In spite of the intentions of the poststructuralist critique, language can bring us to the zero point only by itself becoming a negative meaning, an apocalypse of nonbeing; and this unprogressive claim has an implicit ontology in it that contradicts the vision of language as a field of forces always in motion. So this would-be deconstruction is not a final move, but is—or would be—a final claim (or rather a final anticlaim). As what comes to be a negative metaphysic, it has all the metaphysical force of the positive metaphysic it would undo. It is not the end of arguments about progress, then, so much as it is a counterargument that reminds us of our logocentric illusions. Nevertheless, after we have paid these illusions due regard, we find the same problems about progress in the arts still there confronting us: the failures in the language we have been using to resolve them have not dissolved them after all.

If semiology cannot deconstruct our problem out of existence, it is because the artwork itself is continually reconstructing itself. The poststructuralist critique permits us to recognize that progress in the arts is, as a notion, self-contradictory: to the extent that there is progress—any of the sorts of progress that have been proposed—the term *arts* becomes increasingly unstable, even to the point of utter decomposition. The more progress, the less confident we should be that there is *an* "art" which undergoes it. But if there is no such constancy of term, then clearly there is no progress in what becomes of it, but only a constantly shifting field of differences. The (so-called) arts produced by the several cultural moments necessarily represent such different functions and thus take such momentarily different forms that it would seem self-mystifying for them to claim the same generic term. But there is "art" as a deceiving collective term, and there is the individual work of art.

Theory and Institutions

The first may shift about without substantive meaning, but the second is constant. After all our semiological involutions, the single utterly complete work of art, as it reappears in each cultural moment, is the same work, no matter how differently each culture perceives and conceives it, and the persistence of its presence lifts it beyond the destructive power of our demystifying instruments.

Progress and the Work of Art

No matter how I have turned our question around in this essay, no matter how I have tried to alter our subject, I always come back to that individual work of art. At first we observed the resistance to applying the idea of progress to the arts and found the work itself at the base of every argument used to press that resistance. Then, as I sought definitions that might permit more affirmative answers to our question, none of the alternative definitions could finally displace our original concern about the comparative judgments of works of art produced through the centuries. And when I finally made the reflexive move of turning against the question by showing it was linguistically misleading and at odds with itself, still the substantive issue—and the individual work—remained. And it remains with us now.

But this is just what the work of art has been advertised to do from the beginning: to establish for itself a permanent presence with us. It recurs and recurs and will not go away. It may be that we can use this unique function of the artwork, its continuous presence—so at odds with all our other ways of thinking and writing—to make a last effort to rescue our subject, though in an unexpected and perhaps distorted way. If we have not been able to look from the work outward—to society, to critics, to genres and artistic movements, to our deceiving language—perhaps we can look inward within the work. If we do, we may well find there—no matter how early or how late in history it was produced—a microcosmic model for the idea of human progress.

Let us think of the single, complete, aesthetically satisfying work of art as an ultimate "commodity," different from other desirable "goods" in that it is a permanent "good." Each artwork is perceived to be a single, finite, framed and self-enclosed entity, an absolute and perfected version of all those fleeting "goods" in the human economy (including scientific advances). The attainment of these goods in increasing numbers is supposed to constitute progress—except that with those other goods our satisfaction palls with our gratification. But the artwork is an emblem of a lasting power in things which we do not otherwise find because there is, we seem to feel, something terminal about it as its own fictional reality. If we feel dissatisfied with each experience of the work, we are usually dissatisfied with ourselves more than we are with it.

Think of the expression on the face of a colleague, filled with an ecstasy of anticipation, who reports that he is shortly to witness a new performance of *King Lear* (or *Giselle* or a late quartet of Beethoven) which is supposed to be an extraordinary and fully satisfying appearance of the work, as if in this appearance the work has achieved its once-and-for-all finality. (I use the word *appearance* in the Platonic sense because our colleague has in effect become a Platonist who takes this word with metaphysical seriousness, hoping this once to leap with it to the work's ultimate reality.) He is looking forward to the reenactment of a ritual in which yet newer and more highly qualified pretenders will seek again to unmask the god, the work-in-itself. And though his previous experiences suggest that in the end he will sense a failure, he wants to witness again and again the experience—however frustrating—of coming close. In the nonperformance arts (another silent reading of a poem to ourselves, another viewing of a painting), we would find—*mutatis mutandis*—the same kind of promise, frustration, and hope for another occasion. The phrase "work-in-itself" suggests an absolute ontological status that belies the role of the audience in constructing the reality of the work. Epistemological honesty should lead us to admit that the aesthetic form which holds this promise for us is, after all, a system of signs that depends on *our* interpretive energy if it is to become the work we worship. Paradoxically, we have in effect created the completeness of the ideal object which is the standard of judgment for the less complete experience we have also created.

There is, I grant, something fetishistic about what we feel about those highest members of the canon of the elite art in our culture. Matthew Arnold was in part right about art's functioning as a substitute for a defunct religion, precisely because (as we saw Hume suggest) it can—with a merely fictional commitment—outlast the obsolescence of the doctrines in the world that produced it. So these idolatrous expectations do suggest a fetishism, with each work seen as sacred even if our experience of it is not: each work is seen as containing its own Platonic archetype which any appearance (that is, any experience) of it permits us only to approach inadequately. As I have repeatedly observed in this essay, from this point of view, even technique (and progress in it), like criticism (and progress in it), is only an illusion since the beckoning absolute of the work itself contiues to retreat and remains teasingly beyond its reach. Yet each time we approach the work, through another performance or another private experience, we open ourselves to it as the source of an always elusive ultimate satisfaction toward which it promises to lead us if we can but get beyond our imperfect experiences of it.

I have already observed that this is hardly a function our contemporary art would care about, and that many of us who respond to this art do so while reserving to ourselves the right to seek in older masterworks the idolatrous satisfactions I have been describing. We sanction the new antielitist alternatives, the egalitarian translation of everything into art (or art into everything), presumably as a reflection of our culture's freedom; but we do so in large part because we have the assurance of another sort of art that persists, though that art is now torn away from the cultural values that produced it and is serving our culture which, with another revolutionary "art" of its own, probably needs such works more than ever to fall back on.

The value of each of these works to us and our culture rests upon the dream of its perfection which I have spoken of. Its completeness, sufficiency of self, and the special satisfactions these promise, all these derive from our sense of its internal teleology, that special, disinterested purposiveness of which Kant spoke. This leads, in Kant, to a "finality of form" which suggests the "final things" of eschatology. And I want to suggest that there is something eschatological in what the work's finality (as we project it out of our experience) promises us: an end to history's incompleteness by a final breakthrough that transcends historical contingency, replacing it with its own system of absolute relations. Of course, the work can do so because it *is* free of history. Its finality is possible only because—as our aesthetic habit constitutes it out of the signs before us—it is a fictional finality; and the claim that the work of art is freed as well as limited by its fictional character has been central to criticism since Matthew Arnold. Its eschatological promise allows the work to become the emblem of the conquest of alien elements by the imposition of form, the emblem—in other words—of the breakthrough to utopia, a microcosm of satisfied ends, difficulties overcome, and problems resolved, so that all that threatens as the random is now overwhelmed into an ultimate teleology. It thus becomes an emblem also of the idea of progress, the fiction of progress in the real world, which gains mythic authority, thanks to the internal completeness of the individual work of art in which progress does occur and does lead to a utopia of ultimate satisfactions. We find progress in the joint relations among the elements within the work as we continually seek to put them together to satisfy its promise of utopia; or at least this is another fiction we entertain as we see ourselves moving from one imperfect experience of the work to the next, coming closer and closer to its own Platonic archetype. And yet again it gives us the progressive dream of a world that is an aesthetic improvement over our own in the completeness of its system of satisfied ends.

So the work of art comes out of history, seems to violate our present by managing to make itself into *its* present—an always-now—and thus leads us into itself as a continuously circular history. Yet it points to a future beyond our grasp—another experience of it in which its Platonic archetype can at last be realized—thus beckoning us toward indefinite progress, toward utopia, a totally humanized utopia that demands our total indulgence and receives our partial failings—though we like to think each time less partial—every time we experience it. The work's capacity to achieve its own fullness of power, irrespective of its "progressive" place in history or its "progressive" role in the history of its art or its genre, by itself can transform the idea of progress. The "free play" of total breakthrough achieved in the work (free with respect to history and to the empirical world) yet leads—as it caters to our perceptual habit of seeking completion—to the realization of the teleologies latent in the human power to impose form, the power to create an order we cannot find. Art contributes to the idea of progress, then, not as a result of its own historical sequence of artifacts but through the very process of fabrication within each object. This may seem to be mere aestheticism, though I think not. It is more profoundly anthropological than that in its giving to the arts a major role in maintaining, and perhaps transforming, our capacity to imagine an idea—a narrative—of progress. As the emblem of its own quest, art represents the dream which, as a model, it presents. Its very being thus keeps alive the human habit to narrate progress and imagine utopia. And it is this habit that keeps alive the humanity in the rest of us.

3   From Theory to Thematics:
The Ideological Underside
of Recent Theory

In this essay I confine my observations to a number of critics on the American scene. My objective is not to conduct a survey but to examine, through a few examples, a persistent and unintended consequence of the recent antithematic direction in theory which would have us avoid the thematizing act in its search for a purity that would celebrate method while suppressing substance, that would celebrate structural functions while suppressing ideology. Such an emphasis, with its fear of the ontological and its consequent suppression of the worldly references of words, has led to an imbalance and, in some quarters, a smugness that regards with disdain the critical concern with the moral and ideological consequences of literary works. My use of the term *ideology*, I hasten to add, covers a spectrum of commitments far broader than the political— indeed the entire range of moral-thematic belief systems—although in the end most of them may be seen as having political consequences.

It is difficult, if one reads and believes even a small part of much currently fashionable theory written in the United States, to continue to take seriously the question of literature's explicit moral and ideological meanings, however ideological the motives behind the writing may be.

This essay is a substantially revised version of my article, "In the Wake of Morality: The Thematic Underside of Recent Theory," *New Literary History* (issue on "Literature and/as Moral Philosophy") 15 (1983): 119–36. My focus here is more sharply upon ideology as the parent of moral concerns.

Having retreated from the notion that posited moral philosophies can be taken at face value, as if they meant what they claimed to mean, and having questioned the notion of literature itself as an exclusive selection of privileged texts, one is more likely these days to turn on the question and spend one's efforts attacking its obsolescence. Perhaps I can suggest a sense of this attitude by recalling a moment of self-definition that was pressed upon me several years ago, while I was being introduced as a speaker before a major university audience. My introducer repeated to us the words spoken by another theorist, a well-known critic identified with the school of deconstruction, who had preceded me on that podium some weeks earlier. Looking forward to my appearance which was to follow his, he was said to have reassured his audience that, if its members felt unreceptive to his hard message, they could wait for the more agreeable pieties that would issue from me as a representative of "the moral gang." As I heard the phrase, I found it (and still find it) reminiscent of "the gang of virtue" (those in the service of an unfeeling Western ideology) named—though by an unsympathetic character—in Conrad's *Heart of Darkness*; and it is similarly condescending, if not contemptuous.

I mean to spend some time here discovering the extent to which I deserve that attachment, but more important, discovering why the current critical fashion can see it as quaintly archaic, an approach that these days has presumably been interred for good by the skepticism of semiotic studies.

I suppose the moral gang of which I am supposed to be a member contains most of the major critics in the history of our dominant literary tradition in the West. It is hardly news to report that Plato, despite his fear of, and opposition to, the arts, set the terms of moral obligation which were to be taken up by critics to come, whether their discourse was intended to support or disagree with Plato's position and—consequently—to defend or undermine any or all of the arts. The responsibility of the critics—and through them of the arts—to the moral realm was from that beginning unquestioned, whatever the questions that might be brought about the nature of that responsibility. Even Aristotle, whose *Poetics* (and, even more, whose *Rhetoric*) seeks at times to evade an immediate relationship to moral consequences, never—perhaps because he is working in the shadow of Plato's issues—lets loose of an at least tangential contact with the moral realm, so that we cannot assess his total impact as an aesthetician without invoking the *Nicomachean Ethics* and allowing that work and the *Poetics* to furnish mutual illuminations upon one another. And others of the ancient treatises on the arts, as we move into Latin works, treat moral concerns far more openly and directly.

But it is in the tradition of the Renaissance *Art of Poetry* and the Renaissance *Poetics* that, whether claiming allegiance to Horace or to

Theory and Institutions

Aristotle, treatises on literature seem to become unabashedly aware of criticism's moral obligations (as well as those of the art being criticized or theorized about)—probably as a result of the Platonism that pervades these works and that moment in our intellectual history. In the work of a wonderfully talented and varied horde of sixteenth-century Italian critics and their brilliantly urbane heir, Sir Philip Sidney, the moral function of poetry—as an experiential extension (and thus a rhetorical demonstration) of philosophical principles—is an almost automatic assumption. Nor would it occur to them to consider making a distinction between what ought to be the moral objectives of poetry (whatever may be the shortcomings of individual poems) and the moral objectives of the critical discourse that is to instruct poems about their proper mission. It is a major advantage of Platonism, once Renaissance Platonists turn it positive (that is, once they invert Plato) so that they may defend poetry rather than condemn it, that the oneness of moral attraction in universal goodness—as it gathers beauty and truth within itself—can allow all kinds of discourse to lose their distinctness as they reflect the single idea.

Though the metaphysic changes radically, Enlightenment and neoclassical poetics retains an inevitable moral flavor, with regard to both its own character and the character of the poems which are its objects. In a gigantic critic like Dr. Johnson, we find some degree of struggle as he seeks to maintain the primacy of the moral,[1] but—despite some wavering here and there—he can hardly be said to maintain anything else as primary. His predecessors and contemporaries were for the most part more single-minded in their didactic concern. In them, as in critics for centuries before, the meaning of literature is dependent upon the unquestioned universal precepts furnished to its particular fictional examples by moral philosophy. Indeed, literature was to be kept morally secure by being brought by moral philosophy into its firmly held ontological precincts.

Beginning late in the eighteenth century, the inflated humanism of romantic and postromantic consciousness seeks to replace the guidance of a metaphysically ordained morality with emanations from the poetic imagination of the man-god-poet. But though the source of morality may shift from the cosmos to the single (though crucially representative) mind, the overriding character of those formal impositions—which are moral impositions—upon human experience, and thus human art, is unchallenged. Whether it comes to us in the subtle delicacy of Kant's claim that

---

1. I examine at length Johnson's struggle with the moral in "Fiction, Nature, and Literary Kinds in Johnson's Criticism of Shakespeare" and " 'Trying Experiments upon Our Sensibility': The Art of Dogma and Doubt in Eighteenth-Century Literature," both in my *Poetic Presence and Illusion: Essays in Critical History and Theory* (Baltimore: Johns Hopkins University Press, 1979), pp. 55–69 and 70–91.

"the beautiful is the symbol of the morally good" or whether it is trumpeted in Shelley's overconfident pronouncement that "Poets are the unacknowledged legislators of the world," the common elements of this aesthetic still put forward the signs of membership in the "moral gang" by insisting on the dominance of the formal impulse and on the inevitable place of the moral within the formal. For the making of forms *is* the making of laws, human laws which, as forms, capture and tame the vagaries of wayward human experience. In its bewildering variety of manifestations throughout the nineteenth century, formalism—even at its most extreme—maintains itself as moralism, whether blatant, surreptitious, or inverted.

Still, I do not mean to underestimate this shift, beginning in the late eighteenth century, from cosmic forms to forms invented by human creators as the source of moral authority. Though it seemed to leave the moral function intact, this shift of authority, with its loss of ontological security, carried that which eventually would threaten the moral function itself. And it did from the first imply the separation of that moral function from the well-ordered precincts of moral philosophy, with its conformist ideological consequences. For it was a shift from the authority of moral philosophy as a body of universally binding doctrines whose justification must ultimately be theological, to the authority of an individual poetic imagination. Of course, since the latter was sanctioned by a transcendental idealism, it was trustworthy and not just wayward, so that a quasi-theological authority was still at least implicitly present. Nevertheless, the essentially humanistic metaphysic has been proved by history to be far more flimsy, leaving, in our time, no objective supporting structure to which poetry's moral claims can be tied. But my brief historical survey has not yet brought us to this, our present desperate moment.

The freeing of literature from its subservience to moral philosophy—and hence to the ideologies of system—did for awhile produce a new, and profoundly vital, moral function for literature as a replacement for a philosophy whose potential for private guidance had been discredited. We have seen that the criticism of older, more secure times, confident of the truths of the moral philosophy behind it and confident, too, of the authority of philosophical universals to bring the errant particulars of human experience into line, could assign to literary works the role of presenting, in their particular cases, exemplary demonstrations of those general truths. It was the obligation of those works to show those particulars as having been brought into line, shaping the fiction accordingly in order to tame them. But more recent criticism—specifically that twentieth-century criticism that inherits but trans-

Theory and Institutions

forms the project initiated by the romantic and idealist thinkers—sees literary fictions as subverting those universals through the painstaking development of its particulars as autonomous particulars. This is, essentially, the move we associate with the New Criticism.

That move seems to come out of the notion of aesthetic disinterestedness as originally developed by Kant. That is, Kant is taken as defining the aesthetic by distinguishing it from practical reason, as well as from pure reason—practical reason being the realm of *interest* as guided by the human faculty of *will*: in short, the realm of the moral. To define the aesthetic by its functioning apart from any interest external to it—to define it as disinterested—would appear to exclude the realm of the moral and hence the ideological, from art. But in the hands of the post-Kantians of our century it has worked quite otherwise.

It is surely true that writers as different as Schopenhauer, Yeats, Croce, Bergson, Hulme, Ransom, and Tate treat the will as fatal enemy to poetry, thereby separating the aesthetic in literature from Kant's notion of the practical, from the satisfaction of human interests. The suspension of the will—which is for them a proper consequence of the aesthetic—leads to the rejection of moral philosophy as a system of universal principles to guide action, since it must be seen to be an unwelcome intruder whose authoritarian nature would disrupt, and then distort, the free play of particularity which only aesthetic disinterestedness can permit. Literary works, then, demonstrate their aesthetic freedom (from interests, as defined by ideological systems) by exploiting the errant (that is, the system-defying) nature of their particularities, by subverting the potentially applicable universals that they may bring to mind. And these subversions occur not only within the fictional action but also within the language, the artistic conventions, and the very tropes of the work as these strive to establish a unique system of aesthetic play.

But such a subversion of ideological universals has important consequences for our moral awareness, especially since twentieth-century thought has provided an alternative tradition of making moral claims that can arise only where moral philosophy proper has been subverted. I am referring, of course, to the existentialist-personalist tradition that flourished some decades back, a tradition that thrives only on the anti-Hegelian rejection of universals. It sees the moral universals of systematic thinking as denying the unique subjectivity of the person, imposing a death-dealing totalitarianism of spirit that rejects different-ness, settling for a conformism projected outward to posit an ontological structure of enslavement. In an analogous way, it sees the universals of normal language as similarly life-denying, so that they must be subverted by the playful deviations of language-become-literary in quest of its own uniquely particular—that is to say self-justifying—authority as a verbal system. By blurring the analogy, modernist critics in this line of thinking find a natural alliance—indeed a similarity of interest and, finally, a two-sided identity—between the post-Kantian aesthetic assault on moral will, with its consequences for a too-controlled language, and the existentialist-personalist assault on external moral authority (or, as they might prefer to say, on universal authoritarianism).[2]

This union of interests between a post-Kantian aesthetic and an anti-Hegelian existentialism leads on both sides to a flight from moral imperatives, at least from giving those imperatives the role of emerging—without being undermined—from literary works. But this is not, as it might at times seem to be, a flight from moral sensibility itself as the appropriate atmosphere in which the work is to draw its breath. Indeed, in the existentialist-personalist context it is anything but such a flight. It is, instead, a claim that literature is the only discursive equivalent for experiential particularity; that is, it alone is faithful to our moral experience in its infinite contingency, the only language created to match that experience. In this view, literary works are to furnish paradigms of the self-defeating fraudulence of universals, thereby precluding the extraction of any moral proposition upon which practical decisions can be based. But, it is claimed, only the irreducibly unique case can provide authentic moral insight, and only literature has the language and the narrative manipulation to confront the irreducibly unique case and to protect its irreducibility.

So, far from being divorced from moral considerations, literature is seen to have an indispensable moral function, one now its own since it no longer requires the external authority of a universal proposition to sanction its particular case. Literary form, viewed from the limited vantage point of moral universals, is seen as grounded in a structure of oppositions in which neither side yields—provided we interpret fully enough—so that each would-be universal claim is undermined by its antithesis, and there is no all-resolving synthesis. In this way literature does find a moral objective in the wake of the abandonment of any possible universally applicable moral philosophy, for there no longer are any categories that dare speak an imperative. Yet, of course, this is for literature the most ambitious and exclusive claim for a moral

---

2. I provide a detailed study of the collision of these two traditions in "The Existential Basis of Contextual Criticism," in *The Play and Place of Criticism* (Baltimore: Johns Hopkins Press, 1967), pp. 239–51.

function that any discourse could make, even if it is one ideologically slanted toward the alienation of individual rebellion. Since my book of some years back, *The Tragic Vision* (1960), arises out of such a post-Kantian-existentialist posture, at once formal and thematic, there is little question that—however much its existentialist energy depended on the exploding of moral structures—it most strongly maintained me as a stalwart, if defiant, member of "the moral gang," though hardly an ideological gang like that specified by Conrad.

We see, then, how completely moral philosophy has been removed from its ideological role as guide to otherwise errant literary fictions, but also how completely the removers, our romantic and postromantic critics, still the moral gang, retain their commitment—however heterodox—to both the moral, and hence ideological, function of literature and the moral function of their criticism. If moral discourse is seen as an empty and fraudulent exercise of a failed language, literature is salvaged for language as the one kind of discourse in which words still struggle toward creating a fully human meaning.

It is just this privileging of literature which our newer criticism these days would deny, as it would extend the demythification of language from philosophy to all writing, including what had been set aside as the special mythic preserve of literature. Just as the combined post-Kantian and existentialist tradition, as I have described it, would empty moral philosophy of meaning while keeping only poetry full, so its theoretical successors would empty poetry as well, demystifying it with other discourse, and on the same principles. We are now to be wary in literary works as in philosophical ones of a naïve logocentrism that persuades us to ascribe reality to the references of words as if it were literally contained within them. (This is another version of the warning against "existential projection" from the order of words to the order of world made by Northrop Frye in another context some years back.) Consequently, the literary work must be deprived by them of its claim to illuminate our moral experience, as it is seen to join other discourse —including moral philosophy, of course—in only pretending to a revelation (or at least reference) from which its semiotic character actually shuts it off.[3] So much, then (shall we say?), for the relation of literature to moral philosophy as a live and fruitful subject, now that both of them have been disposed of as claimants to moral knowledge of human existents. Has all that the history of criticism took so seriously

---

3. I use the term *semiotic* in this essay not as it is used by technical semioticians for whom it addresses the mutual relations between signifiers and signifieds, but as it is used by American poststructuralists who address only the play among signifiers itself.

for so long been demythified, demystified, and deconstructed away? Is there nothing left except for us to examine the history and the nature of our deceptions and self-deceptions?

I must admit that, in this newly changed theoretical moment, I have modified my own claims to which I have before referred, so that I speak now less of the existential and more of the anthropological—that is, I speak less of poetry's license to reveal the actual moral contingencies that the ideological abstractions of philosophy must ignore and thus misrepresent, and speak more of poetry's license to create complex illusions which provide us with visions of the shape that our own action-guiding fictions, private or collective, may take. This may seem to be a niggling difference, though I see it as an important theoretical change that permits me to concede a skeptical view of the revelatory capacity of language, even literary language (if we can still distinguish a literary function), the need to shift from the meanings of words to the dizzying and obfuscating functions of words. But it is also my way of suggesting that—whatever recent language theory may do to deny the humane missions we confidently used to give to our several kinds of discourse, and especially the literary—the moral and, yes, ideological spurs to our speaking and writing are still with us, leading us to smuggle in those concerns, even if we do so under alien permits that might point toward excluding them. Such an assertion might itself seem to be a self-serving anthropological assumption of mine, except that I believe it is justified by careful reading. Even in those theories that most try to lock textuality away from the world, within itself, those theories that are least permissive about what texts can tell us about their ostensible referents, we can find at work indirect claims for privileged philosophical and ideological meanings, though—as with deconstructionists—they may be negative ones, representing unspoken negative visions. In the hands of a daring and ambitious critic, I mean to argue, poetics does not remain purely descriptive or semiotic; instead, it narrows into the realm of privilege and spreads into the realm of the thematic. It subliminally invokes attitudes that we can think of as moral, or even ideological.

I am speaking about the thematizing that occurs even within those theories apparently least concerned with, or perhaps most concerned to deny, any legitimate thematic dimension for literature or its criticism: I mean, then, to turn antithematic theories on themselves, to watch them turn themselves thematic. And, having suggested the thematic underside of a number of theories, I will then move on to propose some thematic genres for them. I now suspect I may have been more accurate than I knew in describing more theories than my own—many not yet invented—when, years ago in *The Tragic Vision*, I described "*thematics* as the study of the experiential tensions which, dramatically entangled in the literary work, become an existential reflection of that work's aesthetic complexity."[4] Of course, in most current theories the situation is the reverse, since in *The Tragic Vision* I was centrally concerned with "thematics" while today theorists are ostensibly concerned with the verbal level of writing at the expense of existential reflection. But I believe my observation holds: purely semiotic studies, those that perceive the textual or intertextual as a systematic sequence of signifiers, seem to impose even upon the most stubbornly antithematic commentator, even today, a thematic analogy, often unguarded, that thrusts itself into the critic's company. The difference is that my own existential interest, a couple of decades ago, allowed me to be more candid and less embarrassed in seeing it there. Indeed, in my desire to escape the charge of escapist formalism, I wanted to see it there.

Today, though my semiotic awareness makes me also more distrustful about the poem's revelatory powers, I remain all too aware of the thematic implications of my own aesthetics of illusionary presence. I now mean my criticism to dwell upon the literary work as a self-conscious fiction: to dwell upon the ways by which the work, operating within our moment of aesthetic perception, persuades us of a metaphorical identity among its elements while reminding us, through its self-reference, that this feat can be worked only within such a moment and with the reader's complicity. It is, then, an identity that calls itself illusionary, that acknowledges another (also illusionary?) realm of difference that affirms its aesthetic power of presence while denying itself any ontological substance. In effect, it warns against our projecting it beyond itself and into the realm of human existence.

Yet how can I not acknowledge that such a theoretical approach favors those literary works which are most self-conscious about their artifice, those works which most emphasize the elements of their reality which would dissipate themselves into the transient evanescence of phantoms, thereby dissolving our certainties and loosening our grip on our world's heavy furniture? Can I refrain from seeking to turn all the works I treat, insofar as I wish to make them worthy of my admiration,

---

4. *The Tragic Vision: Variations on a Theme in Literary Interpretation* (New York: Holt, Rinehart & Winston, 1960), p. 242. In this passage I take great pains to divorce "thematics" from "theme" (which I there define as "the so-called 'philosophy' of a work, that series of propositions which we supposedly can derive—or, better yet, extrapolate—from the aesthetic totality that is presented to us"—p. 241). So we are far from moral philosophy, locked in a language context that still, in its subtle network of internal relations, relates to our existential condition, and hence to our moral state.

into works tending in this direction? Can I refrain also from imposing certain privileged themes that reduce reality to appearance, accompanying them with a privileged metaphysic or antimetaphysic, and finally a privileged conception of paradox as the moral problematic, dwelling on moral dilemmas and their inevitability? All these of course have ideological consequences, leading to an implied liberality of moral judgment, the anti-authoritarian consequence of seeing the harsh, repressive inadequacy of universals, each undone by a paradoxical countermovement.

Further, there is in my theory an implicit demand for aesthetic form that calls for the fulfillment of the obligation—the moral obligation—upon man as form-maker to impose shape, however fictional, upon the unformed data of experience. As with Matthew Arnold, poetry becomes the last resort for a culture whose moral psychology, after the death of its gods, requires the soothing power of myth, though now accepted only as myth and no longer as a falsifiable fact. So, however much in retreat, I represent "the moral gang" still, and in this variety of ways. I am being confessional about the thematic underside of my own theorizing in hopes that this lengthy recital can set the example for equally unwelcome suggestions that create similar doubts about other recent theories, which may be at least as anxious to avoid the charge of thematizing their linguistic or semiotic claims. I should like to propose similar suggestions about a number of these theories.

In light of my earlier discussion, it should not be hard to establish that extensions of the New Criticism—however outwardly formalistic—would be heavy with thematic implications. Ambiguity or paradox as a New Critical verbal and structural principle can easily become thematically overdetermined and slide into a description of how things are in the moral and metaphysical universe, as all of existence turns duplicitous. These days this seems obvious enough. More significant, perhaps, is the spatialization of the temporal in the New Criticism, which can turn into the thematic mythification of history.

For example, Joseph Frank's well-known claims about "spatial form" may be seen shifting all too easily from words to existence: from the effect of simultaneity achieved by the juxtaposition of successive verbal units to the collapsing of several historical moments into the archetype of an ever-returning eternal present. Following the example of Eliot's poetry and applying Eliade's religious mysteries, Frank blurs and then substantializes the analogy between the breakthrough of time by poetic words seeking form and the breakthrough of time by history seeking a transcendent eschatology. Thus for Frank the poem works "to undermine the inherent consecutiveness of language, frustrating the reader's normal expectation of a sequence and forcing him to perceive the elements of the poem as juxtaposed in space rather than unrolling in time." In this way "Past and present are apprehended spatially, locked in a timeless unity that, while it may accentuate surface differences, eliminates any feeling of sequence by the very act of juxtaposition." But in this second quotation the terms are becoming ambiguous, in that they can refer either to simultaneity as it affects verbal sequences or to the actual dissolving of historicity. ("By this juxtaposition of past and present . . . history becomes ahistorical.") In the passage that follows, Frank completes the thematic transfer: "What has occurred, at least so far as literature is concerned, may be described as the transformation of the historical imagination into myth—an imagination for which historical time does not exist, and which sees the actions and events of a particular time only as the bodying forth of eternal prototypes." It is, he adds, "the myth of eternal repetition and, in the last analysis . . . the abolition of time."[5] I have paused over Frank's work because I thought it would be useful to observe so clear—if naïve—an example of the unannounced transfer from the formal to the thematic. But we may not be surprised to find such an appeal to the spatializing mysteries of simultaneity in this metaphorical projection of the New Criticism.

The more recent deconstructionist strain of American poststructuralism would seem to present a greater challenge to my claim that even purely verbal theories end by thematizing themselves, a greater challenge because deconstructionism so strenuously rejects our conventional referential expectations of how words function. But we can point to examples in this criticism in which the apparently unintended glide from purely verbal matters to those that make claims about the human condition is all too similar to Frank's, however great the doctrinal difference between Frank and them. I think especially of Paul de Man's "The Rhetoric of Temporality," largely because that essay is as vulnerable to this sort of analysis as it has been influential.[6] It seems to be the inverse of Frank's, though it no less easily falls into the thematic realm. De Man makes as exclusive claims for the temporal as Frank did for the spatial, attacking just that spatialization or collapsing of time which we observed in Frank.

---

5. Joseph Frank, *The Widening Gyre: Crisis and Mastery in Modern Literature* (Bloomington: Indiana University Press, 1963). The first quotation appears on p. 10 and the others on pp. 59–60.

6. Paul de Man, "The Rhetoric of Temporality," in *Interpretation: Theory and Practice*, ed. Charles S. Singleton (Baltimore: Johns Hopkins Press, 1969), pp. 173–209.

For de Man's favored mode, allegory, what is celebrated in a word is its "pure anteriority," which renounces "the desire to coincide" with "another sign that precedes it" and instead accepts its "temporal difference," "its authentically temporal predicament" (pp. 190–91). But the last word, "predicament," opens language outward to the human condition: the fate of being only temporal starts by belonging to a sequence of words but shifts to the consecutive, unrepeatable moments of our lives. And with the prohibition against the spatiality of a return, against any simple repetition, the moments can only run out, following one another to death. So the consciousness of death is in each moment, as from each we fall into "the temporal void" (p. 203). It becomes the obligation of each of us—and, even more, the obligation of the authentic poet—to acknowledge the separateness of the human subject confronting the "unbreachable distance" (p. 209) in his temporal predicament, and with it the void, in effect his own death. This he must acknowledge without forgoing its facticity for a mystifying fiction, without—that is—seeking the simultaneity of the repetition that would, unauthentically, spatialize time and so redeem it. Instead of symbolic mystification, allegorical demystification; instead of spatial constructs, temporal deconstruction.

These terms prefixed by *de* force upon language a negative relation to human existence, but also—not altogether intentionally—create a negative vision of existence. Still, de Man tries not to yield up his primary dedication to a language that is shut off from existence, as he seeks to remain a linguistic, and not an existential, critic. He would have us retreat from a notion of the "original self" to the " 'linguistic' subject" (p. 199), trading the "empirical world" for "a world constituted out of, and in, language" (p. 196), a language in which "the relationship between sign and meaning is discontinuous" (p. 192). For language is hopelessly differentiated from the world and cannot bridge the chasm between them: the temporal void is revealed "in the narrowing spiral of a linguistic sign that becomes more and more remote from its meaning, and it can find no escape from this spiral" (p. 203). Consequently, we are told, applying verbal knowledge to the empirical world is an "impossibility" (p. 203). Accordingly, the poem is to yield to this referential incapacity of language. But since it is also an allegory of man as subject, the poem is being allowed by de Man, in spite of himself, to find a bridge after all, and cross over to thematize itself by illuminating our "temporal predicament" as existents. The semiotician in de Man cannot abandon the existentialist in him: treating the verbal sign as that which keeps us from touching our existential fate, he is simultaneously showing that language can contain that existential fate, though as a negative vision.

It is true that the later de Man tried to eliminate the too visible thematic shadow that I have shown trailing his semiotic claims, as he turned the written text more and more within its textual problematic, turning it into its own "allegory of reading." Still, this later position, though more markedly influenced by Derrida and free of terminology we associate with existentialism, is not discontinuous with what I have found in his earlier work. That "narrow spiral" of language has become narrower and is more consistently shut off from the "empirical world," so that there would indeed seem to be "no escape from this spiral" (to use the language of "The Rhetoric of Temporality," which seems applicable with greater force now). But there is still an appeal, though it is more submerged, to the implications of a negative existentialism, and with it a moral appeal to the human obligation to confront the nihilism of the "void," which, beginning as linguistic, still extends beyond to our "predicament." The text before us, trope within trope, trapped within its own figurational turns, returns us always to the problematic of its verbal character and, anticipating our struggle with it, becomes yet another in the endless line of "allegories of reading," tightening this narrow spiral within which texts—together and apart—wrestle with their own textuality. But in doing so it still reminds us of the nihilistic ground—or rather *un*ground—which permits the spiral to turn. The crucial word *allegories*, which de Man retains, will not permit the thematic to be excluded: once allegories are let loose—even those of reading—the spirals they spin tend to escape their own confines.

Hillis Miller, writing in the spirit of de Man and Derrida, substitutes for the metaphor of the narrow spiral the equally tormenting one of the *mise en abyme*. It represents the principle of infinite regress, what Miller calls "the Quaker Oats box effect."[7] Taken from heraldry, where it represents a shield containing an image of itself, which contains an image of itself, etc., the figure here obviously is to characterize the function of the word within the endless march of words we call textuality: in this infinite regress of words, the word cannot escape its network, and can have no appeal except to what de Man called "pure anteriority" or "unreachable anteriority." Once again it sounds as if what we are hearing is only semiotics and not at all thematics. But we cannot ignore—any more than Miller would want to—the existentially loaded

---

7. J. Hillis Miller, "Stevens' Rock and Criticism as Cure," *Georgia Review* 30 (1976): 5–31, especially pp. 11–12.

notion of the abyss in the word *abyme*. Being cast into the abyss by the metaphor, we must grant to the word *abyme* its full density as it describes a verbal crisis that is a reflection of our crisis as living creatures.

Nor does Miller flinch from the consequences of verbal gaps and blanks being characterized as an abyss, but a special abyss of the paradoxical sort the heraldic phrase reminds us of: "The paradox of the *mise en abyme* is the following: without the production of some schema, some 'icon,' there can be no glimpse of the abyss, no vertigo of the underlying nothingness. Any such schema, however, both opens the chasm, creates it or reveals it, and at the same times fills it up, covers it over by naming it, gives the groundless a ground, the bottomless a bottom."[8] This formulation clearly reveals the heavy freight of thematic content Miller is carrying, no matter how strongly he protests that it is a purely verbal structure and not a content he is accounting for. The elusiveness of discourse traps and displays itself, so that the inevitable linguistic movement toward infinite regress slips into the concept of infinite regress—whose home is in the abyss—with its conseqences for our existential vision. Strangely, despite the extravagant differences between the two movements, the now-you-see-it, now-you-don't paradox of this peculiar abyss sounds like an echo of the New Criticism, but so—I believe—does its thematic consequence. It may be an echo also of the early Miller, whose doctrinal allegiance was quite different from what it is now, but whose concern about "the disappearance of God" still haunts his theorizing.

We now can describe how thematization—of theory and, through theory, of criticism—takes place: As we watch, what begins as a pristine instrument of verbal analysis takes on substance, projects itself into a metaphysic that sets out the guidelines of the existential universe which circumscribes first this literary work and then every literary work worth talking about. The analytic method thus is analogized, but the two halves of the analogy invade one another, so that the analogy is allegorized. And the critic's guiding allegory works through figuration until his text becomes its own *figura*.

Viewed this way, the critical text is its own object as much as it is a

---

8. "Stevens' Rock and Criticism as Cure," p. 12. Miller's paradoxes remind me of Thomas Mann's in his *Doctor Faustus*. There Mann describes Adrian Leverkühn's late music, *The Lamentation of Dr. Faustus*, in which "the final despair achieves a voice," silence achieves an echo and "abides as a light in the night." (The translation is that of H. T. Lowe-Porter [New York: Knopf, 1948], p. 491.) The similarity—the paradox that allows negation to ground itself—is for me evidence of the intrusion of a lingering modernism in Miller's postmodernist enterprise.

commentary on a textual object outside itself. But this is very much how recent critical schools, committed to textuality and intertextuality in ways I have described, see the critical text: as no less sovereign than what we used to think of as elite literary texts and as in competition with them. We should note that, in the reflexivity of his essay, Miller goes beyond his literary subject and applies the *mise en abyme* to "uncanny criticism" and to his own work.[9] Once it turns "uncanny," criticism plunges into the textual swim, joining—as one among equals—the poem, its precursor poems, and fellow "uncanny" critical works.

Though I have elsewhere rejected the equal primacy (or equal lack of primacy) of poem and critical commentary,[10] it is useful to proceed here as if this now widely held claim had merit. For it is by accepting critical texts as occupying the same level of creativity as the poems they presumably are *about* that we can pursue the moral and ideological implications of recent critical modes. From the beginning of my historical survey in this essay I have been aware that, for the most part, critical theory too often makes no distinction between the question of the ideological claims for poetry and the question of the ideological claims for criticism, so that the first of these two issues is the only one addressed, the latter being dragged along automatically. But the elevation of the status of the critical text, at the expense of the poetic, permits us to ask about the ideological demands it makes as well as those it responds to. And we have seen in what subtle ways criticism has addressed concerns it had thought it taught itself to exclude.

Because I have focused here on the implied thematic interest of theories presumably committed to other interests, I can further isolate that interest by classifying a few critics and movements, placing them—in effect—in thematic genres normally appropriate to literary works. I would suggest, for example, that, trapped in the abyss, the negations of deconstruction represent something like the thematic side of the tragic, or perhaps only the pathetic. I propose this for de Man or Miller. Or, in a theory of spatial form the attempt to transcend history through the all-inclusive moment of myth may be seen as seeking an epic-like totalization. I propose this for Frank. And my own cherishing of self-conscious illusionary play in language and fiction displays some of the harmless, if hardly innocent, character—I like to think—of a thematic version of pastoral, the genre I propose for myself. The lyric? If I

---

9. Miller, "Stevens' Rock and Criticism as Cure, II," *Georgia Review* 30 (1976): 347–48.

10. See "Literary Criticism: A Primary or a Secondary Art," *Arts on the Level: The Fall of the Elite Object* (Knoxville: University of Tennessee Press, 1981), pp. 27–48.

were to include in my discussion the all-absorbing, triumphant romantic ego of a theory of influence like Harold Bloom's, I believe we would be exposed to the critic's version of the lyric. And if, to thwart all of these as well as the very idea of genre, I took account of Bakhtin, we could begin to talk—through the idea of carnival—about the critic's subversion of genres and his thematic dedication to *genera mixta*. Each of these suggestions of possible generic associations, of course, carries thematic and thus ideological implications with it. The history of literature amply demonstrates that formal genres, overdetermined thematically as they are, emerge soaked in the ideologies that spawn them.

But I would like to cut short these mere hints of possible generic equivalents before I seem to be advancing them literally, for they seem rather overschematized. Still, I find it useful to consider them. I have meant only to indicate the extent to which subliminal thematic pressures tend to shape the theoretical and critical texts of our contemporaries in directions not unlike those we find operating in primary literary texts. As I have suggested earlier, these pressures also shape what critical commentary, anxious to reinforce its theoretical commitments, makes of those literary texts it chooses—in response to its own character—to work upon. Commentary proceeds to thematize the text that it first selects and then reflects, thereby becoming—or rather remaking itself into—the thematic genre of the text that preoccupies it. But, since it is also commentary, it is a thoroughly self-conscious version, reflexive as well as reflective. So the critical text can move from the coyness of a pale image of its object text to the arrogance of a full-bodied substitute or even replacement—or such, at least, is its pretension, one that I have momentarily encouraged here. However autonomous the critical text is licensed to be by current theorists, we still must concede that its object is what—at least ostensibly—gets it going on its self-assertive, and thematic, path.

This self-assertiveness and its deviousness open criticism to being deconstructed by recent theorists of a very different sort from those discussed so far—social theorists, usually strongly flavored by political concerns. Speaking strongly for itself from motives that derive from extralinguistic, or even extra-aesthetic sources, what I have been treating as thematic—and, ultimately, moral—criticism becomes an object of study for those theorists, Marxists and some of those influenced by Michel Foucault, who have been hunting for hidden motives, mainly social and political, behind what texts are apparently seeking to perform. They would extend considerably—indeed exclusively—the suggestions I have made about the thematic and ideological underside of theory. For them no critical claim is as nakedly forthright as its explicit argument tries to make it appear to be; none is to be taken at face value, as limiting its argument to its stated intentions. Instead, what criticism has been presenting to its readers is treated as a complex linguistic device whose structures function as subtle instruments of social enforcement, repressing and excluding on the one hand, privileging and crowning as elite on the other.[11]

In this essay I admit I have been suspicious of theorists whose intentions seem directed away from thematic and ideological matters toward purely linguistic ones, and I have tried to expose in them allegiances not openly proclaimed. But the thematic implications I have sought to expose I see as emerging out of the language of the critical texts I have examined, as claims being assumed by the claims being made, and thus as themselves claims also being made. These are still textbound, then, and part of our interpretation. But, for the social critics I am now introducing, one is to break through what a critical text appears to be saying—its structural, poststructural, or thematic claims—to the political subtext that is really speaking through the apparent system which it controls. Reality is power, and social critics are Platonists breaking through appearance to reality. So theorists committed to uncover struggles for power nourish (and would foster in others) darker suspicions than mine—suspicions of conspiracies, largely unconscious, on behalf of social-political forces working through texts. After all, I do not complain about thematizing: I do not say that it is bad, only that it is inevitable, so that it is better confronted than denied in one's own work or in the work of others. For my observations here strongly suggest that all of us, one way or another, are part of "the moral gang."

But the theorists of social-political power are far more invidious in their suggestions about the primacy of ideology. Indeed, under their tutelage others have learned to treat the history of criticism (or of literature, or of discourse itself) as a disruptive series of disguised struggles for mastery and institutional domination through the use (or abuse) of the word. And they have introduced the study of texts exclusively as verbal emanations of historic institutional forces either

---

11. If this were an exhaustive study, as it is not, I would want to include, as a separate but related group, those Freudians—especially those influenced by Jacques Lacan—whose search for hidden subtexts is psychological rather than political, deriving from private rather than collective drives. But analysis turns thematic—and ultimately ideological—here too. In a representative critic like Shoshana Felman, the commitment to see through the text to a healthy reordering of master-slave relations between the sexes leads to a dissolution of otherness (through sexual self-difference) reminiscent of the French personalist ethic of the 1950s.

seeking or holding power. Ironically, it is a study that is itself repressive, in effect expelling, without embarrassment or self-consciousness, the more conventional study of texts as arguments capable of being attacked or defended on the weakness or strength of those arguments, as if they meant what they said. Instead, the text must always be given the lie by a political subtext that is allowed to overwhelm it. What has emerged is a method of writing critical history that is a radical alternative to what had been the usual way: instead of the history of the succession of argumentative structures that succeed or fail in solving the problems they address, we are to trace the history of the struggles of institutions to gain and maintain power through the manipulation of the discourse they create out of their need.

To return to the ground I so hastily surveyed at the start, we need not search far, in examining writers from Plato to Pope or even Johnson, to find in the mimetic structures and metaphors of their criticism privileged reflections of the social order, as they would have it: the structures and metaphors of their culture, as they would preserve it. Their reification of objective systems, metaphysical and moral, which then solicit imitation by poet and critic, serves social-political needs effectively. Still, we must today be concerned about the vast difference between our asking of a theory, what it means to say, explicitly or implicitly, and our asking of it, distrustfully, on whose behalf it is saying what it does. The first question assumes a theory to be a systematic representation of claims, while the second would deconstruct that representation, would break through the theory to hidden claims whose representation is being suppressed or disguised, though they are being secretly advocated. To ask the second is to produce an ideological suspicion that leads to a suspension of our interest in the first, more straightforward, question. If we wish to exhaust the meaning of critical arguments by citing their causes in their collaboration with institutional (or anti-institutional) powers, then our history of criticism can be considerably simplified—and reduced.

Viewed this way, the old New Critics, speaking a language formed by the totalization of nineteenth-century organicism, can be shown to resemble their forebears in harboring reactionary social functions for literature, though these serve a later historical moment. They would foster the privatization of vision, though collectively—if only subliminally—propagating and extending the ideological imperialisms of which Edward Said and Fredric Jameson have written. And more recent criticism, "after the New Criticism," similarly performs its surreptitious service for a retrograde culture when it is carried out by the

Theory and Institutions

"mandarin" critics stacked together for attack by Frank Lentricchia.[12] The notions of irony in the New Critics and of textual self-deconstruction in the Yale School are seen as acting similarly to reinforce the status quo by inducing the paralysis that stifles action. Everywhere the "political unconscious" is seen as writing texts that are responsive to its will to power, the varieties of strenuous argument lost in the sameness of retrograde service to ideology. Even current anti-ideological theories are seen to have their sources in ideology, so long as we look with the eyes of this kind of social critic. The intention of such negative theories is converted, for the ideology-seeker makes positive use of all things and all persons—and all texts.

Although through Foucault they maintain their own poststructuralist connections with the realm of semiotics, the ultimate appeal of these social critics is to historical realities beyond language in the social structures and their material basis, as these determine human behavior. This is the source of their struggle against all text-bound critics from the New Criticism to deconstruction. Hence, as social-political, these are, indeed, the most moralistic of all the theorists we have discussed. We need not strain to force them toward a thematic statement when they make such statements openly as the other side of any semiotic claim they may make. If I wished to find a thematic genre for them in the literary classification I tentatively put forward earlier for the others, I would have to reach beyond the genres of poetics and assign them to rhetoric, in Aristotle's sense of that ancient art as one devoted to the powers of persuasion and the persuasions of power. Their political interest guides their analysis of the work of others—whether of poets or of critics—especially work which most often is seen to violate that interest, as it guides their own work, which apparently seeks to serve it. But presumably their habit of going right for the subtext, whatever the diversions of the text proper, gives them a nose for the rhetorical function both of the texts on which they comment and of the texts which they write. The difference between the two is that their own text, sponsored by their awareness of the rhetorical secret beneath all discourse, is obliged to be self-conscious—whether in fact it is or not—as it unmasks those other texts that presumably do not know themselves. As master explainer, their own text must explain the ground for all texts,

---

12. Among other places in the writings of each of them, see *Orientalism* (New York: Pantheon Books, 1978), *The Political Unconscious: Narrative as a Socially Symbolic Act* (Ithaca: Cornell University Press, 1981), and *After the New Criticism* (Chicago: University of Chicago Press, 1980) for Said, Jameson, and Lentricchia, respectively.

including itself, thereby joining the others within a Dantean circle of language, in which all are damned, and none innocent. And the ground which that text has explained falls away, for the deconstructive urge cannot find a place to bring its activity to a halt.

This final turn that should make their own discourse reflexive—and my present one as well—exposes us all to the *mise en abyme* that traps even our motives within language with its many false bottoms. Discourse, deconstructed, is turned inward upon itself again, an insulated, reflexist textuality. Still, the ideologist will remind us, there remain, outside, those desires that would shape language to themselves as they seek to shape history in their direction. These desires would subjugate the text to themselves, the subliminal masters that make us distrust all that is said. But when we try to reduce an alien discourse to desires, as they are turned into words they are themselves ungrounded, becoming just another ideology of discourse. On the other side, as we have seen, even a skepticism as profound—indeed, as abysmal—as deconstruction's does not foreclose ideology. Thus there is the continually mutual undoing between the deconstruction of texts to extratextual motives grounded in material reality and the deconstruction of texts into the vortex of textuality—though this is a move that can also be seen as ideological, just as the ideological, in order to assert itself, must convert desire to textuality.

All this is in the background while there remains also the old-fashioned urge to apprehend what the undeconstructed text is trying to claim, were it given a chance, to apprehend that claim and to judge it as a claim to be true. The text may be seen as a devious ideological instrument indeed, *and* it may be seen as just one verbal stage in the reflexive series within an unending spiral; but would we still not do well—after registering and remembering our reservations—to let it make its claims and to examine them on their own, as if they were disinterested stabs at the truth? What I have sought to demonstrate here is that, whether as a rhetorical manipulation of language needing to have its subterranean motives unmasked, or as the infinite regress that undermines the very project of verbal representation, or as a series of words making a claim to meaning which asks to be apprehended and agreed with, literature and the critical language that surrounds and competes with it work their confusing way into the realm of thematics, make their moral demands, and have their ideological impact.

In the critics upon whom I have commented in detail, words and verbal sequences, at the semiotic level, cannot (or, at least, for these and other critics, do not) form the pure subject of criticism but become an analogy—ultimately a *figura*—for experiential commitments (indeed, ideological commitments) which they would subvert, but which they manage only to submerge. If I were to generalize from these examples, I would observe that, like its predecessors from whom it differs so remarkably, modern theory, sometimes in spite of itself or sometimes self-righteously, turns thematic. To thematize is to moralize; and to moralize is to ideologize, even if in the negative way of denying any escape from language. Ideology, masking itself as morality—if not moral philosophy—remains very much alive among us and, indeed, within us, capturing us all for "the moral gang" even as we undo the ground on which that gang can plant its flag. Still, as an act of human will, how can writing itself be other than a moral act, and its objects (yes, objects!) be conceived as other than fellow moral agents, companions to us all?

Literary Invention, Critical Fashion, and the Impulse to Theoretical Change: "Or Whether Revolution Be the Same"

Dialogue

The desire to universalize our experience, to affirm the unity of *being* over the ever-changing variety of *becoming*, is as old as the philosophic urge, an urge we as thinking creatures have known since the dawn of humanity. Trapped within what our own experience permits us to see, we retain the need—as old as Plato's in his war against the Sophists—to try to account for what we must believe is outside those limits, ready to be experienced by everyone. But the philosophic urge in us seems opposed by what Bergson saw as the temporal flow of our experience, which is constantly differentiating itself, though the universalizing impulse wants to prevent us from seeing that differentness. So we tend to reify the common elements we presume to find, treating them as universals that enable us to freeze the ever-changing flow of experience, and then we congratulate ourselves for our philosophic perspicacity.

But this universalizing is exclusively spatial because the very notion of time and its changes is enemy to the desire of our intellect to contain and give structure to the varieties of historical experience. Indeed, the intrusion of a precise and discriminating historical conciousness has long been a deconstructive act because, in introducing change, it gives the lie to our

This is a revised and considerably enlarged version of a paper delivered at the plenary session of the sixteenth Congress of the International Federation of Modern Languages and Literatures (FILLM) in Budapest, August 1984.

universalizing ambition by relativizing it, that is, by subjecting it to its place within our necessarily partial and contingent perspective. Change thus makes our universal claims no more than creatures of our historically determined needs; it reduces theoretical grandeur, built on a single, time-defying, all-inclusive structure, to the culture-bound relativism of permanent revolution. In the realm of pure temporality it is as hard to clutch at a constant as it was way back in the realm of paradox ruled by Zeno. For when it comes to our grasping at solid things, the realm of temporality *is* the realm of paradox.

To the extent that our theoretical ambition is undercut by the historical persistence of change, we must see universal claims downgraded from the truths we attribute to nature to the deluding reifications projected by the partisan interests of historically conditioned institutions and their agents. So change replaces theory, institutional sway replaces nature. And the language of theory, for all its ambition, is seen as responsive only to its self-serving assumptions rather than to the external data it pretends disinterestedly to account for. It can be treated, then, as just another expression of an archive preserved by its moment in history; it is not permitted to step outside that archive even long enough to explain either that moment in history or anything else. Where all is historically contained and controlled, there change will reign, an enemy to all universals but itself. Of course, the claim that change is the only universal is a self-denying one in that the dynamics of change should not allow even that single universality, since that would acknowledge a sameness about change. Still, our time-bound condition seems to encourage us to affirm change, in all its ever-changingness, as the only timeless truth we would, though with some embarrassment, allow to stand.

I have been assuming an either/or relationship between theory and change—to admit one is to exclude, even preclude, the other; but one could seek to bridge this disjunction by proposing a theory *of* change, such as the theory of progress or of cyclic repetition. There is a special temptation to absorb history's moments within one narrative form or another. But I would put aside such proposals by pointing out that they *are* simply other theories, disguised versions of spatial thinking constructed out of closed, all-encompassing metaphors.

It is hardly new to observe the scholar's necessary habit—because he has a theory—of converting history's accidents into pattern. Once it has happened, history does appear irreversible. I prefer to treat change more radically, as a temporal particular which represents the errant moment in its momentous potential to disrupt the formation rules that govern all theories, antihistorical theories as well as theories of history.

Words themselves are major perpetrators of our self-deceiving habit of reifying our experience, freezing its temporality into their own ontological space. Their very being militates in favor of theory and against a fluid experience. The substantives we use, with their deceiving implication that one word represents one thing, suggest constants beyond history's changes. Even as we may describe radical changes from one historical moment to another, we retain the generic noun and with it the sense that it is a common, *essentially* unchanging entity that is undergoing minor, though untransforming, alteration. If we ask, "What is it that changes?", the language of the question itself persuades us to a single, constant "it," whether it be "art" or "the aesthetic" or "poetry" or "drama" or "fiction" or whatever, as we allow the nominal subjects to trick us into essentializing them. It may be, as some poststructuralists might argue, that the generic term, representative of a static nominalism of language, has indeed induced us into a false essentialism, so that we have, not the changing single entity (the "it") we think we are talking about, but only a constantly shifting field of differences which we carelessly mislabel as if it were one thing.

Still the theoretical impulse in us persists and need not be altogether denied. Our discourse requires those very universals which may render that discourse untrustworthy because it blurs the facts of change. Nevertheless we can, in our antinominalistic description, point to the fact that culture *does* function and establish its continuity by means of the verbal genres it holds onto in spite of the shiftings of time. Culture takes its generic nouns seriously, even literally; it allows those generic nouns, as its linguistic norm, to shape its development: from the inside, culture uses its myths to function and to produce more culture. These are effects that the historian and the theorist must take account of, regardless of what the demythologizer may persuade us is really going on outside the comforts of those productive, if deceiving, constructs.

But I have now, by way of language, moved these issues into the realm of literary history and literary theory, and in no area is the conflict between continuity and revolution, between the designs of theory and the randomness of invention, more evident. Seen from the ambitions that give rise to it, literary theory exists to create a discursive unity that can accommodate history's variety, to synchronize the diachronic. Making transhistorical claims, literary theory seeks systematically to account for a broad variety of works of many periods and literatures, flattening out the changes—even the apparent revolutions—that occur among them. Until recently, without self-questioning, literary theory has traditionally assumed that there *is* literature, and thus that there are peculiarly literary works; that consequently there is a legitimate discourse that creates a system to illuminate the performance of each of these works and—by extrapolation—of that body of works lumped

together as what we create as our literary canon. Critical discourse and theoretical discourse about criticism were thus legitimized, and the criteria for our judging the relative value of this discourse rested upon those secure assumptions concerning the primacy of those literary works to which such secondary critical discourse or tertiary theoretical discourse was ultimately to be beholden.

But these so-long-secure assumptions have been not only put in question but also utterly undermined in recent years. Instead of judging the face-value claims made by rival aesthetic systems to account with consistency for the special kind of writing to which they were responsible, we are to see these claims as contingent upon other-than-theoretical objectives. There has been a shift in emphasis from questions about the *inside* of theory—what does it account for? what does it leave out? does it, in the relations among its terms and propositions, argue acceptably?—to questions, apparently from *outside*, which put in doubt the theoretical enterprise itself: what are the pressures leading to the position taken? what is the relation between its principles and its favored literary works? what nontheoretical subtext leads it to the critical judgments it asks us to make? in other words, what are its historical contingencies, however transhistorical it wants its claims to be?

This shift reflects the recent transfer of interest from what we have called *literary* theory to what is today called *critical* theory. The earlier secure ambitions of literary theory have been turned problematic by the critical theorist who deconstructs it by exposing its contingencies. But as we gave vent to that deconstructive impulse, which I have here related to our consciousness of temporality, we created a theoretical discourse beyond what we had earlier thought of as theoretical discourse—a metatheoretical discourse, the only discourse that is now allowed to be genuinely theoretical. From this high ground we could view earlier so-called theories as bivouacked within their unchallenged parochial assumptions, assumptions that now could be demonstrated to be historically or linguistically or institutionally contingent; they could no longer be assumed without self-deception, the self-deception of a pretheoretical naïveté. (For example, a movement that thought itself as theoretical as the New Criticism did can now be declared *un*theoretical in that it failed to undermine itself by acknowledging its own extratheoretical motives.) So *critical* theory (or metatheory) these days, perhaps in imitation of what the critical philosophy of Hume and Kant did to the metaphysics of the eighteenth century, means to put what we previously thought of as theory out of business by ungrounding it. And what we used to think of as "extraneous" issues, as issues irrelevant to the theoretical project, become those that are central to our concern.

Theory, then, is no longer to be treated as an insular, self-directed enterprise. Of the many kinds of pressures (social, political, literary, or whatever) that help shape what may masquerade as the pristine theoretical claim, rendering it anything but pristine, I'd like—in view of our subject here[1]—to concentrate upon the influence of literary fashion in creating critical fashion, upon the role of literary invention in helping to justify critical invention. Literary and critical fashions can be interrelated, and their recent sequence traced, even as we seek to avoid an easy overall narrative for them. Since I earlier ruled out the assimilation of change—and hence of changing fashions—to an all-consuming theory of history structured according to any myth of progress, I must treat them—without hindsight—as a sequence of wayward accidents, each subject only to local forces and not to a rationalized, timeless pattern. In our present theoretical context, it is not impertinent, or an indulgence in idle academic gossip, to concern ourselves with fashion and, consequently, with the politics of criticism and even the imperialism of critical movements, along with their invented theoretical justifications.

Indeed, we can look at the history of recent criticism—especially as it is related to the privileging of one or another kind of literary work—as a succession of would-be empires, movements that have gone through similar stages in their rise and—too soon thereafter—their fall. If we take the word *movement* literally, in thinking of literary and critical movements, we find in it this group commitment to change, to forgo rest for activity itself. This need of a movement to keep moving finds itself in continuing conflict with its desire to establish itself as a dominant, unchanging institution.

Each movement, as a would-be empire, can be seen as deriving its force for change more from the kind of literary culture it wishes to bring into being than from its commitment to advance its internally directed argument toward theoretical truth. It is thus related to literary change as the latter stimulates the rise and fall of literary fashions, with a subservient literary criticism anxious to defend and expand the influence of a particular brand of literary invention. Does critical or theoretical invention follow upon literary invention in its attempt to justify it, does it anticipate literary invention, or is the relationship between the two symbiotic, the interplay of two sides of a single inventiveness? The answer to this question can hardly be determined, and in any case it is probably less important than our need to recognize the contamination of theory by the world of literary fashion.

---

1. The general subject of the Congress was the relationship among literary change. linguistic change, and critical change.

Theory and Institutions

Some years ago Emerson Marks introduced a phrase, "pragmatic poetics,"[2] which I find extraordinarily helpful. Marks used the phrase to describe those poetic theories which derive much of their motivating force from the special kind of poetry that they are trying to license. This seems obvious enough: one cannot know Dryden without recognizing that much of his criticism was intended to validate specific poetry styles, that his "Essay of Dramatic Poesy" was written in part to justify the changes he introduced into dramatic styles and forms. Nor can one read Wordsworth's 1800 "Preface" without seeing the extent to which it is meant to serve as a document in poetic politics, so that it has the pragmatic function in the end less to create a new theory than to make way for a certain kind of poetry, a kind of poetry which Wordsworth is writing and which is not being admitted into the canon, to create—in other words—room in the canon for entries like his which are otherwise likely to be rejected. In order to change the criteria for entry into the canon, one must transform the theory, because each theory authorizes the inclusion of certain works and the exclusion of others.

Early in our own century T. S. Eliot's criticism undertakes a similar task. Eliot's important essay on the Metaphysical poets, his review of the Grierson anthology, sought to persuade readers to take this anthology and these poets seriously, although room had to be made in the canon in order to justify our seeing them as having a place within it. And this was the task of Eliot's essay. So, viewed from the role it seeks to play in the history of literary taste, poetics can indeed be seen as pragmatic. Though the critic's text is apparently addressed to the solution of theoretical problems—to finding adequate and coherent descriptions of the poet's creative act or the reader's poetic experience or the poem itself resulting from the poet's act or stimulating the reader's, together with the function of all these acts in society—it may actually be meant to create a taste which can sanction transformations in the kinds of poems that are written and read, to prepare poets to write them and audiences to read them. In such critical works we can glimpse the dream of literary empire.

Let me use the fortunes of the American New Criticism as a model of the history of critical empire. As I said, the movement begins by seeking to make room for a kind of poetry that until this moment has not been accepted, to authorize and justify changes that a new school of poetry is seeking to introduce. But first it has to get rid of the kind of poetry that has been the most readily accepted. So it attacks texts of that

---

2. Emerson R. Marks, "Pragmatic Poetics: Dryden to Valery," *Bucknell Review* 10 (1962): 213–23.

kind, as Eliot and those who followed him into the New Criticism attacked poems of the romantics and Victorians and Edwardians and Georgians, viewing all these as a continuous hardly changing development without a disruptive theoretical moment in it. To counter these they reintroduced an entire school of poets, in this case the Metaphysicals, which had not been taken seriously as candidates for the canon for a long, long time. One could not take them seriously while holding the canon based on romantic and Victorian poetic values. And for the New Critics the two kinds of poetry seem mutually exclusive. Their preferences require and are accompanied by a literary theory that justifies them. If I seem to be cynically reductive in this account of the genesis of the New Criticism, it must be remembered that I am talking now as a historian might when he looks at the succession of critical movements rather than as a theoretical scholar might when he surveys a number of rival seekers after aesthetic truth. Still, the symbiotic relationship between revolutionary developments in literature and in literary theory seems hard to deny.

We can note, for example, that one of Eliot's major doctrines is that of impersonality, the need for the poem to avoid reflecting the autobiographical poet, so that when the word "I" is used in the poem, it must be seen as referring to a dramatically conceived character rather than to the poet's person. This is just the doctrine needed to reject the one kind of poetry—the romantic—in which the poet seems to invest himself autobiographically and immediately, without dramatic distance, in the "I" of the poem. The "I" in Shelley's lyric seems to be Percy Shelley himself and not an invented persona, just as the "I" of "Let us go then you and I" in *Prufrock* does *not* seem to be the living, breathing T. S. Eliot. Justifying this shift is a theory of romantic poetry in which the relationship between the "sincere" author and his poem can be utterly unproblematic, so that we can slip easily (too easily for the New Critics) from "the man who suffers" to "the mind which creates" (in Eliot's words). It is this distinction which, Eliot argues, the modernist poet must use his medium to reestablish. Since, for this theory and the contemporary poetry that accords with it, Donne and Marvell are much more acceptable precursors than anyone who wrote in the nineteenth century (or in the eighteenth, for that matter), what must follow is a rewriting of the whole history of English poetry with a new set of heroes and a new set of villains, and with a new poetic canon emerging out of it. The first step in the creation of the critical empire has been taken—knock down the old gods to set up the new—following the model of political revolution.

This opening stage of empire is forcefully undertaken by the New

Critics, as just about all authors from Milton to poets immediately preceding Eliot are newly excluded from the tradition which, having moved through the Renaissance poets to the Metaphysicals, is seen as having been suddenly disrupted, and, after a gap of centuries, at last as having its continuity restored with the coming of the modernist poets. This radical rewriting of the history of English poetry is formalized in 1939 by Cleanth Brooks, the model New Critic. In *Modern Poetry and the Tradition*, his last chapter, "Notes for a Revised History of English Poetry," is just the revision that Eliot licenses, with everything from the beginning of Milton until the beginning of Eliot somehow a mistake, a tradition gone wrong. But with Eliot we have a refreshing of what should have been the tradition all the while, so that we can now move along with it.

The first movement of the empire, then, is the most radical one. It is youthful, it is vigorous, and it is incautious, if not—from the distance of a future moment—a little silly, but it gets the job done of putting the new empire in place of its predecessor. Only eight years after *Modern Poetry and the Tradition*, Brooks published *The Well Wrought Urn*, and in this book we discover a second phase of empire. Eliot is just in the process of recanting his own attack on Milton, and Brooks is recanting many of the exclusions of his earlier book. *The Well Wrought Urn* is devoted largely to those poets who were excluded before: between the opening with Donne and the closing with Yeats, we find Milton, Pope, Gray, and even Tennyson himself. (I have overlooked Shakespeare and Herrick, poets who had always been acceptable.) Those previously exluded poets have now become candidates for *The Well Wrought Urn*. But we note that Brooks's first chapter is on John Donne and bears the title "The Language of Paradox." It sets forth a model for the striking discovery that Brooks has made: that he should not have excluded these other poets since they really were in the tradition after all, but only because, if one looks closely enough, they can be made out to be just like John Donne in being filled with paradox. The same names are now seen to have produced profoundly changed poems, though they are poems with the familiar titles and words.

Here is the second stage of empire: the empire relaxes, it learns to include, though always on its own terms. Those that the empire in its early vigor had turned out it now absorbs by way of a totally new reading controlled by the terms established by those privileged writers to whom those being newly admitted can be assimilated. The appearance of catholicity rests on a universal rereading, so that all literature reveals a universal sameness, a sure sign that the movement is about ready to disintegrate.

Catholicity, then, is a disguised form of hegemony: scholars working in every literary period on all sorts of poems are now enabled to find a renewed critical awareness, can write endless "reconsiderations" as the monolithic method accumulates its all-too-consistent interpretations. The ensuing weariness leads to a restlessness that will produce countermovements. We are well into the third stage, with the empire in decline. The pretenders to a successor empire derive their motivation from the desire to restore to primacy those poems at first rejected or at least neglected and later brought back only under what subsequently appears to be the false colors of an alien standard.

In the case of the dying moments of late New Criticism, it is the need to recover romanticism—in its unbounded vision and spirit—that stimulates first dissent and then overthrow. The year 1957, with the publication of Frye's *Anatomy of Criticism*, is properly thought of as the turning point. From this time onward there is a continuing desire for newer, revolutionary movements, although a common interest in opposing the New Criticism and recovering romanticism is at work in them all. In order to recover romanticism, it then seemed, one had also to recover the author, recovering consciousness as well as vision, so that in the late fifties and early sixties the interest in Frye is accompanied and surpassed by an interest in the "critics of consciousness." Frye and those who tried to create a school of Frye rejected the study of individual texts as microsystems, the New Criticism's self-sufficient contexts. Instead, for them literary works were conceived of as displacements of the universal archetypes themselves, all by-products of the single-quest myth that assimilates all works to its universal dream. This dream, the grand collective that is literature, must be treated as the capacious haven that converts all apparently particular works into its categories.

But Frye's prodigious project, despite the efforts of the apostles that it managed momentarily to capture, was challenged almost at once by the critics represented in America by Georges Poulet. J. Hillis Miller displays his conversion to the so-called Geneva critics from his work in the late fifties—at least until he is converted away from Poulet and to Derrida in the early seventies.[3] Miller and other "critics of consciousness" are interested almost exclusively in just those questions that the New Criticism would have ruled out, namely, the extent to which the

---

3. A good place to spot this shift in the very process of occurring is Miller's "Georges Poulet's 'Criticism of Identification,'" in *The Quest for Imagination: Essays in Twentieth-Century Aesthetic Criticism*, ed. O. B. Hardison, Jr. (Cleveland: Case Western Reserve University Press, 1971), pp. 191–224.

Theory and Institutions

work reflects authorial consciousness, becomes part of a phenomeno-logical horizon, projects the author's "feel" of his reality as it figures itself to him. There is a rhapsodic union among the author, the world of his work, the characters he creates, and the reader, as all pour into one great bath of consciousness. The critic ought not to distinguish for analysis the reader's experience from the author's consciousness, or either from elements in the literary work, because they all blend into one another. Such blending, such absorption of represented events and characters into a fused consciousness, is characteristic of the appeal of that romantic imagination which the New Critics had outlawed and which criticism in its wake was seeking to recover.

Shortly afterward, structuralism, borrowed from Paris, entered the scene as the new movement. It was committed to *difference* as its governing linguistic principle, and thus rejected the emphasis on identi-ty fostered by consciousness critics, their bringing together of author, work, and reader into a single undifferentiated consciousness. Structur-alism, in its reaction against existentialism, had to reject consciousness itself as a mystifying point of origin. The structuralist is committed to the primacy of language, so that, in his flight from origins, he sees the "I" not as a representation of authorial consciousness but only as the grammatical subject of an utterance that calls for a predicate. Instead of all verbal creation being traced to its origin in the author's *cogito*, as in Poulet, it is—as Roland Barthes would say—language itself that writes texts, so that texts are created by other texts, thanks to a notion of intertextuality that quickly turned structuralism into poststructur-alism.

Each of these movements that follow the New Criticism has its own imperialistic ambitions, so that each begins by appropriating works with which it is most comfortable at the expense of others. Indeed part of the reason for the theory to press its claims is that it wants to account for the spirit of works that have been left out of the corpus associated with earlier criticism, especially the New Criticism. We know how exciting Northrop Frye is on Blake, and he should be, since it *was* his interpretation of Blake that expanded into his general critical system. The last portion of his book *Fearful Symmetry* sets up in miniature the categories out of which his *Anatomy of Criticism* will grow. So Blake is the figural subject for Frye, as will be other writers engaged in what he thinks of as the quest romance. While he deals persuasively with such writers, it is more difficult for him when he turns to Milton or to those works of Shakespeare which are less conducive subjects for him. Still, Frye and many of those who follow him put themselves in jeopardy as they move into the imperialistic stage of their enterprise, seeking to extend what works so effectively with certain literary texts to authors and works we would think of as less hospitable and try to make them work as well. Or we may observe that Poulet seems to be writing over and over again about his ideal subjects, Proust and Mallarmé, even when his nominal subject shifts—even to as apparently alien an author as Balzac. In the transformation that Poulet—with imperial confidence—works upon Balzac, all becomes misty as Poulet dissolves Balzac's heavily furnished social reality by absorbing it into an airy vision formed through his primary commitment to other writers.

I do not mean to suggest—as perhaps I have—that it was the desire to supplant and reverse the American New Criticism that got these movements going. Some of the European origins of these movements occurred without any knowledge of who the New Critics were or what they were doing. And there are ample philosophical reasons related to developments in aesthetics, as well as in psychology, linguistics, and social theory, to explain why these movements came along as they did and when they did. Still, on the American academic scene the adaptation of these movements for domestic use in the classroom can be related to a general and severe reaction against the New Criticism, and, even more, a reaction against its privileged texts or its rereadings of texts to make them privileged, in favor of other texts and other rereadings.

In the United States structuralism moved to poststructuralism so quickly that the structuralist vision itself almost never took hold on its own. Beginning with a widely attended international seminar on "the structuralist controversy" held in the autumn of 1966 at Johns Hopkins, the transformation to poststructuralism was taking place. At that conference a young philosopher named Jacques Derrida, only a year before he was to publish three books that were to institutionalize deconstructionist thinking, delivered his blockbuster essay on "Free Play," and poststructuralist deconstruction was here before structuralist construction could finish its work. From this point most writers whom people might identify as structuralist were busy demonstrating what made them *post*structuralists as they dissociated themselves from what they saw as the somewhat mechanistic works of theorists like Genette or Todorov or Eco. The previous drift toward diagrammatic method and toward the false security of the social sciences turned another way; and to the name of Derrida the names of Michel Foucault and Jacques Lacan—a considerably older thinker suddenly now brought to center stage—were added. Foucault gave us a new way of thinking history, returning history to the structures of language that shape it in the

Theory and Institutions

directions toward which the rhetoric of power presses its forces. Lacan gave us a new Freud by rooting the unconscious in sign functioning.

But it was the Derridean and post-Derridean versions of deconstruction, as adapted to the literature classroom, that made the serious bid for empire in this country, carrying many newly won followers with it. And it is not difficult to find among many of those seeking to implement this thinking the desire to license some writing that the New Criticism would not permit and that the modernist movement in literature would not sanction. As our modernist giants seem to call for the New Criticism as a way of getting themselves read and adequately interpreted, so the experimental postmodern forms we encountered after World War II now seemed in the deconstructionists to find a theoretical justification.

We see the easy companionship of modernist literature and the New Criticism as early as the work of T. S. Eliot, their major precursor and announcer both as poet and as critic. In Eliot and in his followers modernist poetry and the criticism that licensed it walked hand in hand. Further, the kind of poetry being sponsored in the university writing workshops and the rapid growth of the workshop as an agency for writing "official" poetry as well as novels reflected what was being called for in the English departments by the younger New Critics who had taken their place in the academy. But as the literary movement grew tired, rich with its successes, other young scholars became as tired of the so-called academic poets as they were of academic criticism, having had a surfeit of both. They were ready to welcome a kind of criticism which could license a poetry that had freed itself from what were looked upon as our most neoclassical modernist formulas for closure.

The deconstructionist critics seemed to provide the justification for finding a new, opening voice or—what became more common as the movement grew—for imposing that newly discovered voice on those older works we thought we knew under other guises for so long. In their earlier days what happened, in effect, was that Wallace Stevens as a modernist model was out, and William Carlos Williams as a postmodern model was in. Similarly, the Ezra Pound associated with Eliot was out, and the Pound associated with Williams was in. That is to say, they abandoned the modernist tradition of poetry emblematized as the well-wrought urn—whether the golden bird of Byzantium or the Chinese vase of *Burnt Norton* or the jar of Tennessee. This was the tradition that developed from the French symbolist poets through Yeats and Eliot to the late formalism of Stevens, whose poetry represents in a special way the modernist poetic because, as the ultimate act of closure, his carefully wrought poems quite self-consciously become their own poetic. Instead, they embraced the radical postmodern attempt to turn poetry into a much freer, looser, open association of relaxed words, not so much wrought as merely talked, and thus, in their discontinuities, more closely in touch with everyday life and language. So the poetry that is sanctioned moves, as I have said, from the kind of verbal intensity found in Stevens to the casual prosaics found in Williams.

It must be conceded that in the modernist critical movement there was—for Hillis Miller, for example—another, more modernist version of Williams, less unfit for the company of Stevens, as later there would be for him another, postmodern version of Stevens. Indeed, for Miller both Stevens and Williams are his subjects, and made to serve his critical interests, at the several different stages in his theoretical development. These divergent readings of major modernist and/or postmodern voices, like the alternating emphases given to the widely varied work of Pound, help mark out the succession of literary and theoretical moments for other poets and for critics.

I can trace this theoretical succession, with Stevens and Williams used as respective model poets, more easily by using Joseph Riddel as our exemplary critic. Like Miller, Riddel had early been deeply influenced by the work of Poulet, writing his book on Stevens out of that attachment. Shortly after Miller, at the beginning of the 1970s, turned against Poulet to endorse the newly discovered Derrida, Riddel followed, turning to Williams and writing his second major book, *The Inverted Bell: Modernism and the Counter Poetics of William Carlos Williams* (1974), in which the treatment of Williams is introduced by a lengthy and controlling chapter on Heidegger, surely an unlikely precursor for Williams. Williams is presented as the "decentered poet" who practices "the poetics of failure" in order to counter the poetics of modernism. The replacement of the previously idolized Stevens by the previously neglected Williams is the expected first move toward empire. Riddel and others who share his deconstructionist commitment now license many writers—for example, a newly conceived Pound—and repress others.

But the second stage follows, that of imperialist expansionism, as they rediscover (among others) Wallace Stevens himself, who, it now turns out, is really postmodernist more than modernist, a riper subject for the deconstructionist than he had been for the New Critic or (later) for the consciousness critic. James Joyce, a modernist superstar, similarly becomes a welcome postmodern subject for other poststructuralist critics, for example, for Riddel's student, Margot Norris. Even Ralph Waldo Emerson finds himself subject to Riddel's transforma-

Theory and Institutions

tions. So the canon, which is enlarged or even exploded at the start of the movement, tends after awhile to turn out to be not so different after all, even though the readings within it *are*. By now, in a development of this revolution that makes it all too like the earlier revolution of the New Critics that it seeks to undo, just about everything seems to have become grist for the deconstructionist's mill as the movement starts its decline. Examining work after work in the infinite openness of literature, or of criticism as literature or theory itself as literature, the deconstructionist finds in the very nature of writing the tendency to turn against itself, to suffer—through "troping"—the necessary burdens of "erasure" and "double inscription" (their terms) so that the deconstructionist can do his work on an immense variety of subjects in the different writing genres throughout the several historical periods. Through the hegemony of theory, universal sameness conquers once again, and the impatience of readers of criticism that leads to overthrow seems sure to follow. And the newly reborn social-historical critics have been waiting in the wings.

I acknowledge, however, that I myself have been guilty here of turning recent academic experience into a theory, reducing history's sequence of changing moments into the march of sameness, thereby denying each marcher's claim to be different. I have converted the temporal into the spatial structure of *my* narrative forms. For the human mind cannot allow history to unroll without projecting a form upon it: our formal, universalizing impulse would make theorists of us all. The need to proclaim the differentness brought by each agent of revolutionary change is always in conflict with the sameness of the enterprise that proclaims it. This need is in conflict also with the imperialistic desire— and hence the program—to impose this special version of differentness upon others, thus making it their sameness. There is always the temptation to allow the commitment to the phenomenon of change to freeze into the commitment to a single, privileged change in an often self-deceived attempt to universalize it.

The threat to the newness of present change by the compelling uniformity of the past reminds me of Shakespeare's Sonnet 59, the twelfth line of which, as the climax of its three quatrains, expresses succinctly the theme of this essay.

If there be nothing new, but that which is
Hath been before, how are our brains beguiled,
Which, laboring for invention, bear amiss
The second burden of a former child!
O, that record could, with a backward look—
Even of five hundred courses of the sun—

Show me your image in some antique book,
Since mind at first in character was done,
That I might see what the old world could say
To this composed wonder of your frame:
Whether we are mended, or where better they,
Or whether revolution be the same.

"Or whether revolution be the same." It is indeed a most fitting title for me. The proclamation that something new has occurred, in light of which nothing can ever be the same, that here is a change that transforms history, is always threatened with the grudging concession that it has happened before, with as much ardor, and just this way. The Adamic dream of a new origin, though based on the denial of older "myths of origin," has its unintended inner irony too easily exposed. Even the specially strenuous claims of recent deconstructionism that it has undermined the ground for all previous thinking has been followed by a more skeptical awareness that sees it as a continuing element in history instead of as history's undoer.

The tendency of the self-proclaimed revolutionary to become the imperial expansionist reminds us that literary history and theory can—especially these days—be seen as slipping into the realm of the fashionable. Indeed, my own earlier reduction of theory to the contingencies of its extratheoretical motives has emphasized the dependence of theory on the historical march of changing fashions. It is this march to which I have already denied the rationalization of a progressive shape. Each new fashion, undermining theory as a stabilizing force by privileging only the most recent disruptive change, leads to the idolatry of the new, especially the new-as-revolutionary, as the changer, though by now our skepticism should keep us from thinking it necessarily, or even probably, better than what it seeks to replace.

Probably it was the New Criticism that initiated this obsession with being fashionable some decades back, just as the succession of rapidly moving theories—most of them with short lives—began only with the demise of the New Criticism. Fashion, as an extraneous but significant stimulant for theoretical allegiance, probably entered American literary institutions with the New Criticism by the late 1940s and the 1950s. That is, the New Criticism was the first of the movements to attract followers to itself as *the* fashionable movement, the movement of the moment. By the mid-1950s, large numbers of young people, often with uncritical alacrity, were jumping on the New Critical bandwagon, turning out explications by the dozens, like eggs. I suspect that was the beginning of the major role played by "fashion" in stocking movements in American criticism with followers.

Theory and Institutions

The New Criticism was the last theoretical movement that enjoyed the great good fortune of having no important theoretical competitor on the scene, perhaps because it was the first American critical movement that meant to found itself on an explicit, though often poorly formulated, theory. To be sure, there were early versions of Freudianism and Marxism that offered themselves as alternatives, but these—in the early forms that marked their entry into literary criticism—pretty well wiped themselves out by being rather superficial and often simplistic in their claims and their readings. They are not to be confused with recent, theoretically serious uses of Freudianism and Marxism that coexist with poststructuralism and have become important participants in the theoretical debates. But their earlier versions were hardly competitive. So the New Criticism had the scene pretty much to itself and exercised a dominion that for years brought aboard it (or behind it) larger and larger numbers of derivative scholar-critics. The major arguments then used against the New Criticism were, almost entirely, arguments against theoretically based criticism itself, usually in the name of historical scholarship or social relevance, rather than arguments for an alternative theory.

Once past the New Criticism, perhaps we felt instinctively that we had made a mistake by trusting in one movement so long and so fully without any competitor. That may be one reason why we have, after the New Criticism, changed allegiances so often during the recent succession of movements I have been tracing here. A more likely reason is that once theory, having been introduced for the first time to an American academic audience, found itself in the academy, it began to pursue its concerns with such intensity that, inevitably, a considerable variety of competing theoretical kinds was to replace the relative hegemony of the single theory that the New Criticism represented. Once, thanks to the New Criticism, the Pandora's box of critical theory was opened, we became too overwhelmed by the flood of questionings and self-questionings for a single set of answers to satisfy very many for very long.

So either we learned not to be so monolithic in our theory and thus sponsored an increasing variety of competing theories, or our increasing interest in theory simply prompted more and more varied theoretical proposals to vie for supremacy. Or both. Whichever the case, since the decline of the New Criticism there has been this rapid succession of competing movements. Only a very few years ago many of us believed that finally a movement had thrust itself upon us—the first since the New Criticism—that might claim as general a following and as unquestioned a dominance, however vocal its antagonists. I am speaking, of course, of the deconstructionists, represented in the United States most vividly by the so-called Yale School.

It did seem for awhile that deconstruction might well achieve the kind of broadly based following and lasting control that would permit it a reign that would last a little while, even if not as long as the New Criticism did in our earlier innocence. This succession was made the more ironic since some antagonists presently accuse the Yale deconstructionists of domesticating Jacques Derrida's practice of deconstruction—subjecting it to the Western literary canon and to American pedagogical habits—thereby turning it into a newer, if more reckless, version of the New Criticism. However, those expectations of an extended period of dominance by deconstruction were short-lived, because it has now become clear that it does not sustain anything like the sway that the New Criticism had: having barely arrived, it is already, I think, showing signs of being on its way out, even in the United States, which has held onto it longer than Paris did. Right now the threatening successor is a new social criticism, sometimes referred to as new historicism, which usually derives from the work of Michel Foucault and is sometimes reinforced by a neo-Marxism. Though Foucault clearly specifies his serious differences from Marxism, his work is seen by many Marxists as being compatible with their interests, even when they are anxious to assert their disagreements with him. These groups have been doing battle with the deconstructionists, treating the latter as lately arrived formalists trapped within textuality and hence cut off from the sources of social power. In its aggressiveness this group appears clearly to be in the ascendancy.

As we would expect from theorists so concerned with the role of power, the new historicists and their methodological allies—whether Foucaultians or neo-Marxists, or feminist versions of these—can be seen as also moving through the earlier stages of empire in accordance with my narrative model. Much of their initial energy was spent seeking to reshape the literary canon by introducing into it works previously excluded. From here they were led to question the grounds for the inclusion of all its members. They reviewed the canon in order to sensitize us anew to the role of dominant discursive formations in the shaping of its individual member-works, so that the latter are to be seen as reflections of the historical dispositions of power. Armed with these political claims, they could dispute the grounds used by our culture to support the selection of the members of the canon since these would require value criteria that were now to be rejected as politically suspect. The canon, erected on hierarchical principles, was seen as privileged by a power structure that excluded all that would challenge its dominance,

Theory and Institutions

so that a newly arising power could persuasively argue for introducing works previously repressed by the supporters of the canon: from feminist, minority, and Third-World writings before excluded by sexist, racist, and ethnocentric pressures within the dominant culture. Now, these theorists were, presumably, not arguing for such writings to be canonized since they rejected the very notion of canonical value as an elitist deception. It would be a crucial tactical and historical error, they argued, to try to show that these excluded works shared desirable properties formerly seen only in works of the dominant culture, so that they could be admitted to the club only on the old terms. Their argument means to be far more destructive of their predecessors, all now seen as so many minor alternations with a hegemonic discourse serving a political unconscious in need of being confronted and redirected.

An egalitarian principle, on the other hand, would insist that these works be admitted for reasons of justice and the need to compensate for a political repression that previous claims of aesthetic value had served to disguise. Yet these moves have been following an imperial strategy like the one I suggested for the others: they begin by reshaping the list of works to be read and studied, and then, with an expanding ambition, enlarge upon the arguments for this reshaping in order to reread all the texts in the canon, re-creating them to accord with a universal claim that would change the way we approach all texts by revealing the primacy of the political unconscious. Of course, there seem to be reasons to think that the new historicism represents a movement more revolutionary than previous ones because it would undermine all the distinctions that allowed those others to vie with one another, seeing them all as trivial distinctions, inconsequential varieties within a middle-class series of competitive dances now unmasked by historicist analysis. But we have before seen such radical claims of total deconstruction (of all that preceded) appear from the distance of time as less than utterly disruptive after all. Rather than the undoer of previous theories, then, this one, too, may turn out to be only another competing theory to join the ever-enlarging dialogue.

So the conflicts among divergent critical theories in the United States continue, and we are not likely again to have a generally recognized commanding doctrine for an extended period of time. Too many of our younger would-be theorists, anxious to be in fashion, do not know which way to jump, or for how long. They too often try to be sure that it is onto the latest thing moving. Thus I have been led to take that word *fashion* seriously, however trivial it seems, because the trivial *is* serious in this matter so long as one is trying to record the history of contemporary critical theory in the American academy, in which fashion, and the idea of the new, have become important motivating forces.

Our recent concern with whether or not a particular critical perspective is in "fashion" makes us argue over whether or not it is "new" or whether it used to be "new" but now is old, whether it has been superseded by a perspective that is "newer," and whether the perspective I am about to pull out of my pocket is "newest" of all. It is amusing—but, I fear, more than that, too—to observe the failure of self-consciousness and of historical awareness in our critical theorists or historians of theory as they throw about that adjective "new" in dealing with the "old New Criticism," the "newer criticism," or—as some defenders of the Yale School (or those who would already claim to succeed them) sometimes use the phrase—the "newest criticism." The adjective can be thus thrown about as if the user were not fated to live long enough to watch it fade, with the passage of time, into a joke that history helps it make upon itself. At earlier moments in the history of criticism, other movements of course have thought of themselves as new and even called themselves "new." But it is self-evident that only the failure of a historical perspective could permit the pursuit of being fashionable—the latest thing going—to sanction the absurd appellation "new" which history must render vulnerable almost as soon as it is uttered. Only because what we used to think of as the "New Criticism" is now old is it necessary for its successors to be thought of as "newer" or, most absurdly of all, as "newest."

The use of the qualifier "post" is at least as bizarre, if one views it within the precincts of history. "Post" has had to be invoked mainly because of the historical naïveté that permitted the use of other words, like "new," which already represent the latest thing. But, once the latest has become only belated, something must come after it in order to give the lie to the most-up-to-date-ness of the word now being passed by. The now of the new has become then, in which case the new must become old. But since the word new is not changed, we now have to have something that is—paradoxically—post-new. Thus we have the "post-New Critical" or, more strangely, the current discussions of "postmodernism" as our rebellious successor to "modernism." Those literary movements, I have suggested, are accompanied by the fashionable and new doctrine of "structuralism," which has been succeeded—as we all know—by the post-fashionable, post-new doctrine of post-structuralism. What sort of conception of time is required to conceive of a postmodernism—as if modernism were not newness enough—I find difficult to describe, although it is clear that our commitment to the pursuit of the newest fashion—in literature as in critical theory—has permitted us to use these terms without the embarrassment they ought to bring with them. Yet with the latest "newest" or the last claim of "post"-ness, must history stop now, now that its eschatology has been announced by the superlative beyond which there is to be no further "post," nothing newer? For we must note that the prefix "pre-" is *not* in use, since there is no sign that current movements, for all their commitment to a continuing temporality, want to look beyond their own present to a future they might prepare for. After Matthew Arnold critics have not—like him—offered to sacrifice themselves for a movement yet to come. We rather have wanted self-consummation, not mere *pre*figurings.

Here we return to the central irony for all fashionable movements at the height of their imperial power: the rejection of the past for the new, newer, newest, and post-newest is accompanied by the desire for change to have a stop with this last—very last—change. So change does indeed seek—in each instance—to universalize itself. Even in its most radical undoing of the universal pretensions of theory, change manages to make a claim of its own privileged truth, applicable generally beyond the limited perspective, the time-bound contingencies it would impose on others in bringing itself into being. It is in this form that the theoretical urge persists even in its antagonist, even—that is—in spite of the antitheoretical critique which is a metatheoretical critique that would subvert this urge. And even the critic who as antitheorist would be a metatheorist, the critic who would use the contingencies of change to make the insulated objectives of theory no longer tenable, finds himself playing the theoretical game.

So whether in literature, in the theory that would accompany it, or in theory-*as*-literature, change is the blessed creature of invention, beyond all theories to predict; but fashion is the seductive betrayer of change, leading it into dogmatic fixity—and hence into theory—in spite of itself. Given the appetite of our theoretical urge, which victimizes would-be antitheorists as well as theorists, how could we not expect fashion, despite its dependence on temporal changes, to seek—however vainly—to bring change to a stop, to want not to be surpassed? Even the speaker in Shakespeare's sonnet, having come down to the defeatist concession, "Or whether revolution be the same," nevertheless concludes—in the spirit of the myth of progress—by affirming in the couplet the superiority of the newest arrival: "O sure I am the wits of former days / To subjects worse have given admiring praise." We can reinforce this conclusion with the stronger claims of other sonnets

(Sonnet 106 is perhaps the most brilliant example) that the superiority of the latest arrival makes him an ultimate consummation, a permanent realization, the end to history:

> I see their antique pen would have express'd
> Even such a beauty as you master now.
> So all their praises are but prophecies
> Of this our time, all you prefiguring.

"Permanent revolution" has been converted to a revolution for permanence.

Whether in Shakespeare's sonnet or in theory, where the claim to continuing difference thus ends in a single model for emulation that would produce sameness, a mental construct has been put forward, beyond history's contingencies and secure against further change, with all the risks of that daring, positive act of construction. With each new movement, history is eventually revealed to have had a hidden agenda, a suppressed desire for an eschatological finality realized only now. Revolutions are not fought—with all their disruptions of the past or what is now being turned into the past—only to prepare for further revolutions that would turn this privileged present also into the past.

However, as in Shakespeare's sonnet, the word *revolution* may be read another way, promising not disruption but the patterned turning of the earth itself in the circular movement suggestive of universal order. We have spoken of "revolution" only as the noun deriving from the verb, "revolt"; but by etymological accident it is also the noun deriving from the related verb, "revolve." Though the act of revolting asks for no more than one turn—one reversal—it may be seen as but a part of a larger revolving which goes beyond by bringing the turns around, and turning yet again—and again. However paradoxically, "revolt" and "revolve" may equally claim the noun "revolution" as its own—or rather the noun "revolution" may be seen as encompassing both, absorbing the disruption of one into the larger continuity of the other.

So, "revolution" may, in spite of itself, be converted into the routine, taming change by taking its *dis*continuity out of it. Where "revolution" in this sense is found to be "the same," there theory can with some dubious confidence begin again; and change—for all the temporal disruption it threatens—can, we hope, be accommodated after all. But even in going this far I speak not as a champion of theory so much as its victim, though a willing victim.

Theory and Institutions

Because I am theory's victim, I must carry these oscillations to one further swing. My treatment of these post-New Critical fashions in theory has emphasized their narrowly political character—that is, it has emphasized the role they seek to play in the politics of criticism in the academy and the rival claims to power within that limited domain. But within those modest, intramural, clubby empires, we have seen imperial ambitions shaped also by a serious and honest concern with the workings of literature, though workings shaped as each competing theory would shape them. Still, these interests, like the pragmatic poetics that they foster, enable us to view these movements not as attempts to answer theoretical questions within their own realm so much as attempts to re-create a history of literature and take control of the interpretation of literary texts.

Recent social and historical theorists, in a rush to replace the deconstructionists with their own new prominence, would be quick to point out that I have too narrowly restricted the extratheoretical motives of these movements to matters of literary preference, to questions about which works were to be valued and what in the works made them worth valuing. In other words, social theorists would charge that I treated the "pragmatic" in the pragmatic poetics that concerned me earlier as exclusively literary, despite the fact that many other pressures related to desire—social-political pressures, economic pressures, psychoanalytic pressures—drive critics to shape their theories as they do and, they would argue, are more crucially causative. We can see literary criticism and theory as the more deluded about the purity of their theoretical quest as we move the subtext of that quest further and further from the "literary" sphere, but critical theory in its social-political dimension is to set us straight. So these days the pragmatic motive is offered the more insistently as it leads us away from the ostensible objective of literary theory. Perhaps I have implicitly acknowledged as much in my free use of political metaphors (words like *hegemony, empire, domain, revolution,* etc.), thereby confirming the ease with which the literary slides into the political and the political into the literary. The role of power in creating acts of repression and exclusion in the social-political metaphoricity of our language has been well established by Foucault, and recent theorists boldly expand his insights and ally them with Marx's in order to bring deconstruction back to the material realms of power from the play of intramural textuality.

Having conceded as much as I have to the pragmatic as it diverts us from theoretical pursuits apparently addressed to problems strewn across theory's path, I still want to suggest the value of examining theoretical problems, and proposed answers to them, in their own right, as if they were independent of the hermeneutics of suspicion. In doing so I have been assuming that these are questions worth discussing in their own right, as if the critical texts, with their theoretical implications, had a speculative objective that made one more satisfactory than another: as if, in other words, the theoretical game is one worth playing. Yet my own earlier concern with the pragmatics of critical theory, and especially of recent critical theory, might well suggest that the hidden agenda or subtext undercut the pretensions of theories to mean what they ostensibly mean and to accomplish what they ostensibly accomplish. Does the interest in pragmatics, especially when shown to be insidiously directed by social-political institutions, preclude the theoretical enterprise as one that can be undertaken without self-deception?

This question becomes the more urgent with the increasing dominance of the new historicism[4] as the latest post–New Critical theoretical fashion. Its own social-political focus leads it to see all theory as a surreptitious rhetoric, pursued out of a desire not to solve problems but to manipulate attitudes. At a colloquium in the School of Criticism and Theory not many years back I recall Stanley Fish (a new pragmatist more than a new historicist) exclaiming, "Power is the only game in town," and Edward Said—from the other end of the political spectrum—shouting his assent. As we in the American academy saw in the late 1960s and early 1970s, it may not have been unreasonable for students to make the charge—and for faculty to respond sensitively to it—that the treatment of literature that bestows privilege upon self-consciousness and irony seemed a shrewd and efficacious tactic for ensuring political paralysis by undermining the clear lines of programmatic doctrine upon which political commitment and, ultimately, political action rest. Such a criticism, after all, permits in its canon of works only those whose thematic complexity ensures the evasion of any ideological commitment. Hence the New Critical theorist was seen as the servant of the status quo and of the military-industrial complex that guarantees the status quo. The poststructuralist school of textualist deconstruction today inherits the political charges previously leveled

---

4. I remind the reader that I want to apply this phrase to a group far broader than those Renaissance and other scholars in sympathy with the so-called *Representations* group. For my purposes here, various theorists, not only Foucaultian, but also Marxist and feminist, are included in my use of this term, despite important differences among them. For they share methodological similarities in attributing a deterministic role to the power relations within a culture that impose themselves upon its texts.

Theory and Institutions

against the New Criticism, thanks to its own entanglements in the web of self-undoing meanings which, it is claimed, cuts textuality off from the world. But, as we have seen, the charge of the social deconstructionist is still broader, claiming that the history of Western theory, up to and including textualist deconstruction, consists of so many staged debates all locked within a common set of exclusionary political assumptions that trivializes their differences.

This attempt at social deconstruction, which claims a rising popularity these days, would bring the enterprise of literary theory to an end altogether by relegating its announced mission to the realm of bad faith. For this rhetoric of power is, of course, using its argument to make its own bid for power, whether political or merely academic. The one difference between it and its predecessors is that its devotion to pragmatics as agent of both deconstruction and its own theory means that its bid for power is more naked than that of its rivals.

The arguments that could be used against such political reduction are the ones we have become familiar with when others have made similar moves in the history of theory. They depend, I fear, on resurrecting the author as a willful "subject," if I may use a term now rejected as obsolete. Granted the hold that our moment in history and history's institutions have upon us, have we no freedom of will to formulate and address a problem, and to construct our discourse in order to cast light upon that problem? Granted that we are often self-deceived in our belief that we think and write as utterly free agents, granted that the subjects we choose to write about are not "natural" subjects for us so much as they are institutionally imposed, is all that we work so hard to make our texts say only a disguise for the attempted manipulation of a reader by the subtext? If an effect of our reverence for literary interpretation should be that master texts would complicate the desire for a life of political action, does this destroy our analyses by turning us into agents of the counterrevolution? Even if it could be demonstrated that one extraneous effect of a given theory was that it restrained the revolutionary impulse, are we justified in arguing that such an effect was actually the reason the theory was being put forth, leading us to reject the theory as having been maliciously conceived as part of a general conspiracy? Or should we examine a theory's claims, even if the hope of doing so disinterestedly is a scholar's naïve ideal? To vitiate those claims by inpugning their motives, and to impugn their motives by calling a subsidiary effect a primal cause—and, consequently, to impugn our motives as examiners—is to revert to a determinism that has been effectively refuted in the past. In other words, is this recent social theory, beneath its newly sophisticated language, finally distinguishable in the thrust of its argument from the political reductionism we remember from the "vulgar Marxism" in the America of the 1930s?

The easy dismissal of manifest content, the result of the writer's labors at the surface and the interstices of his text, in the interest of the latent content supposedly unearthed by the highly motivated, strongly programmed interpreter, justly arouses the suspicion of other interpreters, although these latter had better also beware of their own motives, whether they search for other latencies or focus upon the so-called text itself. Our propensity to misread texts willfully in order to make them serve our goals, like the writer's similar propensity to write texts that way, need not preclude our possibility of saying something about the text as our ostensible object, or the text's possibility of saying something about *its* ostensible subject. Surely, we are the farther from those possibilities as we deny ourselves the chance to read the manifest text by asserting that only the latent text, together with the power relations to which it points, is "real." The unabashed Platonism that denies manifest appearance for latent essentiality is no less objectionable for assuming a politically fashionable shape. Nor does the adding of a psychoanalytical turn of the screw help much to allay our concern for this rejuvenated simplification of the problem of verbal representation.

But what about the capacity of the text to generate a complex of oppositional meanings? In response to this, the best of the new historicists, like the best in any movement, are far less doctrinaire about their reductions. Many of them are sensitive to the problematic character of verbal representation, so that they would avoid the naïve simplism of the deterministic claim that a text must be treated as a reflection of the subtextual political pressures that create the dominant language of which it is an example. They prefer to respond to the capacity they find in a text not only to resist the hegemonic discourse, but also, through its own internal play—free play, perhaps?—to subvert it. I find such a response, in the spirit, say, of Theodor Adorno, persuasive, but is it still what is today called the new historicism? Such a conception of texts, and especially of literary texts, as internally cultivating their language of critique has been vital outside this group, to theorists whose concern with history and society is enriched and deepened by textual analysis rather than the other way round. I am thinking of those influenced by the rediscovered Bakhtin and his interest in the dialogical function of texts, in their carnivalizing effect, as they move toward the heterogeneity of the novel, the latter seen as both literary antigenre and index to social dispersion. It is this constant press toward textual resistance and opposition that has more recently been extended in the work of

Lyotard, a major voice with a significant following. Here, too, there is a ubiquity of political metaphors, though they are generated by the *différends* of the text.

This response to the text's power to sponsor resistance to the dominant discourse argues for a relationship between history and text that treats the text more as an agent and less as a servant—counter to the thrust of much new historicism. Still bound to history and its language, the text is yet free to affect, indeed to transform, history and its language. Of course, most new historicists would accuse those who would attribute this power to the text with cultivating aesthetic paralysis, with indulging in a flight from commitment all too similar to that indulged in by those in the tradition of romantic irony from Friedrich Schlegel to the New Critics to Paul de Man. (They might also have to include among these their apparent ally, Adorno.) So we must confront in the text either the reflection of the totalizing discourse of ideology or permanent revolution through the multiplication of discourses of opposition: either words to support action or words to create continual blockage, not so unlike the old doctrine of aesthetic equilibrium. Today we are witnessing a debate between these versions of textual relevance to political power. It would be bracing, if perhaps old-fashioned, to feel that we are free to choose between these latest competing bids to set the fashion.

I have made my way back to my concerns about the pursuit of fashion, the quest for the "new" which, once it becomes old as it shortly must, is followed by the quest for the newer and then the newest. And on and on, fostered by its historical naïveté, it will go. But the stakes become higher when, with an intolerant presumptuousness, the newest bidder for fashion would, like some of the new historicists, end the game altogether. In effect, they would put theory out of business: they would reject for good the claim of any theoretical discourse to possess an about-ness. Instead, this rejection of theory would wrap critical discourse about itself, narrowing its circles within its own hidden motives as revealed by its subtext, thereby creating its own form of closure from which no gleam can escape to illuminate what claimed to be objects of independent thought. Should we not resist allowing the power of fashion to dictate the end of our earnest habits of continuing our philosophic questing and questioning, whatever the limitations of an operation that has always proceeded *as if* it can indeed shed more light upon the old and new, but still dark, shadows of our doubts? I have respect for the fictional force of the "as if," but I have more respect for the not altogether forlorn hope of light, even of the merest glimmer.

A Meditation on
a Critical Theory Institute

Well, here we are. We have persuaded an always resistant institution, the university, to create an unlikely, indeed a threatening, institute in its midst, one dedicated to questioning the status of every academic discipline. Yet critical theory has developed so far and has aroused so wide a following that, despite its potentially subversive character, it is being allowed institutional status by the institution that is its host. But I must ask—perhaps painfully—which has infected which, and, as a consequence, which of the two must we fear has allowed itself to be undone: the granting (if grudgingly granting) institution outside, because of the critique it now looses upon itself, or the newly licensed institution, ours within, because of the self-contradiction its new status brings with it? But let us worry about ours, about the extent to which our institutional status marks the end of our theoretical discourse as we know it in its struggle to maintain an anti-institutional character. Thus this paper is to combine celebration with warning: to combine cheers for our becoming an institutional entity, able to bestow all the goods that go with it, with questions about whether—as self-sustaining gadflies—we should have allowed it to happen. Indeed, I had considered putting slash lines through the last three words of my title (Critical Theory Institute) to indicate that

---

This essay was delivered to open the colloquium held in April 1987 at the University of California, Irvine, to celebrate the founding of the Critical Theory Institute on that campus.

each of them might be cancelled under the pressure of the others. Still, I decided not to in order to remind myself that my intention here was to be more optimistic than that and was rather to emphasize the possibilities for coexistence among criticism, theory, and an institute, so that even in the presence of the others, each might survive, and even thrive.

Still, this occasion reminds me of my doubts about our enterprise. As I have said, when I meditate upon *critical* and *theory* and *institute* as interacting with one another, I find that, in what should be their mutual mediation, each threatens and is threatened by the others. And I believe that the recent history of our theorizing has only exaggerated my sense of these dangers. Let me look at this history as it impinges on these three terms and affects our hopes for their coexistence.

In isolation each of the terms seems secure enough. So I'll begin there, and with *theory*, but taking the word as a substantive rather than as a modifier of *institute*. Coming as I do from the domain of literary scholarship, I look there, and I see the emergence of theory some time back—say, around mid-century—as the attempt to systematize developments in literary commentary. When a few years ago I suggested the framing structure, "words about words about words," to describe the generalizing sequence leading—in reverse order—from the individual literary text to a single commentary on it to the theoretical grounds for that commentary, I was characterizing the way in which the theoretical interest was first attached to a literary study that had for so long tried to do without it. And this was the conventional way in which theory was imposed upon (or rather was seen as growing out of) our critical and reading activities. On the American academic scene, it was the New Criticism that sought to systematize the ways in which we were to read individual literary works and to read them with a critical eye. Slowly, this critical practice persuaded the wary and resistant world of literary scholarship to accept such ways of reading, as well as the critical values implied by them, and to recognize that, insofar as they were systematically controlled, they were being guided by a general literary theory, an aesthetics of literature, a poetics. Theory, then was seen as a supportive structure for critical practice. It was to account for how criticism proceeded, or should proceed: a theory for criticism, a theory of criticism, a theory—then—justified by how well it served criticism and—through criticism—the world of canonical literary works always standing in need of illumination in order to serve its culture, as it would if criticism as its handmaid functioned appropriately. And criticism would function appropriately if *its* philosophical handmaid literary theory, furnished justifiable supports. So the academic licensing of criticism freed up the theoretical faculty to operate and to be open for inspection, though always to be mindful of its obligation to the literary text. Eventually flaws were discovered, not only in the theory itself but also in its claim of authority over criticism and text, flaws that broke the hegemonic hold of the New Criticism and left theory free to move on its own, less subservient to the interest of "close reading" that first sponsored it.

The profession then became more conscious of the ubiquity of theory, no matter how its members chose to conduct their literary business. No longer beguiled by the delusion that the sequence from the reading of a text to the critical authorization of the reading to the theoretical placement of the criticism moved in an empirical direction from experience to judgment to justification, we increasingly recognized that the movement may well have been in the other direction, despite our most faithful empirical intentions. But if our theoretical assumptions, the leftovers of our previous readings, had to be already there to shape the present reading of this text, then the critical enterprise might well be a sham, merely confirming what we already had coming in. To reverse direction is to reverse priorities, and in a way that puts in doubt the entire succession of words about words about words, with its easy referential assumptions. The upward movement from the reading of the literary text to the setting forth of an authorized reading (criticism) to the systematic rationalization of that authorized reading (theory) had set up a series of origins and dependencies, of receding references from the primary to the secondary to the tertiary text. But once that movement was inverted, so that what had been thought of as the tertiary text was already present to condition—and thereby to deny—the primacy of what had been thought of as the primary text, our theoretical awareness could break free of its dependence on critical practice. As long as the canonical text had stood authoritatively *out there*, we could justify bringing theory into our critical function as another serving discipline that would help us to perform our more immediate serving discipline more effectively. But theory's epistemological rebellion against this subsidiary function allowed it to claim not only independence from but also mastery over the several acts—separate or collapsed—of reading, interpreting, and judging texts since only a theoretical subtext could have constituted the text for us to apprehend in the first place.

At this point theory begins to detach itself from literature, which is now itself denied as a distinct kind of text requiring a special criticism backed up by a special theory (poetics). Theory has developed a new set of words, a fourth level, as it were, that rejects the ambition and the hopes of all the other words about words about words that had concerned critics and theorists in the heyday of literature's and criticism's authority. Having originally been justified as a support for literary criticism, theory came to undermine it, to deny it as an act of good faith, to unpack its deceptive or self-deceptive maneuvers. Theory, then, is no longer theory *for* the criticism of literature or—more precisely—theory *for* a criticism that is *for* literature. Indeed, theory is no longer *for* anything but itself, although in the process it has become the agent of its own critical faculty.

The detachment from theory itself—insofar as it consists of texts that set forth a structure of argumentative claims—must soon follow. Theory is no longer *literary* theory but has become *critical* theory, theory that turns against itself. Rather than a philosophic system expounded to enclose a group of texts in order to open them to an attendant criticism, it has become a mode of *critical* philosophy in Hume's or Kant's sense of the word *critical*. Rather than presenting a fixed theory, it does not go beyond a theoretical thrust that, critical (might we say "deconstructive"?) in its workings, would unground the self-assured discipline it represents, represents only while assailing it. It would make us see what claims to be a one-way referential activity as no more than a self-sustaining circular one that has already created what it then takes pains to "discover." This sense of "critical theory" may be seen as a widened version of the Frankfurt School's use of this phrase—widened in that recent critical theorists have at their disposal a broad range of undermining weapons, of which the social-political is but one. In effect, this sort of theory, *critical* theory, undermines not only literary criticism (in the most usual forms we found practiced in its heyday during the New Criticism) but also theory itself, insofar as it was a literary theory, a theory that grounded the criticism of literary texts. In the view of recent movements, then, once you bring theory to bear, you can no longer sustain criticism; but once you bring the critical faculty to bear, you can no longer sustain theory. "Critical theory" is really, by now, "critical of theory." This is how far the mutual antagonism has developed between what had been two self-assured disciplines.

The antitheoretical tendency in recent theoretical writing can become quite extreme when we view it in work from Stanley Fish to *Critical Inquiry*, new style, to *Representations* and the Berkeley pragmatists and new historicists. In the place of theory we find various, though similar, programs of critical moves aimed at the authority of theory—indeed at the very possibility of theory, or at least the possibility of any theory that was not self-deluded about its claim to authority. While any theoretical system would have to claim some universalizing applicability—that it may be applied with a warrant beyond the contextual confines of its own discourse—that claim is denied in advance by the demonstration of historically conditioned textual contingencies that prevent its breaking out. A theory, in other words, must seek to transcend the conditions of its own formation; but the contingencies in which it is embedded keep it from rising beyond them. Any hidden assumption of its own disinterestedness is undercut by the interestedness of the historically constrained circumstances that define it.

Of course, the constraint upon our thought imposed by historical contingencies is hardly a new discovery, and the claim that the transcendent pretenses of theory are only rationalizations produced by the disabling enclosures of historical circumstances has often been made before, although we are now being forced to accept the extremest consequences of such truisms, as we had not before. Would-be systematic thinkers have long worried that they had to utter their theories as if they were not themselves caught in the epistemological trap and in the trap of language—in the egocentric and linguocentric predicaments burdening philosophers at least since the critical philosophy of the later eighteenth century. They have built systems and sought to apply them generally despite the knowledge that their own historical circumstances, the conditions of their discourse, seemed to foreshorten its reach: these create a hermeneutics of suspicion that should close down their operation by precluding its theoretical ambition. Recent theoretical writing, as antitheoretical writing, insists on pursuing the limitations imposed by our epistemological and historical self-enclosures to claim the total incapacity of the theoretical enterprise. It would leave very little, if anything, standing of even the most self-consciously cautious constructs of those would-be theorists who tried their best to transcend their prison house even while acknowledging it. Not that these antitheoretical claims are not themselves theoretical in character. Obviously, I believe that the theoretical urge will not down, that theory will and should persist, if only in a critical form that threatens all institutions—and institutes. So I assume that I can still speak of "theory" though I now refer, not to an inclusive global system, but to the critical view of theory adopted by theorists in their antitheoretical intent.

We can observe this slippage of the *literary* from *literary theory* and the *theory* from *critical theory* in the shifts that occur from the New Criticism to structuralism to poststructuralism. Literary theory, which we have seen to support the New Critical procedure, is generalized by structuralism into undifferentiated textual theory, though still global—indeed, even more global—in reach, with the *literary* dissolved into the generally textual. It is the poststructuralist moment, whether psychoanalytical, social-historical, or linguistic, that de-globalizes all theoretical vain-glory into the unsettling notions of deconstruction. I can, then, summarize the recent history of the mutually cancelling relationship between criticism and theory as a movement from theory of (or for) criticism to theory *as* criticism of the practice of criticism and from there to theory as criticism of theory as a system. We have moved, in other words (or in the same words but with radical changes in their meanings), from a theory of criticism to a criticism of theory, although today it is theorists who practice the latter, whatever its self-destructive (or self-deconstructive) propensities.

We see, then, that the collision between the first two terms of our title, *critical* and *theory*, would eliminate both of them as substantives in order to turn them adjectival, however secure their nominal status once seemed to be in isolation from one another. Of course, it is as adjectives that these terms in our title precede that firmly erected and solidly standing proper noun, *Institute*. But it is this word *Institute* that will unsettle the other two even in their already unsettled state (or rather their state of motion, or *unstate* of motion). For to create an institute is to reify those forces, once more ontologized, that criticism and theory, in their mutual undermining, have sought to keep from fixing themselves. And an institute is the ultimate fix. At this moment, then, ours would have to be an institute dedicated to the anti-institutional—in effect dedicated to its own undoing—if we are to allow its two-headed epithet, *Critical Theory*, to use the forces of mutual antagonism to impose adjectival restraint upon the noun for which it is responsible.

It is clear that there is something in the notion of an institute that seems alien to the individually subversive tendencies that have marked the efforts of many recent theorists. On the other hand, an institute would seem justified if we applied the organizational model of scientists banded together in commonly agreed-upon goals and criteria for achieving them. The scientific is a collaborative model that permits disagreements, but although these disagreements may reflect differences in proposed hypotheses, they do not for the most part shake an unquestionable agreement about elementary, or basic epistemological, conceptions of the very character and function of the collective enterprise. About these there is to be consensus, and on this consensus the scientific institute, with its common purpose, is jointly founded. An institute in the humanistic fields might thus be assumed to follow the scientific model by sharing such an idea of consensus. Not surprisingly, it was theory in its older, more systematic sense that is seen as representing as much of science as the humanities could be expected to sponsor, and so as the obvious discipline on which to ground collaborative work in those areas. What, then, could be more natural, if there is to be a single discipline leading the humanities into the communal life of an institute, than that theory, science's undercover agent, be thus singled out?

But I have been claiming quite the contrary: that the deconstructive spirit of recent humanistic inquiry argues against this role for theory because it precludes this definition of theory as the architect of the systematic agenda for agreed-upon areas of study. To the extent that our theoretical activity has been impelled by the critical impulse, it is denied the status of theory-as-humanistic-science. In the earlier naïve versions of theory that I have described, when it was—with confidence—assigned the task of bringing order to the fields of humanistic discourse, it may well have been seen as the overseer of "the sciences of man." Now, under the deconstructive critique, this is a task as obsolete as that phrase. Indeed, in its recent forms theory appears to be as calculatedly opposed to scientific objectives as Kierkegaard's *Concluding Unscientific Postscript*, and on not altogether dissimilar grounds. Consequently, it would seem to be in flight from the idea of an institute that it would see as deadening in the ontological threat that mutually supportive theoretical activities project. For, as with Kierkegaard, it is the ontological from which theory today is primarily in flight. And it is precisely the ontological to which it is exposed in spite of itself once the theoretical school, as a collective, institutionalizes itself.

As we have observed, the theoretical spirit these days sponsors critical moves that must continuously resist the fixity of critical movements, and it is just such movements that, tending themselves toward institutionalization, an institute would seem to foster. Even the resistance to the institutional, once it turns collaborative, is itself in danger of becoming institutionalized, whether as a common quest for knowledge or as a questioning *of* the quest which, once made common, makes its own claims as knowledge. These claims would result in a positive status for knowledge from which recent theoretical inquiry, perceived as a negating discipline, must recoil. We can conclude that the model in the sciences of the group experimental laboratory, exerting its collective pressure upon those participating in its mission, hardly serves the single private humanist, armed only with pen, typewriter, or word processor, in order to do battle with the blanket ambitions of theoretical zeal. At the same time, it must be conceded that, as soon as the words "single, private humanist" are uttered, they rebound with awareness that all theorists write only in silent conversation with the texts of others, predecessors or colleagues. Consequently, to have such fellow voices turn into live companions in an ongoing present dialogue, as in an institute, can only be exhilarating. Still, even if any claim about

Theory and Institutions

the humanist's isolation proves self-deceptive, his or her relation to the work of cohorts must resist the easy collaboration that may characterize the expectations of an institute in the sciences.

We can recall how brief was the sway, at least on the American theoretical scene, of movements with scientific pretensions. I think, for example, of the aborted influence here of structuralism and of semiotics, with their ambition to establish a participatory role for our theory within the social sciences. This aroused a critical response that cut short their life by exposing them to deconstructive activity. It is true that these movements used the precision of their quasi-scientific instruments to deconstruct *their* system-building, nonscientific predecessors, but the global ambition of those instruments left them vulnerable to being deconstructed in turn. One might argue that our theoretical health has been re-created again and again by the continuing sequence of deconstructors deconstructed: by the successive deconstructions of what had been deconstructive moves, which, in seductive moments of self-aggrandizement, succumbed to the lure of collective power, becoming frozen into a movement. Used this way, the word *movement* is false to itself since the more a movement arrives, the more all movement in it ceases. Each new move takes its turn in saying, "you too have fallen into ontology" to the movement it would displace, although it then uses its success to replace its predecessor, achieving the institutional status that renders it similarly vulnerable to the new deconstructor waiting in the wings.

With or without institutes, then, the drive to move a movement toward institutional status has formed critics into the collective projects we think of as "schools," whether we associate them with a university or with a journal or merely with individuals working collaboratively, though separately, to consolidate their insights into fixed positions. The critical propensity of recent theoretical probing must keep us alert to our oppositional, indeed subversive, mission: an obsession with temporality that dissolves all fixity, even at the risk of precluding the communal. Can we preserve this alertness within the cooperative establishment of an institutional structure? An institute imposed upon by criticism and theory as we know them now would dissolve, while this criticism and theory, imposed upon by an institute, would congeal.

I can summarize the changes and conflicts I have been tracing as a series of institutional moments, each undone by the spirit of opposition: literature as an institution, succeeded by criticism as an institution, succeeded in turn by theory as an institution, and all of them finally (for now) succeeded by history as an institution. Is it not time for the anti-institutional spirit of opposition to rise again, even if it means circling back to literature, though we have now learned to extend that term to cover all writing that we bring within the range of our analytic instruments, many of which have been forged through our encounters with literature?

Before suggesting how the three entities—criticism, theory, institute—may in spite of themselves manage to coexist, let me ask what the agenda for theory now is, as we try to pursue its restlessness in isolation or as we allow it to enter—warily—into the collaborative functions of an institute. I am going to suggest that in our universities theory, recently licensed as an autotelic enterprise, is in danger of so far outrunning the practice of textual interpretation as to threaten itself with losing all influence after it had for awhile helped change the shape of humanistic studies. So I ask that we put high on our agenda the need to confront our own activities as readers and responders more questioningly, the need to slow down to see what we may have passed by too quickly in our haste to press forward our skeptical denials.

How can the literary scholar-critic carry on what are still necessary activities when these rest upon assumptions that have been stripped away by the theoretical activity licensed by a new critical awareness? How can our daily work as readers and teachers of texts vibrate to any such succession of critical undoings? How many habitual but indispensable assumptions do we still proceed upon, assumptions that we should acknowledge, even though we have delegitimated them, or even have theorized them away altogether? There are many of us, I think, who still guard our affection for some canonical literary works that are especially precious to us through our repeated experiences with them, works whose specialness we prefer not to sacrifice to the theoretical zeal that would desacralize them. We might even like to believe that our affection for them has a ground beyond the historical contingencies that allow them to flourish, even though we know how this belief would resurrect mystifications that recent theory has taught us to do without. It might even raise the ghost of ontological assumptions that we have been taught to bury. If, as has been charged, epistemological evasions and historical neglect allowed us to be hedonists before, making whatever metaphysical concessions aesthetic hedonism demanded, deconstruction has taught us the lean austerity of self-denial. But have we been capable of accepting that denial totally in our practice, or does not a remnant of aesthetic self-indulgence assert itself still against the puritanism of some recent negations?

I am reminding us that there are habitual practices that have not gone away even when they have had the theoretical ground cut out from under them. We must confront, more candidly, and self-consciously than we have, the conflict—often within the same scholar—between the avant-garde of theoretical audacity and the rear guard of reading and teaching habits, habits still seeking to control us as if the deconstructive denials had not occurred. Which guard, avant or rear, then, should correct which? Though recent theory delegitimates our most cherished literary experiences, should we discard our literary responses as reactionary gestures to an aesthetic regime now unmasked and declared outmoded? Or should we, out of a pragmatic interest in preserving these experiences at almost any cost, shut our eyes to the consequences of our theorizing and the deprivations that would follow from it? It is a troubling choice. I am proposing that we relax our theoretical austerity long enough to remember those responses that we ought—theoretically—to be giving up and seek to come to terms with all that we hold onto, almost unconsciously, out of a habitual fealty to what critics used to call our sensibility. Indeed it may be evidence of the ubiquitous force of these habits that we bring what used to be thought of as styles of literary interpretation to a great variety of texts, many of them at a great distance from what we used to think of exclusively as literature.

But what are these habits that still seem to demand recognition and concession, even at this late moment? For one, there is the habit, revealed in the declarative sentences we used to describe and interpret the texts we write about or teach, of treating the work as an authoritative primary text to which the critical text is to serve as commentary. For all our attempts to escape from origins, especially the origin represented by the privileged text, we cannot rid ourselves of the commentator's habit—even as we may wish to rid our discourse of the curse of secondariness—of a self-abnegating referential fealty, full of obligations to truth-telling and corrigibility with respect to its ostensible object. And how we marvel on those rare occasions when we witness a critic's virtuoso performance that, we swear, tells us something we now are sure is going on in the text—or, better yet, when we have convinced ourselves of our own virtuoso discovery. For all our epistemological sophistication, can we, or even ought we, abandon totally our smug conviction that we (though perhaps each differently) have unlocked the hidden splendors of this or that work, that it is indeed as we see it to be?

No theory of "crossing over" between criticism and its ostensible object-text is likely to talk us out of this feeling altogether, however much such a theory may lead us to distrust it. At moments even our most radical theorists tend to slip into this role of commentator upon an entity "out there" when speaking about prior, if not primary, texts. A major deconstructionist interpretation, like Paul de Man's, often sounds like nothing less than an interpretation *of* (whatever text), an interpretation to be argued for (in opposition to others that are to be argued against). More often than not, such brilliantly acute readings leave us with the impression, not that they have deconstructed a naïve text, but that they have sought accurately to describe a sophisticated text that, as language is wont to do, has deconstructed itself—a very different operation indeed. One feels the temptation to treat the text like an untamable animal with (dare we still say it?) a complex life of its own. The interpreter must subdue it with the language of criticism or have that language overcome by *it*. Yet we need not worry, since we can be certain that the critic has set the rules for a game that cannot be lost. We are thus assured in advance that the object is *ours*, as we would have it, indeed must have it, so that our feeling about its status "out there" may well be no more than a mystification to validate our projection—a suggestion that would corroborate what theory has been insisting upon. Still, the habitual feeling of its out-thereness and the referential promise of our observations cannot be altogether argued away.

A second habit leads commentators to look for and find internally related functions for the several moments in the text that they would account for. Though we must grant that today the interpreter may proceed negatively more often than positively, looking for patterns of dysfunctions rather than patterns of functions, the fact that these are patterns may turn centrifugal objectives into centripetal ones. The assumption of a functionalism positively or negatively relating part to part and part to whole forces the resistant critic, perhaps unwittingly, to drift toward a traditional sense of closure that recent theory would prohibit. Still we find it happening in ways that suggest the continuing clutch of Aristotle upon us all. It may even betray, behind our theoretical desire to cultivate the aporia, a perceptual habit of seeking to fill in the gaps, to find or create a configurational unity of the sort Wolfgang Iser has written about so eloquently. It is a habit not easily surrendered even for that theoretical persistence that properly growls at our rationalization of the role played by one or another part, since such rationalization can be seen as a front for implicit totalization.

There is yet a third habitual assumption that we still find haunting our practice as readers and teachers, and this one may appear perhaps even more outrageous to recent theoretical stringencies than the rest. I am speaking of our conditioned response to the aesthetic as aesthetic, however this very term has been discredited in recent years as part of the assault on Kantian disinterestedness. How else can we characterize our continuing indulgence of the special fictionality of literary fictions and our deeply felt, repeated celebrations of the best of them? However broadly we now apply the term *fiction* to discourses ranging from the

Theory and Institutions

realm of physics to the realm of history or philosophy, we do not mean it quite the way we do when we apply it to the once-upon-a-time world of the storyteller's fancy. I am referring, of course, to what Aristotle called an *imitation* in the sense of an *imitation reality*, with its imitation lives and loves and deaths, not to be confused with real ones. But better than *once upon a time* or even *imitation reality*, the phrase to define literary fiction that I find fittest, once we study it a bit, is *make-believe*. The literary fiction is the result of making, and it exists to make us believe in it, but only because the poet has chosen to make it for belief, *as if* it were true but not *as* true since its realm is the realm of make-believe. We are to take it *almost* for real—but not *quite*, and oh the force of *quite*! We continue to distinguish this fictional—and, yes, hence aesthetic—make-believe from the rhetorical make-*us*-believe, make-*for*-belief, since the latter, as persuasion, would assume the power to change our minds, our convictions, about the ways things are or ought to be or about what is to be done. This is the realm of Kant's "will" as practical reason, and the separation from it of the aesthetic-as-the-disinterested stirs the impatience of most post-New Critical theory. It is this opposition that causes the aesthetic response, still naggingly active, to be anti-rhetorical (just as the rhetorical is anti-aesthetic). The fact that we have learned to read make-*for*-belief texts as make-believe only enlarges the domain of literary, or aesthetic, perception while reaffirming it as an alternative to the rhetorical, and its enemy.

Are we altogether free of the spirit of Kant seeking even now to resist the all-sweeping spirit of Nietzsche? When the early Yeats, in post-Kantian fashion, condemns rhetoric as "the will trying to do the work of the imagination," we sense the sneering attack on the imperializing domain of the act being made from the escapist domain of art. The make-believe may—from the perspective of the workaday world of will—be no more than an illusion, the realm of appearance (*Schein*) that defines *aesthesis*. It is also the realm of play, in the sense of Schiller, that major post-Kantian. And play, figuring forth a make-believe world, is a freeing us from the will. If it, too, is an act, it is a free act that defies the grounds for action, an act to be uniquely distinguished from acts performed under the domain of the will. Our residual devotion to make-believe, it would be argued, should not be dismissed as mere nostalgia, harking back to a hedonistic aberration in the history of the leisure class. For the habit of illusion-making, of making believe, in opening us to the realm of appearance and allowing us to explore it unconstrained, in freedom, enables us to *see*, looses our capacity for new perception, even of the willed world in which we function. Here is the tendency that becomes exaggerated into the extreme attacks on the will, in the name of aesthetics, by Schopenhauer, Bergson, Croce, and the New Critics.

But the presiding spirit of Nietzsche has supplanted that of the now outmoded Kant, as the rhetoric of will, now ubiquitous, invades all that would exclude and oppose it. By way of the halfway figure of Hegel, Kant's discrete faculties are synthesized in an indivisible realm of history and its choices, so that, with the invocation of Nietzsche, they come to be condemned as so many deceptive manifestations of the all-controlling will. The aesthetic blurs into rhetoric as the make-believe is to be read as a disguised version of a subtextual make-*for*-belief. I must concede, by the way, that, in Jean-François Lyotard's rereading, Kant would be seen as himself anticipating the others by undoing his own structure of segregated and self-authenticating faculties, collapsing them in the direction of Hegel and Marx and Nietzsche as if he were already under their influence, as we are. Here, however, I want to call attention to the persistence of the more traditional sense of the Kantian aesthetic that would authorize our response to an especially detached realm of verbal fiction. We have lately become aware that even the anti-aesthetic Nietzschean movements provide their own, often unintended, aesthetic resonance. So, however strongly our critical awareness as theorists has taught us to distrust the aesthetic response, perhaps its persistence should persuade us as humanists not to trust wholly any theory that would preclude it. And yet it is, strangely, as theorists that we must distrust it.

Thus it is with all these ghosts of problems past. I still see them as actively engaging us in our textual experience, still needing to be faced, indeed to be met face-to-face, and not merely effaced, as too much recent theory demands in its arrogance. In an echo of Paul de Man, one of the more recent giants in whose shadow (or *with* whose shadow) we still contend, I must remind us to watch out for the blindness that accompanies both our quest for theoretical insight and the insight itself.

So our theory, in its continuing critical character, must be critical also of its own excesses, and it can demonstrate this final reflexivity by worrying anew about concerns it had assumed settled, by readmitting as legitimate many questions that its austerity had led it to exclude. The critical spirit does not stop before affecting ourselves as critical theorists, if we recognize our role, as an echo of literature's, to keep all movement—and every movement—in motion, to move constantly without moving into position. Of course, it is a role we rarely can manage for very long, so that we require one another to keep reminding us of it, and of our tendency to lose our restlessness in the self-satisfaction in which motion ceases. So even an institute can serve the collective purpose of our continuing to unsettle one another, provided we do not fall prey to it.

Our mission, I urge again, requires that we preserve the spirit of secession while seeking to avoid creating a competing republic. And if we are fated to coexist with an institute, even it may be useful, if only by reminding us to struggle against its tendencies, which are reflections of our own ambitions that we must also resist. The widespread sympathetic interest we have been witnessing these days in a resurrected Bakhtin as well as in the vibrant postmodernism of Lyotard derives in some measure from the endlessly subversive principle of opposition that these writers foster: the unleashing of the force of the carnivalizing *différend* and the consequent splintering of regimes, converting the homogeneous into the endlessly heterogeneous. This suggests the liberating force of humanistic inquiry that I have been urging, a force sustained by the duplicity of the theorist's language, echo of the play of language taught us by our engagement with literature. Indeed, that force may well have been set in motion by the alertness to play stimulated in literary perception.

The one thing more freely playful, and hence more subversive, than the theorist-critic's text is the literary text that authorizes its playfulness by providing its model. It is this subversive force that may well enable theory to move beyond the social-historical determinism that many of our currently popular theorists, with an antithcoretical zeal, would impose upon theory these days. This more positive view of theory—as we also find it in the work of Theodor Adorno, for example—encourages us to find that power in literature which, rebounding into subversion, frees what the hegemonic discourse would repress. It is this capacity in language that Derridean deconstruction has taught us how to let loose. The theorist, then, need not serve solely as reflector of established powers in the surrounding society, as if verbal representation proceeded unproblematically, so that mimesis was an untroubled, transparent process. But, the historicist can argue the other side, that this anti-institutional mission I propose, with its attendant freedom from the social context, is only a residue of the aesthetic, a delusion deriving from the assumption of a now outmoded concept of an independent and authorizing self. Further, the call to perpetual subversion carries with it a rejection of the communal, which the political program of social-historical theory would want to preserve, perhaps even to the point of defending the objectives of an institutional collective like our institute. But the language process that would catch us all in its ontological trappings makes willing victims of those who would project extratextual social-economic relations as the origin and seat of power, thus replacing the private self they would obliterate with their own myth of an all-powerful collective self.

On the contrary, I propose once more that we see the theorist as indispensable gadfly, with a language to unsettle any institution or institute before it stands too high or too firmly on a single piece of ground. So, if the progression from the critical theorist's move to a theoretical movement seems inevitable, so too, I am happy to report, is the consequent undoing move by the next critical theorist. Still, any principle that would commit us to apply theory to its own undoing must itself be resisted, like all absolute commands, by the theorist who remains alive to one's discontents both with and without theory. Given such alertness, what harm can an institute do? It may well create an establishment that gives a warrant to what we as theorists should be rejecting. But trust our perverse, gadfly character, whose critical spirit is not long to be bribed even by an institute's resources out of doing its proper work. It can be served by the mutual interplay of the dialogue that characterizes the conferences and colloquia that have greatly increased in number with the increasing dominance of the theoretical perspective in humanistic studies, for it is these that our institute will allow to flourish. So long as this clash of voices continues, it can help us ensure that we use our institute instead of having it use us.

II   *Critical Positions:*
Self-definition and Other
Definitions

First I should like to place my theory between the New Criticism and certain elements of poststructuralism by revealing those assumptions it seems to share with each of these positions, which I see as radically opposed to one another. Despite the fact that my early work was largely fashioned by New Critical predispositions and despite a lingering sympathy with some of their central literary objectives, I have in at least two ways sought to differentiate my thinking from the New Critics. Perhaps these modifications were performed in part to immunize this theoretical tradition from the assaults of those who would see in it undeniable tendencies toward mystification, but I like to think that my own transformations of the New Criticism borrowed from—if they did not anticipate—assumptions about language which poststructuralism has now made commonplace among us.

The New Critical aesthetic rested totally on a prior commitment to formal closure as the primary characteristic of the successful literary object. Its dedication to organicism, or to the peculiar sort of "contextualism" that I have described in many places elsewhere, gave to the

---

This essay was presented as a summary of my position before the Konstanz Colloquium in the summer of 1982, the record of which follows this essay. Besides Wolfgang Iser, who chaired the colloquium, the Konstanz faculty, whose responses are recorded in Chapter 7, are Hans Robert Jauss (French), Ulrich Gaier and Anselm Haverkamp (German), and Jürgen Schlaeger and Gabriele Schwab (English).

poem the totalizing objective of self-sufficiency or of microcosmic perfection which, New Critics would claim, was the ultimate realization of the formalistic tradition from Aristotle to Kant to Coleridge and the organicists who followed. All borrowings from the world of actions, values, and language—as well as borrowings from earlier poems—were to be radically transformed by the poet working in, as well as through, his medium into a world of its own finality sealed from his personal interests as from ours. Indeed, those venerable terms, "disinterestedness," "detachment," and "impersonality," all could be invoked as assurances of the work's capacity to come to terms with itself. And yet, in its casuistic perfection, the world of the poem was to guide our vision by making it normative of our own. Consequently, although the existential was to be re-formed into aesthetic terms, through the work there was to be an existential projection after all.

It has now been a number of years and a number of writings of my own since I have come to reject an exclusive commitment to aesthetic closure of the New Critical kind. The New Critical position derived much of its strength from the claim that organicism is all or none and not a matter of degree; consequently, the poem could not be considered part open and part closed, so that the anti–New Critical move could simply shift the emphasis on closure to the emphasis on openness. But my move has been to introduce notions like self-reference, illusion, and metaphorical duplicity in order to argue for a paradoxical simultaneity of utter closure and utter openness.

The argument proceeds in the following way: those moments during which the fictional world betrays a self-consciousness about itself as fiction remind us of the illusionary nature of that "reality" which seeks to enclose us. By a kind of negative reference, this reminder implicitly points to the world that the poem explicitly excludes—indeed represses—in order to affirm its own closure. The world may be reduced to the stage in front of us, but so long as we are aware that it is only the stage in front of us, there is a world outside threatening to break in. Thus the work of art, as its own metaphorical substitution for the world of experience beyond, is a metaphor that at once affirms its own integrity and yet, by negative implication, denies itself, secretly acknowledging that it is but an artful evasion of the world. This claim to duplicity permits me to allow the work to celebrate its own ways and the ways of its language unencumbered, without denying the ways of the world and *its* language. The work's very retreat from referentiality acts paradoxically to point it, through negative reference, to the world it so self-consciously excludes or represses.

The second essential assumption of the New Criticism from which I

Critical Positions: Self-definition and Other Definitions

came to distance myself was its preestablished commitment to the poem as fixed object—a commitment that has been effectively attacked by much post–New Criticism as mere fetishism. The arguments against such reification as a naïve spatializing of the language process have been often enough rehearsed and are well known. We are by now also well aware of the extent to which New Critics neglected the relation of art to the social process as well as to the psychological processes of writing and reading, defined as these are by the flow of language as a governing force in human experiencing.

I would hope that my own theorizing has reflected these concerns. I have increasingly tried to dwell upon the poem as an "intentional object" only, compounded of the reader's projection of what he has persuaded himself was there to be seen and a stimulus provided by a cooperative author, as anxious to create a closed object as the reader is to apprehend it. And it is the work's fictional character that makes the effect of closure feasible, a secular satisfaction produced by the miracle of metaphor long sustained in the culture's theological and aesthetic linguistic habit. Thus the illusion of a verbal victory over difference, the subduing of the temporal. Yet the work's self-referentiality must resound with the differences of the realm of time that threatens to explode the integrity we momentarily want to grant it.

But I do not suggest that through these workings the aesthetic becomes only a game of now you see it, now you don't. Rather, I see the work as touching and unlocking in us the anthropological quest for that which marks and defines every moment of a culture's vision as well as of its inner skepticism that undoes its visionary reality with a "real" reality which is no less illusionary. The making and unmaking of our metaphors, our mythic equations, in experience as in art only reveal the primacy of the operation of the aesthetic in us all—and perhaps explain the extent to which our drive for art is accompanied by a cognitive itch which even the experience of art itself never quite eases, so that the need to experience more art happily remains.

These differences from the New Criticism allow me, I hope, to escape the difficulties arising out of its epistemological naïveté, leaving me less uncomfortable as I contemplate currently more fashionable theories about language with which I share large areas of agreement. Since the ascendancy of structuralism more than a decade ago, critics in this country have had to come to terms with the Saussurean notion of verbal signs as arbitrary and as based upon the principle of differentiation. Thus what used to seem to be the simple matter of representation in language—the presence of a fixed signified in the signifier—is converted into a problematic. In the view of structuralism, signifiers operate in a dynamic field of differentiation and have only arbitrary relations with their presumed signifieds. A culture's confidence in the identity and inevitability of its verbal meanings, rather than its confronting their differentiation and arbitrariness, only testifies to that culture's self-mystification as it falls prey to the metaphysical habit of logocentrism. The wistful imposition of identity is accompanied by the ontological claim of presence, now to be undone by a shrewder philosophy of language that reminds us of the field of absence upon which the system of differences plays. Hence we have the rejection of metaphor for metonymy, and with the rejection of metaphor the removal of the ground on which the New Criticism rested. After all, how can one retain the central requirement of unity in metaphor—the overcoming of verbal differences by the fusion that overwhelms all boundaries that set words apart from one another—if the very basis on which words function subjects them indiscriminately to the structuralists' "all-purpose differentiating machine" of which René Girard has contemptuously spoken?

Though I may be persuaded about language as the marshaling of arbitrary and differentiated signifiers, I would hold out for the possibility that a single verbal structure can convert its elements so that we read them under the aegis of metaphorical identity with its claim to presence. It is this hold-out claim to what the poem can persuade us its language is doing that ties me still to the New Critical tradition despite my concessions to structuralist theory. I seek to maintain this power for creating poetic identity in language despite language's normal incapacities, so that I do not see structuralism or poststructuralism as precluding a poetics such as the tradition since Kant and Coleridge has been seeking to construct. At least I can entertain this power so long as I recognize its dependence on the projection of my aesthetic commitment, which is encouraged by the self-reference in the poem that reminds us that the identity we find rests on an awareness of difference, that the metaphoric already knows of itself as metonym.

Clearly, what is at stake is whether there can be any claim for discontinuities within the realm of signifiers, whether we can break off and privilege segments of language and call them poems as if they have something special in them. One of the ironies of structuralism, it has often been pointed out, is the undifferentiating way in which it asserts its principle of difference (it was just this problem that prompted the Derridean critique of Lévi-Strauss). Eventually any poetics, but especially one like mine, must create its own ground by seeking discontinuities within textuality, at least for the momentary purpose of our aesthetic experience at the hands of a poem. This recurrent need, in our

Critical Positions: Self-definition and Other Definitions

history, to establish a poetics perhaps accounts for the persistence with which theorists resort to a deviationist principle for distinguishing poems from other texts. And what for them sets poems aside must somehow be related to the power of converting differences into identities, the arbitrary into the inevitable—in short, verbal absence into verbal presence.

But in these last years there have been assaults from several directions on the theoretical deviationism that for many decades had been a basic assumption for the dominant aesthetic. Some of these newer directions overlap one another significantly, and this is about what we should expect since most of them are related, one way or another, to that version of structuralism which—in an anti-hierarchical spirit—rejects the literary work as an elite object and, consequently, rejects any collection of such works as a duly constituted canon.

First, the application of "information theory" is used by some as a monolithic model of interpretation that reduces all varieties of discourse to itself, searching out the cues for encoding (by the author) and decoding (by the reader) of the message which, as programmed discourse, the text presumably exists to communicate.

Second, the analysis of the process of signification leads others to apply their conclusions about the emptiness of signifiers—the absence of all signifieds from them—to words in poems as in nonpoems. They judge the deviationist's claim to find a privileged fullness in poetic language to be a delusion and a fetish, a mystification. In poetry as in philosophy, they would deconstruct the metaphysical assumption that ontologizes verbal meanings.

Third, there are those who see all varieties of language as playing a similar role in culture's history, its way of meaning and of conceiving its reality (and of imposing it upon others). One can use what Foucault calls discursive formations to uncover the several archaeological stages in our development. And there are no exceptions among those discourses contributing to, or reflecting, those formations.

Fourth, as a corollary to the third, theorists may seek to deny the apparent meanings intended by all texts, reducing them to rationalizations of the author's "will to power." These critics are not satisfied with stopping the deconstructionist process once assumed stable meanings have been changed into a textual play among signifiers; they rather pursue that process beyond all texts—until textual pretensions are traced to the political or psychological motive that puts them forward as its verbal disguise for private or social objectives. For these critics, whether they derive from Marx or Nietzsche or Freud, there is no innocent text, no disinterestedness in its production or its reception:

An Apology for Poetics   111 instead, though the text offers itself and its fiction as all there is, the author means to use it to manipulate the actual world, to imperialize the world his way. And poems, again, are no exception.

Fifth, there are those who analyze all texts as originating in tropes or in narrative structures. Such analysis bestows literary categories upon nonliterary as upon literary texts, so that all texts are treated as similarly figured and similarly fictional. Consequently, there is no "normal" discourse from which poetic language could deviate, no neutral sequence of words or events (or events as words) on which we have not already imposed narrative and tropological shape. In effect, all language is deviation and there is no norm. Thus there is no neutral reference, so that we all speak in fictions, whatever truths we deludedly think we mouth. We have gone beyond Molière's Monsieur Jourdain who was surprised (and impressed) to learn that he had been speaking prose all his life; for in this view we have indeed, like all our fellows, been speaking (and writing) poetry—that is, fictions that we had been taking for sober referentiality. Where all are poems, there need be no special gift of poem-making.

Sixth, finally (and this one also overlaps some of the others), theorists can consider all speaking and writing—or even, more broadly, all human activity—as indifferent parts of what I have referred to as the seamless fabric of textuality, of course without distinctions within it: the world of words as text or even the world itself as text (the journal *Semiotexte* or the new, more radical journal, *Social Text*). We cannot, in this view, escape from experience, worldly and verbal or worldly *as* verbal, as a single capacious room composed of wall-to-wall discourse (to borrow Edward Said's phrase): the world as text, all of it just one hermeneutic challenge. Here is the farthest move away from any notion of the poem as a potentially discrete entity.

In all of these cases, the distinction-making power that would create a poetry and a poetics has been cut off. And, in light of the convergence of the several lines of recent theory upon these structuralist or near-structuralist notions, there would seem to be good reason to be persuaded by what they have taught us about the deceptive nature of sign-functioning and about the unified character of our apparently varied discourses at given moments in our culture. But I propose that we still worry about whether we wish to include literary discourse within this monolithic construct. Or, on the other hand, do we rather wish to see literary discourse as achieving a self-privileging exemption from that construct by manipulating all its generic linguistic elements until they are forced to subvert their own natures and do precisely what a structuralist view of language would preclude them from doing: from functioning as signifiers that create and fill themselves with their own signifieds as they go, thereby setting this text apart from textuality-at-large as its own unique, self-made system? Without some such notion, are we capable of accounting for all that our greatest works perform for us? Do we not, further, have to recognize the peculiarly fictional, and even self-consciously fictional—which is to say self-referential—character of our most highly valued literature, even if we wish to grant to nonliterature a fictionality and reflexivity that less sophisticated readings of would-be "referential" discourse did not used to grant? And are not literary fictions, with their peculiar self-reference, sufficient to separate the work that they characterize from the rest of discourse?

By urging the reflexivity and the tropological character of all discourse upon us, poststructuralists have perhaps not leveled literature into common *écriture* so much as they have raised all *écriture* into literature. If these critics argue against the exclusiveness of poems (that is, fictions, "imaginative literature") and rather seek to include a wide range of works by essayists, historians, philosophers, and even social scientists, they do so by treating these works as texts to which techniques of analysis appropriate to literary criticism may be applied. Even more, their techniques of deconstructing their nonliterary texts, stripping them of their referential pretensions and reducing them to their naked fictionality, are to a great extent echoes of what poems have always been doing to themselves and teaching their critics to do to them. It is for this reason that I suggest that, instead of the concept of literature being deconstructed into *écriture*, *écriture* has been constructed into literature. As a consequence, everything has become a "text," and texts—as well as the very notion of textuality—have become as ubiquitous as writing itself, with each text now to be accorded the privileged mode of interpretation that used to be reserved for discourse with the apparent internal self-justification of poetry.

I think, for example, of the work of Hayden White on history writing, in which he sets forth a number of models of narrative structure based on the several tropes (or master figures), modes of discourse that he treats as reflecting the modes of human consciousness. Obviously, his reduction of every historian's truth claim to the illusions of the poet's fictions, his obliteration of the realm of neutral fact and of discursive reference, will not please many historians who take their truth-claiming function seriously. Indeed, it may well seem to condescend to nonpoetic humanistic texts for us to cut them off from any truth claim by restricting them to the realm of fiction and to the metaphorical swerve of private consciousness. Whatever the deconstructive mood may suggest, the historian may well want us to believe his version of history over the version of others, or the philosopher may want us to accept his claims about the nature of language or of reality, so that either may well resent our turning him into a poet *malgŕe lui*. The literary humanist should understand that it may not be taken exclusively as flattery if he brings historians, philosophers, and other humanists under the literary tent, especially since they are so determined to pursue their ostensible objectives. Words like *fiction* and *illusion* should teach us that there is a negative side (from the cognitive point of view) as well as a positive side (from the aesthetic point of view) to being a maker of literary fictions, and others may not be as comfortable with the designation as we literary people are. The sober scholar in the nonliterary disciplines, who does his careful work and makes his claims to its justness, may well feel that his discipline and its distinctive ambition are being trivialized by being treated as a fiction shaped by his tropological bent. And such attitudes, which would protect the distinction between—say—history and poetry, have had the history of literary criticism on their side since Aristotle initiated the distinction between history and poetry in chapter 9 of the *Poetics*. Indeed, even earlier, Plato had inherited and severely contributed to the war between the philosophers and the poets in many places in his work, beginning most notably, perhaps, in book 2 of the *Republic*.

Such questions as those, for example, about the boundary between history or biography on the one side and the novel on the other, and about the applicability of narratological analysis to each of them probably remain serious questions, despite efforts to collapse all discourse into undifferentiated textuality and all textuality into trope and fiction. So let us grant that some fictional obfuscation, with its rhetorical swerving, takes place outside the realm of literary fictions, but let us allow some remnant of the free play of fictional reflexivity to be left to the literary intent, and let us allow historians, for example, to replace it by more precise and clearly aimed objectives. Our temptation to tell the historian what he is doing ought to subside, at least a little, before his own perhaps less subtle sense of what he is about. And the finally free-floating inventiveness of self-conscious make-believe in the literary text should also in the end be acknowledged as a thing apart, despite our best efforts to see in what ways these differing kinds of texts, produced in response to such varying purposes, may reflect on one another. Aesthetic foregrounding may well go on outside poems, but do we not condescend to our writers in all the disciplines when we ignore, or deprecate, the several responses that the body of their works appears to be soliciting from their different readers?

So I suggest we respond critically to the enterprise, currently so common among us, that would undermine the poem's differentness from other discourse. What this enterprise has been seeking to accomplish is a deconstruction of the metaphysical assumptions behind the traditional aesthetic and its resulting claim about the poem's ontology: the claim that the poem is a totalized structure, a self-realized teleological closure, a microcosm whose mutually dependent elements are cooperatively present in the fulfillment of their centripetal potentialities. Instead, the deconstructive move reduces the poem to a play of centrifugal forces such as characterizes general nonpoetic discourse. Gaps appear everywhere—absences and emptiness—and we are to acknowledge these gaps for what they are, resisting our constructive tendency, imposed on us by centuries of self-deceiving habits of literary interpretation with their ontological assumptions, of trying at all costs to fill those gaps. For what we have taken to be the self-fulfilling and self-sealing poem is seen by deconstructors to be, like all discourse, mere vacancy, acknowledging a lack of substance, fleeing all presence as it leads us down the lines moving outward to the intertextual forces that become the code, but that permit no integrity, no free-standing sovereignty, to any would-be body operating within them. In this sense, the poem, as a construction of elements manipulated by art into a presence (according to the traditional older aesthetic), has been deconstructed into absences that can be made to point only to the code of writing itself. It is seen as an *allegory* of reading other writing, not as a *symbol* that reads the world.

But what of the need for closure, an aesthetic need responsive to the habits of our perception which searches for closure in the objects of its experience? Should we not value, and set aside for separate treatment, those specially constructed objects that seem addressed to that aesthetic need? A criticism that preserves its own referential obligation to its literary object can treat poems as dislocations of language that enable language to create itself as a medium that can close off what structuralists have shown to be normally open. Our perception, as aesthetic, seeks to close its object into a form and then to project it onto the object as created by the poet who, presumably, also seeks closure. But both perception and its object also rebound into a self-awareness that recognizes the specious, if highly effective, grounds for the aesthetic and its dependence on what our habits of perception insist upon.

It is under these provisional conditions that we have learned to commit ourselves to the aesthetic response. These conditions also qualify and complicate our sense of presence—of signifiers that have filled themselves with the signifieds they have created within themselves—within the play of words before us. And, despite arguments of both structuralists and poststructuralists, the illusion of presence emerges for us from the written as well as the spoken words before us. But it is always a presence sponsored *pour l'occasion* and coexisting with our awareness of the lurking absences that haunt both writing and speech (*écriture* and *parole*).

As has been suggested in poststructuralist semiotics, the speaking voice may make us too ready to conceive the presence of the speaker, so that we concede too little to the anonymity of speech as it enters the network of all that is spoken or can be spoken; in consequence, so the argument runs, we would concede more if we were confronted by the silence of the apparently anonymous written page. But, on the other hand, a counterargument might claim, speech may seem to be the more firmly tied to absence—the continuing fadings-away linked to temporal sequence—as the sounds dissipate in the air as they are spoken; further, the orphaned page, composed of visible (and invisible) traces left by an absent speaker, may nevertheless persuade us of a spatial simultaneity among its words as it takes its place within the physically copresent book. Let me turn the matter around again by adding that even speech, considered as a sequence of sounds, suggests a sensuous presence in its auditory phenomena that belie our sense of them as fleeting transparencies. As the poet dwells upon those characteristics, heard and seen, that turn words into sensory things, the signifiers can take on the weightiness of substance. In these ways, with the knowing cooperation of the reader-hearer, the word on the page *or* on the tongue can be made the occasion for our assigning a tentative spatial presence to it. But in remembering it also as being no more than word—the trace on the page, the buzz in the ear—we do not deny its temporality within the flow of our experience, worldly and linguistic: its elusive *un*presence despite our attempts to seize upon and fix it.

As I contemplate the possibility of conceiving speech as more likely to sponsor the feeling of absence than writing is, as well as the possibility of conceiving them the opposite way, I am aware that it has been my interest to dwell upon the poet's attempt to persuade us to break through to presence, whichever of the two is the case. I am aware, further, that in my career I have been concerned more with the presence of texts as discontinuous entities than with the speaking presence *in* texts of the authorial consciousness that is their point of origin. This fact only reveals my inheritance from the New Criticism and its obsession with isolated texts as well as my inheritance from the Anglo-American tradition dating from Bacon, which seeks to respond to empirical phenomena, rather than the French inheritance from Descartes, whose concern with the *cognito* and the resulting concern with consciousness can never long be shaken. It may be that the New Criticism has, after all, even shaped my differences from it just as, perhaps, critics of consciousness like Georges Poulet have helped shape the thinking of the poststructuralists who have excluded consciousness as a controlling origin for the text.

There is yet another emendation I would make to the poststructuralist's critique as it affects my claim—an unmystified claim—to poetic presence. I would argue that there is a major difference, not noted in poststructuralist theory, between the generic difficulty with presence in our logocentrism and the special difficulty with presence in the language of poetry. It is not noted because one must distinguish poetic from other discourse (by means of a deviationist aesthetic) before being able to see the different sort of presence constructed by the poem. I have pointed out the usual prestructuralist assumptions about transparent representation—a signified fixed into presence within its signifier—assumptions which, according to poststructuralists, we see our language as making, thanks to its implicit metaphysical assumptions. It is this presence that is to fall victim to the poststructuralist's deconstructive enterprise. As a proponent of a deviationist theory of poetry, I could join in this enterprise while holding out for a special presence that a poem can build into itself by subverting and reworking the materials left it by those discourses which poststructuralists have deconstructed in order to reveal the absences within them. The metonymic character of the usual sequence of signifiers, with their differentiations, can be transformed by the poet (so I would claim), who manipulates his verbal elements so that they may appear to be functioning as metaphorical identities, creating a presentation of signifieds through the generating powers of the signifiers with which those signifieds are perceived as being one. We see this poetic presentation feeding itself into a fullness out of the gaps of the failed *re*presentations in nonpoetic discourse.

If Derrida calls attention to our need to correct the naïve feeling of presence in all texts constructed in the logocentric tradition of the West, de Man—in his critique of some romantics—complains of the poet's arrogant effort to achieve the monistic presence of symbolism (metaphor) instead of accepting the allegory (metonymy) which is the appropriate way of language. Each of these denies simple presence by seeing all language as functioning in a similar way, but though neither would grant to poetry any privilege within the general realm of discourse, de Man's critique does attack verbal presence on rather different grounds, within the province of the self-privileging poet or the overreaching theorist who takes up the fight for privilege on behalf of the poet. And these are the grounds on which my own argument for poetic presence, without challenging Derrida's, can stand as an alternative to de Man's.

But the dream of unity, of formal repetitions that are seen as the temporal equivalent of juxtapositions, that convert the temporal into the spatial through the miracle of simultaneity—this dream persists, reinforced by every aesthetic illusion which we help create and to which we succumb. We cultivate the mode of identity, the realm of metaphor, within an aesthetic frame that acknowledges its character as momentary construct and thereby its frailty as illusion. But it allows us a glimpse of our own capacity for vision before the bifurcations of language have struck. The dream of unity may be entertained tentatively and is hardly to be granted cognitive power, except for the secret life-without-language or life-before-language which it suggests, the very life which the language of difference precludes. In poetry we grasp at the momentary possibility that this can be a life-in-language.

Let me suggest that, in our anxiety to resist the mystification of ourselves, we may concede too much to temporality when we grant it a "reality" that we deny to its rival category, space. Space, presumably, is an invention of the reifying act of mind in flight from confrontation with the world of fact which *is* the world of time. So the mystifications of the spatial imagination are, in the work of Paul de Man, deconstructed by our introduction of temporal facts. But we must wonder whether this deconstructive act is not a privileging of time that sets it outside the realm of mind and language while giving it ultimate control over both in spite of all our inventions. Is time any less a human category than space, to be given a secure ontological space which its very own meaning contradicts? Yet the spatial, as that which redeems time, must be taken as a delusion when considered from the temporal perspective, though—let us grant—this perspective may be no less fictional than spatial. So the poem as language may well seem to have a dual character, being seen at once as canonized text and as just more textuality, as words at once shaped into a palpable form of art and playing an undistinguished role in the network of discourse. This duality should not be broken up into disjunctive choices: either a metaphorical delusion—the spatial simultaneity of the I AM—or the open flow of time that is to set the delusion straight. Instead, it is to be seen as two illusionary ways in which poetic texts seem at the same time to force us to see them as functioning: as a metaphorical world at once constructed and deconstructed. It is this self-conscious duplicity within both response and poem which leads me—despite whatever other

Critical Positions: Self-definition and Other Definitions

changes my theory has undergone—to persist in seeing poetry still as a form of discourse whose functioning separates it from other forms.

In the original "Apology for Poetry," Sir Philip Sidney sought to maintain the place of poetry though it was being threatened by an austere philosophy that shut it off from the truth and would allow it no other proper function. This attack would exclude poetry from the rest of discourse, while our current theoretical movements would too readily absorb it into the rest of discourse. Any theory devoted to poetry must today argue for a separate definition of the poem, thereby justifying its own right, within the realm of language theory, to function as a maker of claims for its subject. Thus my apology here is not for poetry so much as it is for poetics, the theoretical discourse whose existence, resting on the assumption that there *is* a poetry, is threatened with every denial of poetry's separate place. In this way, having begun my career by commenting on the "New Apologists for Poetry," I now find myself an apologist—I hope not altogether an older apologist—for poetics. I can make my apology, I am now convinced, only by making the tentative, self-undercutting moves that separate me from those older new apologists and may seem at moments to align me with those who refuse to grant a separate definition to poetry *or* poetics. But my hold-out separatist tendencies invariably win out, so that, with whatever phenomenological concessions, I remain an apologist after all.

7   A Colloquy on "An Apology for Poetics"

WOLFGANG ISER (chairman): On the occasion of his visiting appointment at the University of Konstanz in the summer of 1982, Murray Krieger was invited to the *Fachbereichskolloquium*, which is an institutionalized forum in the Department of Literature both for presenting work in progress by its members and for discussing the work of prominent scholars in the field coming from outside. The scholar invited is usually asked to submit a paper which reflects the basic tenets of his or her thinking so that the discussion can be entirely devoted to further explorations of his or her ideas.

In Murray Krieger's case, his essay, "An Apology for Poetics," served as a point of departure, and all the arguments advanced in the discussion started out from concepts put forward in this essay. This holds equally true for the following introductory remarks outlining Murray Krieger's position.

If literary theory is to be indentified as a distinguishable type of discourse within the realm of discourse, it is bound to have an object to which reference is made. Even if we were to collapse literary theory into a featureless continuum of ultratextuality, we still would run into differences that mark off distinctive strands of discourse within the continuum and thus involuntarily spotlight traces of distinctions. As literary theory has been a genre for more than three thousand years, history at least testifies to the existence of that special something which is conceptualized by that very discourse. Yet in these latter days of literary criticism, Murray Krieger maintains that a plea for literary theory can be made only in terms of an apology for poetics, reflecting the situation in which the state of the arts finds itself.

In order to substantiate this claim, past orientations for assessing the literary object have to be exceeded and current ones have to be brought under scrutiny. Hence Murray Krieger proposes a stance that is equidistant from both New Criticism and poststructuralism. New Criticism privileged the literary text and poststructuralism made it evaporate into textuality. In criticizing these two alternatives, Murray Krieger maps out his own position which cuts across both of them.

New Criticism favored the idea of closure because the text most valorized reconciled all its apparent ambiguities and dichotomies, thus figuring perfection which, in turn, made the literary work congeal into an object. Instead, Murray Krieger argues, closure and openness pertain equally to the literary text, constituting its basic duplicity. Closure implies a retreat from the world, a status implicitly accorded to the artwork by the New Critics. Yet closure results not so much in harmony, as the New Critics wanted to have it, but in exclusions that rebound on the artwork, turning it into pure metaphor. This reconceptualization of closure signalizes that each presence represented by the work functions simultaneously as an indication of what it has displaced, the absence of which reinscribes itself into the represented presence. Consequently, the work is neither an object nor a pure depiction of a given, but basically a metaphor meant to bridge an unbridgeable gap. Closure, then, ceases to be the ineluctable feature of harmony which the New Critics considered the be-all and end-all of the work, thereby revealing their unquestioned commitment to classical aesthetics. Instead, closure turns into a sign, highlighting a deep-rooted desire in the human makeup for the sense of an ending both in terms of space and time.

In this respect, Murray Krieger conceives of the text's duplicity as a means of charting anthropological dispositions of man, whose cultural activities arise out of a basic duality between closure and open-endedness.

In so deviating from a New Critical position, Murray Krieger appears to swerve toward a poststructuralist one. Yet he intends to be equally discriminating regarding his own position by setting it off from what the poststructuralists had proposed.

First and foremost, he objects to having metaphor replaced by metonymy as the favored trope of those who advocate ultratextuality. Metaphor, he maintains, outstrips metonymy insofar as it is a form of "secular transubstantiation," implying, of course, that whatever representation displaces inevitably bounces back on it, showing it up for what it is: the illusion of presence. In contradistinction to this revelatory capacity of metaphor, metonymy is nothing but arbitrary sign-relationship. If, however, the difference between absence and presence is inscribed into metaphor itself, and metaphor is not only the constitutive feature of the text but also identical with it, then this type of text can clearly be marked off from the continuum and can be identified as literature.

In this respect, Murray Krieger applies the concept of deviation to textuality itself. This attempt carries an implicit irony, as deviation originally had to postulate a norm from which the literary text was meant to break away, whereas here a concept which eliminated distinctions and made them shade into textuality has involuntarily provided a norm from which deviations can again be traced. This is the grandstand view adopted by Murray Krieger for his defense of the specificity of the literary text and of poetics as a means of theorizing both its structure and its function.

The endeavor to establish discontinuities in the continuum is bound to be critical of a great many conceptualizations of textuality that have emerged in the wake of poststructuralism. If the literary text was conceived as a model of communication, its basic duplicity would be resolved in the code-governed transfer of its message. If it was considered as semiosis, a reduction of the technical operations of its sign-relationships would occur. If it served as an index of the *episteme*, it would be downgraded to an illustration of it. As a structure of power or as an assembly of tropes, it would be confined either to an indication of authorial intention or to the pattern of rhetorical strategies. Whatever the frame of reference in the approaches concerned, the literary text is made to dissolve into something other than itself, and should this be the truth of the matter, then, according to Murray Krieger, poetics itself is destined to vanish as it no longer has an object.

However, Murray Krieger sounds a note of hope, especially in view of the now rampant deconstructivist criticism. What deconstruction promulgates has long since been a conspicuous feature of the literary text, Murray Krieger maintains, and he seems to be borne out by the constant return of deconstructivist critics to the great works of literature for tracing the "presence" of those principles in the text that they advocate. Literature always discloses its fictionality and thus brackets both the assertive and the predicative nature of the sentence sequence out of which it arises.

Furthermore, literature as metaphor has continued to act out the game of presence and absence since its inception, a procedure that almost turns it into a paradigm for what deconstruction intends to bring to a greater awareness.

And finally, whenever deconstruction is brought to bear on other types of discourse, such as philosophy and history, the exposure of the underlying reifications does not result in the total obliteration of their distinctive markers; one still can tell the one from the other. If these distinctions were not to persist, how would it be possible to deconstruct historic discourse by means of resorting to literary categories, as Hayden White has attempted to do?

Yet, irrespective of Murray Krieger's own subversion of the deconstructivist argument regarding the uniqueness of the literary text, the basic reservation of the argument still stands: The literary text either symbolizes or represents a presence which appears to be self-referential, whereas each presence cannot help being a sign of an absence.

This fundamental charge against privileging the literary text is countered by Murray Krieger's having recourse to anthropological needs to which the text is supposed to respond. We seem to have a basic desire for closure, the frustration of which in our workaday reality spurs the imagination into action in order to provide what otherwise is denied us. Hence our preoccupation with endings and our constant fabrications of myths result from this ineradicable necessity. The literary text, Murray Krieger argues, relates to these cultural activities that are meant to compensate for our frustrations and deficiencies. He intends, however, to give it a different turn. The poetic medium signifies a presence that is self-referential though it allows the signifier to figure something else in addition. This very duality reflects the nature of language itself, which is both designation and figuration. The poetic discourse brings these two functions into coexistence, thus inscribing absence into presence and thereby making closure illusory. Yet this illusion fulfills the nostalgic hankering after unity; it resuscitates the dream of an all-encompassing wholeness which was lost by entering the symbolic order and which can only be recuperated within the symbolic order by poetry. For Murray Krieger this is the reason why poets manipulate the metonymic character of the signifier in order to turn it into a metaphoric entity. Consequently, each poem is part of textuality and a unique text at one and the same time. The metonymy of its signifiers makes it part of the continuum of textuality; the bridging of differences, however, creates a metaphoric unity, the nature of which is the duplicity of closure and open-endedness.

MURRAY KRIEGER: In order to get things going, but without taking too much time, let me expand on what I say in "An Apology for Poetics" by making only three points. First, I want to remind you that whatever I claim for the poem and its privilege I do not claim objectively: I think everything Professor Iser has said in his introductory statement acknowledges this qualification, but I want to point it up for a moment. I make these claims within the provisional notion of the poem as an illusionary stimulus constructed into an object only by a reader who, believing himself to be following cues provided by the poem, seeks to make that poem one by filling in the gaps and apprehending, he thinks, patterns provided by the poem. The poem becomes poem for us, then, only through an act of complicity made in accordance with the aesthetic habit in our culture, after many centuries that have fed that habit of turning sequence into teleological structure.

The term *aesthetic* itself is literally derived from "aesthesis," whose meaning relates to how we perceive, and the notion of illusion is, of course, embedded in the notion of aesthesis, and of its German equivalent, *Schein*. In our tradition the author often creates in order to provide the reader with what he is looking for, and will find if he tries hard enough, whatever our skepticism may lead us to deny about its ontological status. And questions about its ontological status I do not find interesting or, for my purposes, necessary. In this, then, I mean to make common cause with Professor Iser as I read him. Like him and like Ernst Gombrich, whose work has had an influence on both of us, I am more interested in how we come to see and project poems, and subsequently interpret the illusionary realities that come out of our seeing and our projecting, than I am in deconstructing that projection in an attempt to discover what it is we really have done to ourselves through this projection and how delusionary it may be. I want to account, that is, for the aesthetic from the inside, from inside a culture's perceptions and activities. My interest, as phenomenological rather than ontological, means to be in accord with Professor Iser's. I acknowledge a significant similarity in what the two of us are trying to do as we both attempt to demonstrate the difference between the functioning of "literature" and of nonliterature, seeking out the apparently self-conscious fictionality of the literary in contrast to other discourse, however fictional that other discourse may often prove to be. I feel especially close to the work that Professor Iser is doing right now, and I very anxiously await the projection of some of these notions in the volume on fiction and the "imaginary" on which he is currently working.

That is the first point. The second: despite what others claim about my work, I am anxious to find ways to get from the poem into history, whether it is private psychological history or public—social and political—history. My central concern with metaphor means to extend itself, means to focus, not merely upon metaphor as an all-enclosing and all-inclusive element, but also upon what the metaphor represses and excludes, what the poem seems to know is outside itself and in need of being repressed and excluded to preserve it as poem. I find that the enclosing, totalizing pretension of the poem as metaphor—or rather of our reading of the poem as metaphor—seeks to subject itself to the power of its own illusion, that which would repress whatever threatens to explode the metaphor and undo the poem—which is just about everything outside itself and its all-enclosing elements.

The shrewd, self-deconstructing poem reminds us of this repression by its subtle, barely sensed though self-conscious, smuggling in of the repressed. Now, all this is enormously telling, it seems to me, about the private drives of the poet, but—even more—about the cultural moment: what its vision, its politics, admits or represses, what its words permit, what they see or are blind to, what their hearers are to hear or allow to be wasted on the air.

Such intimations are of great historical importance, allowing us to see what the poet's language hides as well as what it reveals, what role is played by the social as well as the psychological drive for power, a role revealed by the hiding as well as by the saying. They also tell us about the several successive societies of readers, each of which finds both its enclosing metaphors and what by implication it senses as the repressed. Each historical set of readers responds in its own way to the need to fill in the gaps, by means of which each constructs metaphorical wholes for its literary works. Through the history of a literary text, readers have filled it in radically different ways, the different fills, different patterns, answering to good historical reasons, as Professor Jauss has shown us in his contributions to our sense of historical interpretation. Our uncovering of such different totalizations is crucial in unlocking the critical procedure my sort of theory proposes, so that it may open outward into social history from what is too often thought of as a self-enclosed formalism.

One final point, which is meant to direct whatever reading you have done in my work. I want to be candid about the overall objective that grounds and limits all my claims: They are, I remind you, based on the appeal to the anthropological, to the inside of culture. To put it another way, whatever system I have rests upon an agreed-upon indulgence of an aesthetic experience and our complicitous role in creating it. This objective, then, accepts the traditional canon as a given, a canon of works singled out as privileged (as "literary") because they seem to require our interpretation, as much interpretation as we can find for them and claim they deserve.

Now, the members of the canon, of course, should shift about continually, for I hope we are not so locked into a particular group, so committed to any works, that we cannot permit some to be elevated into the canon and some to be dropped. But the requirements for membership reflect the claims of the theory, since these seek to justify such works. The claims allow the interpretations that seem adequate to the works in the canon, the very works that they seem to call for; and, in calling for each work, they remind us what to look for in it and, by the same act, have the work justify itself. Such is the curse of the inevitable circularity of theory. Still, clearly such a theoretical structure does not preclude other kinds of theories that seek to satisfy other objectives outside this limited one created under the agreed-upon constraints of the aesthetic tradition in the West and the works that are there as we have made them there, that seem to have been composed in accordance with it. Perhaps, with too much candor, I should confess that the ultimate value of the theory is that it allows me to keep reading the things I want to read and enjoy, and to have good reasons for enjoying them.

So I return to my acceptance of the idea of a canon, with all that this idea implies about the historical assumptions of cultural acceptance under conditions imposed by patterns of power. Within our Western canon I find works that we see as self-privileging. That is, they internally seem to earn the privilege we bestow upon them. I say "seem to earn the privilege," because I must always remind myself that they earn it within their and our mutual complicity. It is, I say again, this complicity which for me the language of Professor Iser's *The Act of Reading* is so useful in justifying, as we find the clues we are looking for to satisfy the phenomenological search for pattern. For me this is the anthropological given, and I'd rather accept than deconstruct it. It is for me the enabling assumption for an aesthetic that our best poetic creations persuade us to invent. And they deserve nothing less than such an invention.

HANS ROBERT JAUSS: As central to the argument of your essay, "An Apology for Poetics," your critique of the false claims of structuralist theory (especially pp. 112–13) impressed me a great deal. Could one not intensify this critique with the following: (a) The premise of classic structuralism is *de singularibus non est scientia*. Does it not follow from this at the very outset, that structuralist theory is incapable of dealing with literary works in their singularity, or put another way, in their historical-aesthetic difference (*Alterität*)? (b) If structuralist theory seeks to deconstruct the literary work as an "elite object," has it not also fallen victim to the fiction of a closed (and unrelated to the world) universe of signs, which it paradoxically denies poetry? (c) If structuralist theory seeks to deconstruct the concept of literature into *écriture*, doesn't it do this in circular fashion by admittedly deriving *écriture* itself from the teleological concept of the text in the paradigm of written literature? Isn't the world as *écriture* consequently just as much a literary fiction as the semiotic notion of "world as text"?

KRIEGER: I thoroughly agree with you, and especially with your suggestion that the teleological conception of text is in many ways the ground from which the structuralists' notion of *écriture* arises. Hence my suggestion that what is happening is that, instead of literature being deconstructed into *écriture*, *écriture* is being constructed into literature. But your notion of "historical-aesthetic difference," or *Alterität*—as a kind of deviation from the norm—is beyond their consideration. In effect, all texts are seen by them as already troped, so that there is no neutral ground to serve as a discourse to be deviated from. On the other hand, our argument against their claim may itself appear to rest upon assumptions common to the deviationist aesthetic, and these appear to posit the properly disputed claim that there is something to be termed normal discourse. But, I must remind you, I am aware that for me the distinction between normal discourse and deviation is heuristic only, though I think very usefully heuristic. I posit normal discourse as a concept that I can use to describe supposed deviations in order to find the special ways in which poetry is working. So normal discourse is a nice negative reference for me in that it allows a standard which, by the way, does not exist for me any more than it does for those devoted to the notion of *écriture*. We could easily agree about that. The difficulty which deviationist theory presents is precisely that there can't be any deviations unless one acknowledges a normal discourse, and if one acknowledges, under the pressure of recent language theory, that all discourse has tropological and narratological elements, these prevent any version of it from being normal. How can we have a deviation, if we don't have a normal discourse to deviate from? Obviously, what the deviationist critic has done, and I am one, is to create a necessary fiction of a normal discourse which exists only by extrapolation from what the finished poem seems to be. That is, one would have to extrapolate from the poem a supposedly prepoetic discourse from which the poem is to be seen as deviating. As you suggest, this predeviated-from model is all that the structuralists have come along and given us—perhaps the very model which the poet might start out with, but which the poem would never end up as being. So in that sense I like the notion of its being heuristic, though I think some of our structuralist friends might like it less.

JAUSS: I see a difficulty with your notion of "aesthetic need," if you define this as "need for closure" (p. 115). If it is maintained that a theory of perception accords with the need "to close the form we perceive" (p. 115), then it seems to me that similarly a theory of aesthetic perception is able to invest the imaginary object with absolute perfection in order to make perceptions aesthetically meaningful.

And moreover, it is this reception of the imaginary object that enables closed meaning structures (*Sinnstrukturen*) to open onto horizons of new (or repressed) meaning. The "sense of an ending" seems to me much more of a "*structural* apocalypse" with which aesthetic experience can never be satisfied. Aesthetic experience ensues from the transgressive need to challenge the given, which is always grounded in the conventions and norms of a closed world. This transgressive need opens up new meaning possibilities (*Sinnmöglichkeiten*) within the interminable process of telling and retelling, interpreting and reinterpreting. I remind you of Paul Valéry's critique of the classical-organologic conception of the work of art, in which he proposed an alternative notion of *poiesis* which suspends the organically closed form in the never-ending process of form-building (and thus, too, of the plural and contingent forms of poetic structures). The closed form of a work on which you seem to insist would in this view derive from the illusion of a reader who has not seen through the classical prejudice of a work's autonomic status.

KRIEGER: I am again not in disagreement with you in that I freely acknowledge, first, that for me the need for closure *is* consistent with a "theory of aesthetic perception," as you describe it, and, secondly, that the "imaginary" (my "illusionary") object does not rest in closure but, through reflexivity, opens itself outward through its implicit self-denials. So I have no trouble with the notion that we must reopen any aesthetic object that is threatening closure. It seems to me precisely the double movement that I have been trying to suggest. As we work with these poems and as we think they seek to have us work with them, they threaten closure at every moment, but in such a way as at the same moment acknowledging the deceiving character of that closure, the fact that theirs is a fictional closure which must be taken only as fiction, therefore leaving a world of unenclosed materials outside the walls, always banging on those walls and threatening to break them down.

At the most elementary level, every time any of us talks about a poem in class or picks up a poem at home and asks "why" about any of its words or any of its lines or characters or incidents or figures, we are making many assumptions of totalization or of closure, since we assume there is a satisfying answer to be found for the "why." Our habit of reading in a way that is perceiving aesthetically (and here I suppose I am to some extent betraying a leaning toward Gestalt such as Gombrich, Iser, and others have betrayed on other occasions) leads us, when reading poems, to want to make each of them fill in the gaps and come together to find itself a totality. Now, that of course seems wholly in accord with the New Criticism. But what I have learned in the last fifteen or so years—and have become increasingly explicit about—is that in the poem and in our response to it there is a continual self-consciousness about the inadequacy of the games the poet is playing to force closure (and the poet plays all kinds of formal games to achieve it). This self-consciousness leads to the subversive element that you mention Valéry talks about, which I have always sensed as well: it is the duplicity that Professor Iser discussed, that which doubles every attempted closure back upon itself.

Generally, it is, in effect, the dual, self-contradictory "reality" we sense as we contemplate the characters onstage as at once one of us, living lives like ours, and yet utterly apart, in the unempirical realm of repeatable make-believe. And they somehow must be seen as partaking of both at once, enclosed in their own world which, showing itself to us as artifice, opens—by negative reference—to another projected "reality" outside which the inside can never enter, or rather is protected from entering.

Or, to shift from drama to duplicities of poetic language itself, let me refer again to a favorite, because obvious, example I have used from "The Rape of the Lock." The assemblage is about to take their coffee, which is being heated. What is to transpire is nothing but an empty ceremony in this ceremonial world that excludes what we might think of as flesh-and-blood "reality." But the language that relates the ceremony to us reminds us, in its double meanings, of that other "reality" being repressed: ". . . the fiery spirits blaze. / From silver spouts the grateful liquors glide, / While China's earth receives the smoking tide." I take especially the phrase "China's earth," which is violently and brilliantly duplicitous in that it means at one and the same time the refined earthen artifact from China and the earthy peopling process of that populous country. And in the "silver spouts" and "grateful liquors" which become the "smoking tide" received by "China's earth" we have the ceramic equivalent of copulation, the exclusion of the biological by the ceremonial artifice that imitates the fleshly, even uses its language, though only to remind us of what it must not show and cannot permit. The prolific realm of peopling—identified with China in the stereotypes of Pope's "orientalist" verbal moment—lies just beyond the frame of the poem, repressed and excluded, though by means of its language the poem manages with a wink to direct us to its outside, the hidden side of its glorious moon.

Nor is this trick an isolated one in the poem, since throughout its course its language plays similar games, all serving the very notion of the rape of the lock, the only rape possible in this decorous closet of a world which shuts out those acts which its words, from "rape" onward, remind us are *not* taking place. The excluded is constantly there, in the underside of the language, banging on the walls the poem seems to want us to construct around it, trying to get in. But, as we have seen, the poem is also acknowledging surreptitiously the impossibility of the exclusion it struggles toward.

I have not meant to stray from the question. My aim has been to show how a poem that with so much care encloses a fragile world apparently maintained by its metaphors, subverts its enclosures and reveals their emptiness, by indirection opening our vision outward to that fully peopled world it so willfully would ignore. In doing so this poem exposes at least me to a new awareness that eighteenth-century poets (and others) too often dared not admit was there, and it is a brilliantly illuminating anthropological document for producing this exposure.

JAUSS: If I understand correctly, your theory calls for a new dialectical notion of "negative reference," according to which the poetic work does not simply suspend excluded reality, but preserves it as something negated (as the background to what has been excluded), which remains the condition of the work's being understood. It seems to me that Adorno anticipated this when he interpreted Goethe's famous poem *Uber allen Gipfeln ist Ruh* as a text which, although suggestive of a harmony with nature, at the same time evokes by negation the excluded, restless, and unpleasant reality of our world. If I correctly understand the premises of your theory, then would not your concept of fiction also have to be defined as "negative reference," which for example would make possible the narrating of events, thereby enabling us to reflect and gain knowledge of reality?

In your critique of Hayden White, however, it looks as if the use of poetic fiction always fails to deal adequately with the supposed objectivity of historical truth. White's categories of "emplotments" have more than demonstrated their worth in understanding nine-teenth-century historiography. I would argue against the view that White's categories reduce historical truth to the mere illusion of poetic fiction (we can for the moment set aside his claim about their origin in the rhetorical figures of metaphor, metonymy, etc.). Fictional structures, to which the principles of the Aristotelian fable (beginning, middle, end) already belong, by no means transform history into a closed "other" world of fiction, but first make—comparable to Kant's regulative ideas—complex historical reality knowable in meaning contexts. (On this point I enclose my essay, *Gebrauch der Fiktion für Anschauung und Darstellung von Geschichte*.) Wolfgang Iser has himself also set out why poetic fiction must be understood no longer as a world opposed to reality, but as the basis for contact (*Mitteilungsverhältnis*) with and a communication of "reality." The fictive generates meaning as it opens the way for experience. If this should be the case, would one not also have to include poetic fiction in the catalog of metaphysical assumptions to be deconstructed, which already includes different assumptions of the classical ontology of literature? That is, poetic fiction, like these assumptions, could no longer be understood as a totalized structure (a self-realized teleological closure). Would not the communicative function of fictions offer yet another possibility to your "Apology for Poetics"?

KRIEGER: As I understand you, your suggestion rests on a series of epistemological expectations which Hayden White's extreme skepticism could not accept. It is he, not I, who sees only the fictional element in historical discourse and who, consequently, would collapse any distinction between historical and poetic fictions. You would still retain a privileged, prediscursive and extradiscursive "reality" which White has precluded (or pretroped). As a matter of fact, I find White's categories of "emplotments" even further from epistemological issues than I have so far suggested. I remember, when I first looked at the title of the crucial introductory essay to his *Tropics of Discourse* ("Tropology, Discourse, and the Modes of Human Consciousness"), I was startled by those final words, which turn us from any interest that could move outward toward possible historical constructs of "realities" to one that moves inward into consciousness. This is a troublesome overdetermining of White's structural categories, one that makes them substantive, so that as you read you discover he is talking not about emplotments, but about existential projections of modes of consciousness. Consequently, he forgoes any heuristic advantage of the sort that you have proposed.

However, I think we could ignore any difference between us concerning our interpretation of Hayden White, and the force of your question remains to be dealt with. You seem to be suggesting that, by means of my notion of negative reference, poems can be related to reality after all—perhaps no less so than history, even if more obliquely so. Agreeing with me that they betray an awareness of what they exclude or repress—that untamed experience beyond their metaphorical closure—you would have me acknowledge that in this indirect way poetry helps open reality to us. Having insisted that White's historical fictions can be made to relate to an extrafictional reality (by means of something like "Kant's regulative ideas"), you would also refuse to deny poetic fictions their revelatory role. So if White identifies historical and poetic fictions by virtue of a common tropological autonomy that approaches discursive solipsism, you finally bring them together from the other side, through their common discursive capacity to disclose reality, to be instruments of historical cognition. How tempting I find this move as I seek to bolster my "Apology for Poetics" with anthropological arguments. But I must resist.

In my recent writing I have become more and more anxious to show that the realm that the poetic metaphor seeks to exclude in its less self-conscious moments is also in the end just another realm of discourse rather than the realm of experience itself; thus it is also fictional. Next to the poetic enclosure, it may feel like reality, like raw existence itself, but the negative reference that—against the primary poetic thrust—points us toward it is still verbal only: it has us trade one illusionary semantic possibility for another, as in "China's earth," in which the flesh of a mythically conceived population of

China is superimposed upon the ceramics of the mythic refinements of China's art. My constant return to the hobbyhorses of *Tristram Shandy* in recent essays stems from this notion of a multilayered set of verbal and textual illusionary possibilities, with which I would replace your suggestion of the clean polarity between illusion and reality, of fictional enclosure and its negative reference to a privileged, if excluded, world of actual experience. I prefer to bracket them all as variations operating within the linguistic realm.

So, unlike you and White (in what I see as your opposed ways), I still seek to distinguish history from poetry, though hardly on grounds as secure as they were for Aristotle. In a rather obvious and commonsense way, I suggest that, in dealing with history, White and others deal with texts that apparently mean to be something other than fiction: they would hardly present themselves as self-conscious fictions, and most historians would hardly be flattered to be told that they were really fiction-writers. Most of them would wish that they were somehow "truer" than historians who came before them (or than competing historians around them). To that extent, then, history and poetry cannot be treated similarly as fictions. Nor, I would argue as you would not, can they be joined by a similar function of referring, positively or negatively, to reality. I focus rather on the difference between them. The difference is that poetry seeks to justify its fictional status: it not only wants to be a fiction but wants to acknowledge itself as a fiction. Further, as a self-conscious fiction, it provides several sets of perspective glasses and, through them, a collection of conflicting, mutually exclusive verbal realities whose coexistence it sustains. In this sense it remains for me a discourse apart, one that I prefer not to deconstruct. I cannot enclose it within a universal set of narratological emplotments. I cannot do so because, as you have agreed in an earlier statement, that would be to turn poetry into a form of undifferentiated *écriture*, thereby giving up on it as something that deserves to have a poetics written about it.

GABRIELE SCHWAB: Those unconvinced by the orthodoxies of either New Criticism or poststructuralism cannot but receive Professor Krieger's "Apology for Poetics" with sympathy. He seems to do away with the aesthetic ontology of the work as a fixed object (pp. 108–9) and its critical counterpart: aesthetic closure. He objects to structuralist and poststructuralist theories and claims that they have been draining all "*écriture* into literature" (p. 113), "all discourse into undifferentiated textuality and all textuality into trope and fiction" (p. 114). Professor Krieger's insistence on the distinctive character of the work of art, its microcosmic unity *and* its openness to the world, the indeterminacies in work and reception *and* the need for closure, leads to his conception of aesthetic duplicity which makes him a leading mediator of conflicting ideas in the contemporary critical domain.

The challenge of Professor Krieger's position lies in the fact that he sees this aesthetic duplicity to be grounded in anthropological functions of literature. The questions I should like to raise concern the specific nature of this duplicity and its anthropological implications. At first glance it seems that Professor Krieger's conception of aesthetic duplicity stems from a happy marriage of theoretical features normally belonging to rival theories. I should like to summarize four basic arguments which form the core of his new positive model. Two of these focus primarily on qualities of the aesthetic work while the other two deal more with the reception process:

1. The poetical work possesses a self-referential quality which operates as an inbuilt device delimiting it from a surrounding world to which it nevertheless relates. Such self-referentiality permits one to view a work of fiction neither as a self-contained cosmos nor as merging with an all-inclusive background.

2. The poetical work possesses the power to convert differences into identities (pp. 110f., 114f.). This accounts for a constructive tendency in the work, its particular presence, manifested especially in that fusion of differences realized in metaphor (p. 110). This identity is not total and not so much grounded in the object as in the process of reception.

3. In the reception process the reader actualizes the work's potential of identities according to his "need for closure" (p. 115). This need, an anthropological fact rooted in imagination, is fundamental for aesthetic experience in general.

4. Another basic characteristic of the poetic work is its *deconstructive element*, which "keeps it open to the world, to language at large, and to the reader."

Obviously, the anthropological "need for closure" and the work's "power to convert differences into identities" have mainly constructive functions. However, in what way may these be related to the deconstructive element? The "something" that keeps literature open to the world is attributed to the linguistic nature of the work, to the transient and empty character of its signifiers. Created by means of self-referentiality, it will hardly be overlooked by a reader familiar with poststructural theory. The moment of "presence" is thus reflexively broken. Closure and deconstruction may coexist, be it in the form of an act of reading and its reflexion, or in the form of an actual aesthetic experience in the context of a whole series. But it also seems to coexist in the poetic language—a coexistence that results in "the paradoxical nature of language as aesthetic medium."

In all, these four basic qualities of a poetic work and its reception constitute the *fundamental duplicity* which helps to differentiate the work of art from other texts and which, in turn, forms the basis of Professor Krieger's dual aesthetic theory.

However, such an aesthetics of duplicity seems to be somewhat unequally balanced. Granted that there is a "need for closure," is there a corresponding "need for deconstruction" that could claim an equal aesthetic status? And, even more importantly, where may the roots of the anthropological need for closure be found? Professor Krieger relates it to the "dream of unity" suggesting "the secret life-without-language or life-before-language. . . . the very life which the language of difference precludes" (p. 118). "In poetry we grasp at the momentary possibility that this can be a life-in-language" (p. 118). If Professor Krieger describes the "miracle" of closure in such a way, does he not also need a more embracing anthropological model, once he has taken the first step toward anthropology?

I carry this argument even further: Doesn't the power to experience prelinguistic unity as "life-in-language" presuppose a "deconstruction" of "ordinary" language experience? The duplicity of the work would then have to be based on an anthropological model that conceives of two different modes of imagination mediated by the work's double and yet unifying "Gestalt." Yet Professor Krieger insists on not relating his duplicity to two different modes of imagination. But to give coherence to his model, he is still obliged to account for a deconstructive power rooted not in language alone, but—like the need for closure—in anthropology.

One solution would be to follow the historical line of Kantian and romantic aesthetic theory and appeal to reflexivity as an anthropological power when pressed to specify the motivational force behind the deconstructive elements. If he pursued this line of thought, Professor Krieger would have given up a view of the work of art as a self-contained object, but would still remain tied to the old dualism of sensitive and reflexive capacities. Reflexivity, however, as far as its independence and its motivating forces are concerned, has come under heavy attack in our century, especially from deconstructivism.

Thus, the self-reflexive deconstructive power Professor Krieger refers to is not identical with the deconstructivist's deconstructive power, which is turned mainly against the closures stemming from reflexivity.

This problem has even further corollaries. If Professor Krieger, as he made clear in our discussion, wants to avoid grounding duplicity in art on a duplicity of imagination, does that not implicitly lead to a rather Kantian relation of closure, imagination and synthesis, whereas the deconstructive quality of a work would be an additional, but not a basically aesthetic value? Drawing the consequences immanent in Professor Krieger's dual poetics, it seems to me that he reproduces the very conceptual dichotomies of the divisions which he tries to overcome. He has identity, closure, presence, fullness, microcosmos on one side and difference, openness, absence, emptiness on the other. Yet his general sympathy with deviationist aesthetics should also acknowledge that deconstructive qualities may themselves have a dual aspect: They deconstruct ordinary identities in order to construct a new aesthetic "identity," which might indeed evoke or merge with prelinguistic modes of experience. Wouldn't this invite one to connect the "dream of unity" with a poetic language mediating between a primary mode of imagination and a secondary mode of imagination that has its origin in the acquisition of language? Then the "miracle" would lie in the merging of two areas that exclude each other in everyday life.

KRIEGER: I find these comments intensely probing, and as troubling as you meant them to be. Out of my need to address them I may be pressed to say more than I have been able to say before—or at least to say in the paper you have read. I see two related issues as the major ones you raise. First, you ask how I would relate (and must I not relate?) my notion of duplicity to the anthropological and perceptual appeal I make in my attempt to account for our habitual search for closure. This question implicitly requires me to confront a second, one more intimately tied to the practice of criticism, which asks where the locus is of the duplicity that turns closure upon itself, in spite of itself, and, through negation, finds an opening after all.

Let me turn to the second question first. Am I claiming—as I think I am—that both sides of the paradoxical combination of elements, those forcing closure and those undoing it, can be seen as originating in the literary work, or am I claiming, rather, that the closure alone originates in the work, while the countermovement that opens it outward is the reader's deconstructive reaction? I believe you suggest that it is the second (a judgment appropriate to the "reception aesthetic" associated with the University of Konstanz), though in this case I would disagree. But on the other hand I do agree with your observation that in my framework the two moves—toward and away from closure—do not occur in parallel ways, are not analogously related to the work and our response to it, so that there is an imbalance between them as I assign them their functions.

Thus you are concerned that, for me, only the closed totalization, as predeconstructive, is the work's responsibility, while it is language's special character, as it flows through us, that leads us in the opposite direction. But I mean to argue, instead, that it is not the skepticism of the reader's verbal awareness and its inclination toward demystification that turn the incipient closure duplicitous. These (the skepticism and the inclination) may exist in us and are perhaps easily stimulated, but both opposed stimulating tendencies can be traced to the work in its workings. For it is the very nature of the aesthetic medium, as we have instituted it, to look both ways, so that the very act of aesthetic closure provides its own denial that becomes our opening. Again I point—as I did in my reply to Professor Jauss—to the duplicity (in both senses of that word) produced by the stage as medium in drama as well as by language as exemplary medium in all poems. So I claim that the duplicity results not from our need to demystify the would-be totalized closure by opening it to our own realities, but from the verbal intricacies of the work's self-conscious fictionality which doubles its every move upon itself, thereby accompanying aesthetic affirmation with denial, simultaneously a construct and a self-deconstruction.

Yet, if I may return to the first question, it is true that I find a difference in the origins of these doubled (and yet opposed) moves—as these relate to the culturally imposed habits of human response—and this difference, with good reason, disturbs you. I claim that the closure we find, or attempt to find, is related to our perceptual habits as these have been culturally conditioned. So our tendency is to pursue closure, not duplicity. But if the challenge that closure imposes upon itself which, in self-denial, returns us to openness does not—like closure itself—derive from our habitual need, then whence comes it? And is it, then, less firmly (which is only to say less anthropologically) grounded than is the closure?

I am proposing that this countermovement derives from the language itself as—again in accordance with Western tradition in the arts—it has been tortured into functioning as an aesthetic medium. I am claiming not, as some poststructuralists would, that it derives from the dynamics of language itself, but—I repeat—that it derives from language as transformed into aesthetic medium. Duplicity is, as you have suggested I would say, the consequence of a mediation. And whence comes the mediation? Why, from the medium, of course.

Our habit of seeking closure is an aesthetic habit, one cultivated within the Western tradition since Aristotle posited closure as the response to a teleological need not normally satisfied outside the aesthetic realm. It finds a fulfillment for a world of experience and of language normally left unfulfilled. But most of our experience, as nonaesthetic, would evade the tightening restrictiveness of language that has been subjected to poetic pressure. Language itself, functioning within rules controlled by the principle of difference, according to the structuralist model, is already a denial of the possibility of verbal presence and identity, and consigns these latter to the realm of mystification. But our usual reading habits, responding to such a language, are just those which the aesthetic must work on us to suspend, so that we can invoke those other habits we have been taught to carry at the ready when the occasion and the work which helps provoke it seem to summon them to a special response. Then the emptiness of our usual words, characterized by the arbitrary and the differential, is broken into as we transform them into the teleological—and hence metaphorical—fullness of an aesthetic medium. The obstacles of our ordinary reading habits may thus be overcome by the culturally learned, extraordinary reading habits, but as we respond to the self-conscious way in which the work suggests its own as–if-ness, its fictionality, we also sense the return of the emptiness of the words as nonaesthetic, which we associate with the casualties of everyday experience. Not that the sense of aesthetic closure is to be even momentarily abandoned, but it is sustained only in the teeth of its frailty, indeed its illusionary evasions.

Now, there are of course some readers who will not be roused from their disposition to read the poem as if it were the morning newspaper, those who are not alive to the potential sacredness of the aesthetic occasion. And there are some who succumb so completely to it that they put to sleep the deconstructive awareness that permits the poem to remind us of the illusion we are fostering, and those less exclusive ones we are excluding or repressing. Even more, there are nominal poems that do not deserve to be treated as other than a newspaper, although the conventions of the occasion may themselves persuade some readers to argue in their behalf. Then critical debate about the virtues of the poem in question can ensue. Presumably we would be seeking to justify the outside stimulus for the suppressing of one set of reading and responding habits for another. One set may be just about always there for us as we carry on our business, at peace with the absences that empty our words. But the other set is conventionally authorized for us within a culture that has sought to reserve special occasions for exploring what the unattainable dominion of verbal presence and identity would be like, in spite of our persistent involvement—in temporal experience as institutionalized in an arbitrary and metonymic language—with openness and difference, with the consequent emptiness of signification.

In claiming that our aesthetic pursuit of closure is culturally conditioned, I am suggesting that it is a habit that is at once anthropological and perceptual. How both? For the perceptual claim would rather suggest the realms of technical psychology, or at least epistemology. Obviously, however, I am following the lead of Ernst Gombrich in claiming that what we see and how we see it are the results of perceptual habits both created and served by the culture's visual tradition as embodied in its arts. So, for all practical purposes, the perceptual habit *is* the anthropologically induced habit. And within the Western aesthetic this habit looks for—and thus makes, and thinks it finds—closure as its aesthetic objective, although it is also prepared to respond to what Rosalie Colie used to call the *un*-metaphoring (or deconstructive) recoil action also provided by the literary work. The latter may seem to be a contrary accompaniment to the pressure for closure, a counteraesthetic thrust always challenging the aesthetic pressure. Yet the anti-aesthetic must be taken as necessary to the validation of the aesthetic so that it becomes, paradoxically, the integral part of the aesthetic that guarantees it, but only by guaranteeing its irreducible duplicity. This is the argument that leads me to see the poem as a metaphor that has known metonymy but tries to appear as metaphor anyway, without denying the metonymic state of language beyond its moment. Thus that part of the aesthetic which is anti-aesthetic allows us to frame the object while threatening to break through the frame that holds it within; persuaded by the picture, we look, with it, just beyond its own carefully wrought edges, much as we do, for example, in Velasquez's *Las Meniñas*, about which we have had so much comment in recent years.

Yet the anthropological-perceptual pressure to find (by making) closures persistently returns as a way of keeping us in touch with a magical manner of signifying, of having words that can touch or even become our most internalized visions, which are otherwise not available to us as linguistic creatures. I would propose that we readers reach for a prelinguistic or presymbolic level of response which is immediate, unmediated; that is, we feel immediacies of response, though we cannot know them because our knowledge is linguistic and symbolic, and our consciousness of knowledge is linguistic and symbolic. In that sense there is no prelinguistic or presymbolic level, except that we have this feeling that there are pure responses which come, as it were, before—before mediation. Yet everything in language *is* mediation, and with a special kind of mediation—that which is related to its peculiar medium—in poems.

My assumption, like the structuralists', is that where language is, there already reigns difference. And any notion of identity is lost with the loss of language as metaphor, succeeded by the awareness of language as a differential—which is to say, a metonymic—instrument. In the old days the romantic anthropologist used to talk about the primitive possibility of our having a monistic language that precedes "difference," with the natives eating their gods. It is the sort of thing you still get in a historian of religion like Eliade, for whom there is the possibility of linguistic identity, the miraculous collapsing of difference. This kind of anthropology has been exploded, of course, by what structuralists, as linguists, have taught us about the way signs work.

What I am saying is that poetic language, having like all language known metonymy, is not an innocent working for the mystifications of identity; rather, it is already in the realm of metonymy and cannot get out. Is it an act of nostalgia still to cherish identity—an attempt by the aesthetic to recover a lost past? That possibility is not what interests me so much as the attempt by poems to discover a way of speaking, or by us to discover a way of reading, which will allow language to have a primal force. In the aesthetic moment poets seem to be working desperately to enclose some kind of presence, even if only an illusion of presence. We who deal with those poems, indeed with the best of them, have—I think—an obligation to discover how their language is working, working by virtue of words that are doing just what words are not supposed to be able to do: somehow to find a way of capturing the gods. Poets seem to have been aware that language is empty until someone manages to force it beyond its incapacities, and poets seem to have appointed themselves to try for this breakthrough. I am trying to suggest a theory that will help us to trace and justify what they do.

Anselm Haverkamp: Professor Krieger, your own "Apology," as it were, deals with an issue whose tradition is characterized by critical treatment in an apologetic mode, and whose identity over and above

Critical Positions: Self-definition and Other Definitions

the inconsistencies of this tradition could, in fact, only be maintained apologetically. Must the first aim and anxiety of a new poetics continue this tradition of the old, and implicate the realm of literary productions within the rhetorical domain of everyday speech? The rhetorical character of the question is perhaps all too obvious. It surely may be heuristically useful "to distinguish poetic from other discourse (by means of a deviationist aesthetic)." But this distinction still presupposes the very rhetorical continuum of speech (that is, of discourse, as an all-too-hasty totalization of the rhetorical field might suggest), which the poeticalness of literary texts is said to have always already interrupted. What, then, ought the aim (if not the anxiety) of a new poetics be which takes its point of departure no longer from the rhetorical primacy of speech, but from the hermeneutic difference between the discursiveness of speaking (*Diskursivität*) and the textual qualities of written texts (*Textualität*)?

The hermeneutical discontinuity of texts within the field of discourse—that is, textuality as a discontinuous sphere of written texts within the domain of spoken language—functions as an open structure (as open systems are open to surrounding environments). This structure, if I follow your argument adequately, under the influence of a deep-seated anthropological "need," awaits closure, and in the case of literary texts provokes their calculated closings. Poetic texts, in your view, somehow await though resist their own closure. Between the rhetorical (*Appellstruktur*) of semantic ambiguity which provokes closure, and the linguistic potential of a semantic undecidability which precludes closure, you propose a duplicity which enables the possibility of closure and openness, simultaneously closing off and opening up. This duplicity is based on what you call "the primacy of the operation of the aesthetic in us all," or more generally, "the aesthetic need," which is the foundation of an apparently unproblematic complicity between author and reader. You don't subscribe to the naïve New Critical faith in the unifying power of metaphor which satisfies this common need, neither do you propagate the structuralist disillusionment brought about by the metonymic arbitrariness which effectively undermines the epistemological claims of any "organicism." Mediating the conflicting tendencies, you speak of "poetic identity despite language's normal incapacities," and conjure a duplicitous notion of metaphor which metaphorically (if not metonymically) combines metaphor and metonymy, "a metaphor that has known metonymy."

Reducing metonymy to mere arbitrariness, the fashionable predilection for metonymy effaces the seminal distinction of a structuralist poetics, though the very success of it rests largely on, and is in fact the result of the metonymic reduction. The original distinction, however, as developed from Jakobson to Lacan, comes closer to your own intentions than the reductive account of your summary allows. The Saussurean metaphor of projection which Jakobson appropriates, and the Freudian metaphor of condensation which Lacan favors and develops into the metaphor of superimposition, provide models for "a metaphor that has known metonymy." The reduction of the structuralist problematic aligns your own notion of duplicity more closely with formalist concepts of metaphor than is necessary and desirable. Duplicity, as you have it, seems rather an argument for a kind of double closure, or alternative closure which anyway ends up in closing off. It is difficult to see to what extent this duplicity can ever surpass the impasses of a semantics of tenor and vehicle which was intended, though not successfully, as an interactive model as well. Richards's interaction theory, however, leads beyond the inherent limitations of the formalist position, limitations which seem to be maintained in your apology for a formalist dualism. Being attentive to the duplicity within the interaction of metaphor may be a progress beyond New Critical varieties of so-called fusion, but it is not enough to account for what is going on in the activity of reading metaphors. The metaphorical illusion of poetic identity (an illusion of presence, as you admit) is the result of a substitution of signifiers whose insisting force (*Drängen*) originates within, and remains efficacious despite its repression (*Verdrängung*). Where there is metaphor there is presence within absence, to bring Lacan back to Sartre, a dialectics of presence and absence which qualifies the imaginary impact of reading.

However one would like to elaborate these models of metaphor, they could certainly provide for what you call "the poem's differentness from other discourse," but in a different way. This differentness would be grounded not in semantic closure or hermeneutic totalization, as you suggest, but in an aesthetic resistance to the structural coercion (*Strukturzwang*) of the interpretive process, ironically "resisting our constructive tendency," and thereby setting free the aesthetic as functional pleasure (*Funktionslust*). The extent to which even deconstruction, which you use as a counter, can account for this remains to be seen.

KRIEGER: First I should like to pursue for a moment your discussion of the relation of my notion of duplicity to New Critical ambiguity on the one side and to poststructuralist undecidability or instability on the other. What is at stake, of course, is my argument for the distinction—if there is one—between poems and other discourse. The term *ambiguity*, I would say, operates within the New Critical poetic exclusively under the blanket of closure. That is to say, the claim is made that the total poem is enclosed only by virtue of the several disparate, if not opposed, meanings that are working together. It is essentially the Hegelian model in which all oppositions unite, so that it is no accident that again and again these critics use Coleridge's passage from chapter 14 of the *Biographia Literaria* in which the imagination "reveals itself in the balance or reconcilement of opposite or discordant qualities."

So the balancing and the reconciling control the direction of the ambiguities as they intermingle in spite of their polar tendencies. Opposition fuses into a system that is marked exclusively by closure (exclusively despite the inclusive representation of the several-sided ambiguities). Any threatened opening is a threat to the system that would empty it of its poetic character. On the other side, the post-structuralist notion of undecidability or instability suggests that there is no limit to the ever-opening concept of textuality. There is no limit to the mobility of the signifiers which seem to chase themselves across the vast network of language stretching before and after.

My notion of duplicity is differentiated from the poststructuralist in that it treats a single verbal sequence as if it could, *pour l'occasion*, be treated as a discontinuous text which appears to us, under the aegis of the aesthetic moment, to have certain determinate sets of internal relations. This duplicity would differ, however, from New Critical ambiguity because it does not represent a synthesis in the Hegelian model; there is no balancing or reconciling of opposite or discordant qualities. Instead, it puts us on the razor's edge, and yet we seem to fall off both sides, at once into and outside the text as metaphor. It at once is contained within the work's domain and yet subverts that very possibility by entering the language system beyond, which it also finds sanctioned—however indirectly—within the work. And I return to my old maxim that seeks to clarify what the poem asks us to believe—tentatively and illusionarily—when it asks us to believe its metaphor: it asks us to believe in a verbal miracle, in which words are seen overrunning their bounds, their distinctions of property, only while reminding us that we can indulge a miracle only so long as we know it cannot have happened. For if we believe it did really happen, then it's a miracle for us no longer.

But now to your objections. I do not feel the force of your complaints as I do some others, because I think they arise in large part from a verbal misunderstanding that can be traced to the ways our different languages use the term *discourse*—or at least to the way you seem to translate my use of that word. You assume that my interest, as I distinguish poems from other discourse, is to begin with "everyday speech" and then to deal with deviations from it. And your concerns spring from your sense of the inadequacy of the realm of speech for grounding a poetics. Consequently, you ask that I turn from the limiting conception of discourse as speech (your *Diskursivität*) to the different framework produced by the conception of written texts (your *Textualität*).

Not surprisingly, you are suggesting a correction that would lead toward the hermeneutics of reader response, although I believe that I have, in effect, adopted it in advance. For *discourse* is not restricted to speech in English, but can refer to written texts as well, and in my work usually does. "Normal" discourse is not, for me, "everyday speech" at all. In fact, in my essay, "Poetic Presence and Illusion II" (in my book, *Poetic Presence and Illusion*), I have explicitly, and with some care, distinguished between the realms of *parole* and *écriture* and have dealt with the differing considerations imposed by each of them and with the special problems of textual interpretation arising from the collision between them as we read. So, to the extent that your concerns derive from the restriction of my term *discourse* to speech, they are ill-founded. My work, I believe, is as much riveted to the problems of textuality as any reception-aesthetician should require.

Perhaps it is this (mis)reading that leads you to view my notion of aesthetic response as resulting from a "complicity between author and reader." But this is to make the aesthetic interaction a speech act, as I would not, since for me the complicitous relation exists not between reader and author but between the reader and the poem as a written text. Further, the role of the aesthetic, for me, goes beyond the linguistic distinctions of Jakobson to which you seek to reduce my position. For I cannot permit it to rest in generic grammatical notions. I am sufficiently responsive to phenomenology to recognize the role played by our disposition in permitting language to work for us in special ways, and this disposition is not derived from the operations of language itself. What converts grammatical functions into functions that serve as an aesthetic medium (Michael Riffaterre would call them "ungrammaticalities") is the self-conscious fictionality which we are prepared as aesthetic readers to entertain and which the work seems to us to be soliciting us to entertain.

It is under the aegis of this conventional receptivity that those deviations occur which enable us to respond to linguistic forms as aesthetic. It is in accordance with this disposition that we can entertain the illusion of the closed metaphorical construct, though as "a metaphor that has known metonymy," it helps sustain our consciousness of its illusionary, self-created limitations.

Consequently, my argument springs from claims about intentionality rather than claims about a universal grammar or semiotic. I would derive my hermeneutic from—in your words—"what is going on in the activity of reading metaphors" and hence, within an interactive model such as you seem to prefer, for I have more in common with reception theorists than I do with Jakobson. It is the aesthetic intentionality that leads me to the deviations that create the aesthetic medium, that lead me—in other words—to the manipulations of our fictional, our imaginary, stage-space in our self-conscious response to the aesthetic occasion and to the specially made stimulus that sets it off, provided we are willing and knowledgeable enough to be complicitous. And, in speaking of the work as metaphor, I would go on, as I have elsewhere, to discuss the strange commingling of pressure and repression (*Drängen* and *Verdrängen*), much as you have. So, much as I distrust an answer to an objector that concludes by insisting that, at bottom, there is little disagreement, I like to believe that such may well be the case in this instance.

ULRICH GAIER: If one sees, as you do, the poetic as the enticement for the reader to deviate from the continuum of the text, shouldn't one, then, take into account other possibilities of enticement beyond the structure of the text? For instance, such a text as a newspaper article has nothing poetic in itself to entice the reader to deviation; if published, however (as has been done by Peter Handke), in a collection of poems, a newspaper article seems to obtain this "poetic" quality. Shouldn't one, therefore, account not only for the mere structure of the text, but also for the entire communicative situation, including the specific conditions of author and reader (and the variations in these conditions), the mutual presuppositions of the partners, and the media as these are conditioned in and by their historical change?

KRIEGER: You properly remind us, once again, of the governing role of the reader's perspective and the dependence of that perspective upon the context of what you call "the entire communicative situation." And you go on to suggest that, under the proper "communicative situation," just about any text might be seen as displaying what you term "'poetic' quality." No argument there.

For us to see the poem as aesthetic object, it and we must share several different sets of mutual presuppositions (or rather we must have them and read them into the object as sharing them), thereby leading to our sets of expectations for which we seek satisfaction in the work at hand. When we argue with one another about whether or not a particular poem adequately fulfills them we may be able to come to certain agreements, at least about the grounds for deciding. If we think our expectations are being met, we tend to project the appropriate stimulating features onto the object. But the critic in us wants to decide between what feels like a power built into the poem by the maker to control our response and a power we might be projecting onto undeserving newspaper language. Yet it *is* true that the habitual occasion prepares us to read as if we can find the power in the poem, so that we may make a poem out of whatever we are reading—even broken-up lines which are indeed from the newspaper. Whether our projections are or are not justified by what seems to be on display before us is what critics argue about. But that is not at all to deny that we can be fooled by deceptive devices, such as you suggest, which impose upon our habits of reception. Still I think it *is* accurate in such cases to say we are being "fooled," which suggests that the claims being made about the constructed forms, sponsored only by our response to the conventions of the occasion, are indeed our unjustified projections in that they are utterly arbitrary, without any anchoring in the stimulating object. So, while I freely concede your point as it applies to our actual reading habits as aesthetic or would-be aesthetic respondents, for me the question of *ought*—how we ought to respond if we seek an appropriate response to the stimulating features of the work at hand—remains one which any critic still anxious to perform must be honest enough (and pragmatic enough) to acknowledge.

What I have been doing is to install a series of cultural supports—what you call "the entire communicative situation"—as enclosures around our capacity to see. This cultural context constitutes an anthropological ground for what we see, thus replacing the ontological ground our philosophy has been forced to give up, though (I must confess) giving up as little critical ground as possible. We discover or project out of a cultural commonness of language and expectation and history and tradition, and these of course differ enormously with time and place. But still there remains the habit we have, as readers of valued aesthetic objects in our culture and its traditions, of sitting down and opening to a page and reading, and trying to read in a special way; and we get very disappointed if something on the page does not startle and disrupt our make-believe-normal-but-really-not-at-all-normal reading, and send us moving back and forth in the text, trying to watch all sorts of things going on at once. And if spots of text here and there do not start to light up, first singly and then in patterns, we may well begin to wonder whether we are reading a poem or the morning newspaper.

I repeat, nothing I have said is meant to deny that we may well be the sole creators of those flashing lights in our habitual anxiety to find them and respond to them, and that, whatever the case, our attribution of poetic quality will confidently follow. But I cannot believe that this act, when it is especially high in the scale of the arbitrary, is not at times corrigible by reference to the text. Further, I must acknowledge that the kinds of patterns that readers find or create will vary as their expectations do, vary with their language and their language of expectation. Again I refer to the help given us by investigations like those of Professor Jauss, because it is precisely the study of the history of the interpretation of individual texts that helps tell us how to read now by illuminating the kinds of language we have at our disposal. In conclusion, then, I do not see that the fact that we project, sometimes more in complicity with the poem than at other times, should bother us so long as we still agree to make great demands of the poem and to cultivate the fiction that we can discover what the extent of *its* powers over our response ought to be.

JÜRGEN SCHLAEGER: I wonder what "price" you have had to pay for your ingenious reconciliation between two diametrically opposed concepts of the structure and function of "successful literary works." I think that this price can be best measured in terms of historical applicability. It is true, you try to base your concept on the anthropological makeup of the human psyche, thereby implying a methodological shift from an ontological to a reader-response point of view; but, to my mind, this does not make your notion of "the paradoxical simultaneity of closure and utter openness" less normative.

Considering the immense variety of "successful literary objects" the conclusion is conceivable, if not unavoidable, that this variety could be understood and classified in terms of differing relations between closure and openness. There may be literary works the achievement of which consists in the minimalization of that basic tension between openness and closure. There may be others which created and still create aesthetic pleasure by playing upon our need for closure; and again, there may be works whose success lies in the continual subversion of our attempt "to close" them. A strict exclusion of gradation from your concept of literary discourse seems to me to sacrifice too much on the altar of harmony between modern poetological schools.

KRIEGER: Your question assumes that I view all poems as partly closed, partly open, some more one way, some more the other, in a continuous gradation from one extreme to the other, an entire spectrum leading from almost total closure to almost total openness. It is a tempting notion in its friendliness, for it is attractively reassuring in its catholic acceptance—and pleasantly easy, too easy. But it is one I must reject, for it strikes me as a flight from theory with all of its necessary repressions.

Instead, mine is a quite different model: according to it, in reading (as in watching a play) we seek a form that produces total closure, except that as we find each form closing, we find it also—through its apparent consciousness of its own fictionality—opening itself totally toward that which its closure would exclude. So every act is an act of unqualified closing that must in the very process reverse, and thus open, itself. The model is built on an all-or-none, changing into an all-*and*-none arrangement, quite different indeed from the continual eclectic compromising between the ratios that share partial openness and closure.

Still, you must ask, what about those obvious differences among works along that spectrum you observe, running from those that seem most referential to those most wrapped in their own artifice? The question really is, are there poems about whose value we might agree—within broader agreements about our common expectations and so on—which do not persuade us to read them my way in order to earn that evaluation? (Of course, the circularity of this procedure is obvious enough.) What of poems, you may ask, which are largely open on the one hand or, on the other hand, poems which seek closure without betraying a fictional self-reference? (By self-reference I do not mean the obvious operation in which some parts of the poem are referred to by other parts, but rather the poem's referring to its own artifice, to its character as an unreality, as a merely illusionary fiction.)

In order to collapse the differences along the suggested spectrum and so find among them a common tendency to fictional self-consciousness, I recall the perspective given me by Ernst Gombrich, who teaches us to argue for the self-referential character of those artworks which at first appear most explicitly mimetic and hence the least artful. He reminds us that even the trompe l'oeil painting, which seeks altogether to lose its artfulness by merging into the reality it

Critical Positions: Self-definition and Other Definitions

would imitate, calls not less attention to its unreality, but more. It apparently wishes to fool the eye and make us think it is the thing itself—of the world and not of art—but, as it confronts our artistically conditioned attention within a conventionally accepted aesthetic occasion, it functions not to deny itself as art but to proclaim the brilliance of the manipulation of the medium which makes us recognize that we might have been deceived, though of course we have not been. Representative of the most "realistic" possibilities of art, it reminds us, then, of the fictional nature of the mimetic claim of all art. I believe this line of argument answers your attempt to hold out many poems from my attempt to find in them the subversion of the closure they seek to impose.

But of course my every word here confirms your stated fear that my notion cannot be saved from being a normative one. Clearly, I restrict my claims to what you quote me as calling "successful literary works," and I discover these as I find them satisfying the criteria I use to define them—just the circular procedure I acknowledged earlier. But surely I would not include all the texts that you and others might want me to in a would-be descriptive method that seeks to evade the normative. In this and my other answers, clearly I do not fear being normative; indeed, I would not dream of seeking *not* to be. I confess I could not feel any theoretical power in a poetics that does not accept its normative fate, even if I admit the theoretical difficulties inevitably courted by bringing questions of value to the surface of our awareness and allowing them to dominate our argument, as they probably would in any case.

WOLFGANG ISER: *Concluding Remarks*: As I reflect upon the exchange of arguments, two issues figured prominently in the discussion: what exactly is duplicity and how do we conceive of mediation? There seemed to be basic agreement on duplicity as a conspicuous feature of what we have come to call the literary text. Thus, the concept of duplicity as delineated by Murray Krieger was not in dispute; on the contrary, it became the pivot of the discussion around which the interchange revolved. What emerged, however, as contentious was the way in which mediation is to be understood.

Murray Krieger indicated that the idea of mediation loomed large in his argument, for which it provided a basic underpinning. Yet it seemed that what he intended to mediate concerned primarily a fundamental dichotomy, yawning between two diametrically opposed theories regarding the literary object: New Criticism and poststructuralism. His theory reshuffles the New Critical perception of closure just as much as it intends to recast the poststructuralist conception of presence as illusion. His aim in doing so was to establish duplicity as the hallmark of the literary text, in consequence of which mediation was conceived as a reorganization of the relationship between two mutually exclusive theories, epitomized in the concept of duplicity as mediation between closure and openness. And as the distinctive quality of the literary text appeared to be in question, mediation according to Murray Krieger comes to full fruition when the blending of opposite notions in regard to the literary text serves to pinpoint the disputed singularity.

This was the juncture from which disagreement began to spread, which nevertheless was pervaded by the uncontested idea that duplicity and mediation are crucial to the literary text, though their interrelation could not be exhaustively dealt with as long as language was the overriding issue for its investigation. Murray Krieger had to make language his prime concern as he wanted to separate the literary text from other types of text in view of the currently overpowering impact *écriture* exercises on the theory of literature. Yet to ground the specificity of the literary text in language primarily is bound to lead to a feature analysis which turns out to be a last resort whenever the language model is paramount.

This apparent restriction imposed on duplicity resulted from the intertwining of two theories, whose main preoccupation is the poeticity of language in the one case and the textuality of discourse in the other. Duplicity, then—so the discussion showed—should no longer be confined to the "prison house of language" and instead should be linked to other frames of reference, if its claim to being the distinctive mark of literature is to be upheld. And as Murray Krieger himself has opened the gate leading to a realm outside language by tying closure to a human need, the confines of language were exceeded in the discussion.

The concept of closure itself came under scrutiny. Supposing it originated from an anthropological desire which seeks expression in the literary work, what makes it different from that kind of closure which governs our perceptual activities? A pure percept resulting from these activities is not as yet endowed with aesthetic qualities which rather arise out of a gestalt-breaking effort. Now, if the duplicitous nature of the text were to fulfill this very function, duplicity itself would have to be traced back to anthropological dispositions. Murray Krieger, however, did not seem to be inclined to conceive of duplicity in this way; for him it is to be brought about by the verbal intricacies of the work's self-conscious fictionality.

Critical Positions: Self-definition and Other Definitions

Should closure and duplicity really have different roots, the anthropological issue raised will be headed off into an unpremeditated direction. Closure, then, as reflected in the text, tends to appear as an anthropological constant, which is either exposed or manipulated by linguistic operations whenever it is pushed over the threshold of the unconscious into the symbolic order. By unfolding this implication inherent in Murray Krieger's theory, a vital problem of literature's relation to cultural anthropology moved into focus. Is literature merely a mirror of the anthropological givens, or is it perhaps a divining rod for finding out something of our makeup? Instead of being an illustration of such assumed givens, the literary medium might serve as a field of exploration for the workings of the human imagination and promise insight as to why the imaginary potential has been fed back into human reality for the 2500 years since its documented inception.

Cultural anthropology, then, could turn out to be less a frame of reference for determining what literature is, but would emerge itself as an area of investigation for providing answers to questions such as: why do we stand in need of literature and its fictions? In case there is such a revelatory capacity inherent in literature, its specificity should be conceived more in terms of functions than in terms of structure. Structures and features would then become subservient to the functions the text is meant to fulfill, which simultaneously would account for the kaleidoscopically changing forms of literature as responses to existing challenges.

Thus the differences between Murray Krieger's position and that held by the participants in the discussion came out into the open. Murray Krieger made a case for duplicity as the hallmark of the literary text in order to prove that literature becomes literature by virtue of this very feature; if there is literature it must have a specificity of its own which can never be derived from anything other than itself. In defending his position Murray Krieger orchestrated his idea of duplicity which in the end turned out to be an embodiment of mediation itself.

The participants, on the other hand, gave a tilt to this idea of mediation by asserting in different ways that literature has to be mediated with either the human makeup or the historical situation out of which it arose, or with the modes of communication in order to bring out the specificity in question. Thus, duplicity, though agreed upon as an important concept, can only be taken as a heuristic notion for finding out what remains hidden in the workings of the human mind, what is revealed by the responses to a situational challenge, and what allows for the communication of an experience which has never been in the orbit of its potential recipient.

Although there was no basic disagreement about the issues under consideration, the mode of tackling them brought out different intellectual temperaments marked by opposing points of departure: a linguistically and structurally oriented approach on the one hand and a hermeneutically and anthropologically oriented one on the other. Each of them is trying to rescue the text, though on different grounds, either by its self-produced singularity or by the multifariousness of its function.

My title, with its words *literary* and *privilege* and—even worse—its coupling of them in the interest of *evaluation*, may seem to be serving a nostalgia that rival theorists may find quaint. It has for some time been clear that the very possibility of talking about literary value has been undermined to a degree that has become critical. The long unquestioned assumptions that underlay the ordinary language we used to bestow or deny value in talking about verbal objects and our responses to them have now been questioned to the point where the more astute of us have indeed had to change that language.

For one thing, the habit of attaching value to objects, as if it were contained in them waiting to be perceived or—unhappily—missed by us, was undone by increasingly self-conscious epistemologies and phenomenologies. Our interest, therefore, was to shift to the varying needs (and, therefore, the varying evaluations) of a society that produced this oddly elitist habit of granting such privileges to some of its artifacts. In addition to separating values from objects and changing the point of interest from aesthetic value to the sociology of evaluation, we have also dissolved the object itself into the undifferentiated codes of textuality at large or the vagaries of the experiences of its readers. So, already struggling against the denial of value to the literary artifact, the would-be evaluator must confront the disappearance of the very object about which he would predicate the value. In light of these developments, I think wistfully back to those easier days only a decade or so back when the question of evaluation in the arts may have suggested many problems but had not yet become problematic. Today one cannot begin to come at it without first questioning the assumptions that permit the question to be put.

The very possibility of evaluating works of art rests upon the assumption that one work is superior to, or more satisfactory than, another—at least to someone and on grounds that must be specified. With whatever qualifications, then, this leads to the further assumption that there is a hierarchy of value among works of art (or at least a hierarchy of works as valued). It is on the basis of this hierarchy that a culture seeks to establish the selection of works that are most highly valued, that yield an experience found to be most worth repeating, so that their accessibility to that culture's members is most worth guaranteeing. Thus it is that the canon of works in a given art is at every moment being established and reestablished: whatever shuffling there may be among potential members of the canon included or excluded from time to time, there is no backing away from the principle of exclusiveness—yes, let us say it, of the elitist principle—which permits the entire procedure to proceed. And it is our increasing awareness of this principle, with all it implies, that has led—these last years—to our becoming critical of it, that has subverted our impulse to evaluate and has introduced the problematic element that undermines in advance every attempt, like this one, to talk about this subject.

How seriously, or rather how literally, should we extend the social-economic metaphor of exclusivity, or elitism, that is hidden in the assumptions behind the traditional notion of evaluation that has been so severely put into question in the theory of recent years—so severely that, as you have seen, I must open a talk on evaluation in literature in this nostalgic and defensive manner? It is evident that in our recent theoretical revolution there are many who would insist upon just such a literal extension of the social-economic metaphor into the aesthetic realm. Or rather they would deny the existence of an aesthetic realm, reducing it instead to a disguised and mystified form of the social-economic. And from the dissolution of art into economic fact political action should follow.

Once brought down, without discrimination, to the world of quantity, all commodities should, on democratic principles, be egalitarianized. There seems, in other words, to be a moral justification for suppressing distinctions in value among our art objects and between them and other objects. Because these anti-aesthetic theorists are not concerned that they are taking too literally an analogy between a classless society of persons and a classless society of their products, they blithely hold that class structures should no more be tolerated among our commodities than among our citizens. And what, to them, betrays this outmoded class consciousness more than the act of setting apart a few select masterworks into a *canon*, a term whose unfortunate theological implications can now be exploited? In the quantitative domain of commodities there can obviously be no intrinsic qualities to argue for masterworks or for a canon made up of them. Enemies to the aesthetic literalize (and thus reduce to raw economics) the submerged economic metaphors in discussions about the "value" or "worth" of an art object. Similarly, they see political (and theological) metaphors—on behalf of "privileged" treatment of "elite" members of the "canon" as implicit everywhere in older and traditional criticism, and they press such metaphors to their literal consequences since they wish to condemn the aesthetic convention, out of which older cultural moments produced (and cherished) masterworks, for its aristocratic exclusiveness.

As a consequence, such theorists may have to consider those works most admired in the past to be as obsolete as the discarded social and political institutions that are reflected in their elitist pretensions to be "high art." To reject our revered masterpieces, then, is really to reject the political institutions at work in the cultures that produced them. It is as if, by turning against an aesthetic monument, which history and the critical tradition have carefully segregated from—and lifted above—its fellows, the anti-elitist critics somehow can wish out of existence the reactionary political context that may have been thriving when the work was created. (And they find it hard to ignore the fact that much of our highest art has emerged out of reactionary political moments.) Better yet, they are implicitly acknowledging that, if the work should have any special endowments, those endowments require, and grow out of, the undemocratic characteristics of its social-political context, so that, by denying what had been the accepted superiority of the work, the anti-elitists can somehow discredit the political beliefs of the culture behind it. Hardly a sample of "people's art," the great work of "high art" seems to demand the metaphors of an aristocratic body politic even to find the audacity to ask for itself the privileged treatment, the idolatry, the claim to special "value," that has been accorded it.

One important consequence of denying the status of art to specially formed objects is the denial to the object of any kind of formal closure which the critic is to search out and valorize. From Immanuel Kant onward, this formal finality had been the fulfillment of our aesthetic need to find in the object what he thought of as "internal purposiveness." The dethroning of aesthetic object and aesthetic value, and the abolition altogether of the aesthetic realm, destroy the closed sanctity of such objects as self-fulfilled, as fictions, opening them anew instead to an immediate relationship to normal experience, and to normal discourse. With the theoretical disappearance of closure, which is now seen to have been a deceiving myth, all objects, their would-be fictional boundaries dissolved, flow freely into and out of normal experience (all texts flowing into and out of the sea of textuality), now that they are declared no more than a routine part of that experience and that language field. The formal closure, which post-Kantian aesthetics sees art as imposing upon experience, is derived from the human impulse to order, which is behind the impulse to art. And for the anti-elitists, the most objectionable character of the great work of art is its assumption of the absolute value of humanly created order, *its* order. Instead of authorizing the human creator to seek a triumph with his order over ordinary life, the anti-elitist asks for the embrace of the ordinary and the condemnation of any order that would disdain it. And he rejects the suggestion that the ordinary is a crude, brawling confusion which needs rescuing by the refinements of an aesthetic order that permits us to apprehend it. As anti-elitist, he distrusts as politically suspect our every impulse to impose upon the ordinary. For, in relating art to society, he relates aesthetic order to social-political order, and he sees the latter as a characteristic of regressive and repressive moments in our history.

The flight from an elitist concept of order is a flight from value and, as we have seen, a flight from any separatist notion of the aesthetic. It can affect our attitude to older works, if we decline to segregate some of them into a canon and to term them the best we know; and—more crucially these days—it can affect the creation of new works, persuading makers to disdain making art in order to dissolve the making into the value-free (or equally valued) experience of common life. But can these flights from the valorizing of art, flights into the freedom of modern Western experience, actually eliminate the special experience of our enduring interactions with the greatness of our masterpieces (and hence the special value we attribute to them)? And do we not take such aesthetic judgments and such masterworks for granted even as we try to be receptive to the social and anti-elitist arguments that justify an often anti-aesthetic avant-garde? In our self-prompted, postmodernist enthusiasm, we may—at times reluctantly—accept many of the most anti-aesthetic experiments as peculiarly representative of our cultural moment. But we can afford to do so, perhaps, because we feel secretly assured that our older gems of art have already been made and are still with us to be valued in their rarefied separateness. I wonder, when we try to respond to recent electronic music, or to recent "conceptual art" with its war on painting or sculpture as objects, or to the recent instinctual verbal emissions we still call poetry, whether we do so knowing we can count on Mozart or Cézanne or Shakespeare to be there for us to go back to. In other words, for all our attempts to

Critical Positions: Self-definition and Other Definitions

cooperate with the revolutionary art (or anti-art) that may reflect our moment at this end of the historical continuum we may egocentrically view as progressive, I suggest that we quietly rely upon, and are assured by, our antiprogressive commitment to works of art with which the postmodern world usually does not seek to compete, and very likely could not do so if it tried. To the extent that this is the case, there remains the need to evaluate the older works which still—however subliminally—constitute the elite canon that we unconsciously retain for our aesthetic security, whatever the freedom—including the freedom from striving for aesthetic value—which we grant to new works.

The notion that there *is* peculiarly aesthetic value, distinct from other values we impose—and hence "disinterested"—is our inheritance from Kant's *Critique of Judgment*; and the critical tradition that culminates in the now old New Criticism is a development out of Kant's formulation. The reader or spectator—or rather that rarefied version of reader or spectator that we call the critic—is to treat what he thinks of as "the aesthetic object" as an entity on its own out there, an object that he seeks to apprehend in its wholeness, its internal purposiveness. Thus he is to treat it apart from his own interests, and apart from the artist's interests, as an integral artifact, a self-sufficient fiction. It is the doctrine of disinterestedness, as the characterization of the aesthetic, which leads to the need to maintain "aesthetic distance" (distance between object and subject of aesthetic experience and distance between object and its sources in man and culture), and from there to the autonomy and self-sufficiency of the object (through the internally exploited principle of a purposiveness free of any external interest).

The reification of those systems of signs which our interpretive energy converts into aesthetic objects is now complete, and we proceed to idolize them. The objects we have projected into being we have set firm boundaries around (as if we learned, and decided to justify, why we have set frames around paintings); by so doing we have made them into special objects, illuminated by their self-directed purposiveness from within. The objects are thus treated as self-enclosures, as totalizations, with a self-fulfillment that raises them above all nonaesthetic human fabrications (however strong the interest these latter satisfy). In this way objects of art have become elite objects for us, beyond the common level of objects that—responsive to interests beyond themselves—are not finally objects at all but, instead, flow beyond themselves into the interests they serve.

But it is precisely this doctrine which, we have seen, recent theorists must seek to deconstruct, in order to reveal it as no more than a beguiling mystification which uses the disguise of disinterestedness to subjugate its mystified followers to a most "interested" doctrine of power and exclusion. Such deconstructors can point to an obvious coincidence between the world of economics and the world of aesthetics (and we must remember that the very notion of the "aesthetic" was born only in the middle of the eighteenth century, when it became economically fortuitous to have it around): the coincidence between the rise of a peculiar—and disinterested—value for works of art and the rise of museums and art collecting as ways of placing monetary value on works of art as collectibles, collectibles to be coveted. But for a Marxist deconstructor (like the Nietzschean or Freudian deconstructor) there are no coincidences: the rise of a theory that finds a way to put a special value on artworks must serve the economic motive which can turn that value to material use. Connoisseurship ends by serving as investment counseling, as the aesthetic plays its role in the conspiracy of the acquisitive society. The object may be turned into a fetish, but that fetishization does not mask its status as a commodity (and oh, what a rarely privileged and highly valued commodity!) from the piercing eye of the deconstructor.

Nevertheless, we continue to speak as if there is a judgment of aesthetic value to be bestowed upon or withheld from literary objects, so that it remains our anthropological obligation to record our culture's illusion of aesthetic value and, consequently, to grant that illusion a momentary validity as a phenomenon of our social experience to which we must attend and for which we must account. We are thus led to examine the grounds for constituting that value and to place literary works in some relation to works in the other arts as culture has responded to its self-imposed need to impose value on them. I have spoken of Kant's aesthetic judgment as the major systematization of our culture's commitment to an aesthetic realm filled by a canon of properly endowed objects. Such an aesthetic realm is persuasively derived from the notion of Kantian "disinterestedness," objects whose apparent wholeness or integrity—whose status as fictions—can be attributed to a self-generated "internal purposiveness." So remarkable a turning-away from our interests as determined by the workaday world requires a reworking of the world's materials (including its language) away from the patterns they usually assume as the result of our customary need to make our customary use of them.

To the extent that it derives from this aesthetic, criticism in the so-called fine arts must take its method from its need to reveal what makes its special object so special, what turns an artifact into art, with all the exemptions and the privilege conferred by the word *art*. Somehow the artist is to have worked his medium into paths which, in its recalcitrance, it would normally not take; and this deviation opens opportunities for exploitation that allow the object to achieve its unique closure, closure being a necessary and ultimate characteristic for this aesthetic. Criticism must seek to follow and account for this process, in whichever of the arts it is serving. Hence the critic, concentrating on the medium, concerns himself with those tangible elements in the art object that give it its material being, that solid reality which the museum (or the acquisitive individual) collects, thereby setting it aside for us to visit and admire.

Our culture may well have converted these objects into our fetishes, claiming them to be worthy of our secular worship. And museums, filled with them, do indeed become the churches of the secular world. If the objects within have been ripped out of their cultural contexts and collected as autonomous individuals in order to be made into aesthetic idols, then obviously their material reality is indispensable; and the physical media of the plastic arts, as they are manipulated by artists who construct their precious objects out of them, would have to become central features of an aesthetic concerned with accounting for the formal purposiveness—and hence the self-sufficiency, the totalization or the internal closure—of such objects. In other words, the emergence of aesthetic vision out of the artist's struggles with his medium is properly a central concern in any attempt to account for the unique character of the object that we have made elite by segregating it from its culture for worship in the museum.

To those of us in literature, much of this discussion may well appear troublesome. We wish literary objects to share the aesthetic characteristics of objects in the other arts, and, indeed, I am assuming as much when I suggest that the New Criticism represents a final stage in the post-Kantian tendency to create a canon of art objects as fully formed members of an ideal miscellaneous anthology. But the emphasis I have been placing on the art object as a tangible entity capable of being materially valued, of being collected and displayed, would appear to put poems as verbal fictions at a disadvantage, if not altogether out of consideration. The question of the medium of the language arts has always been fraught with difficulties, but never so much before the dominance of an aesthetic that gave so primary a role to the material medium. It is very likely for these reasons that the major literary aesthetic after Kant (say, from Coleridge to the New Criticism) spends much of its energy seeking to create a medium for poetry which, despite its ambiguous nature, will allow it to be treated analogously to the plastic arts in an aesthetic that pays tribute to the human power to demonstrate its mastery over a recalcitrant medium.

Please do not misunderstand: nothing that any literary aesthetician can do is going to turn the poem into a materially precious object. The word's spiritual—or at least immaterial, airy—appeal does not permit us to speak of it as a medium except metaphorically, does not permit us to see the poet working like the sculptor or painter except by rough analogy which must preserve a keen awareness of the differences between the poet and the others. I am only trying to say that the elevation of art objects into precious objects, as the result of the transformed attitudes toward art arising during the later eighteenth century, profoundly affected literary theory by forcing it also to find a way of making its object truly an "object"; that, as the result of an aesthetic devoted to autonomous objects of art, literary theory began, by contagion as it were, to search for a material (or a metaphorically material) basis for the poem even though no one was seriously anticipating turning the poem into a collectible object. (As I have suggested, the post-New Critical anthology of poems is as close to a museum as we are likely to come.) The aesthetic, one might argue, spread out beyond the realm (of materially precious aesthetic objects) in whose special interest it seemed to be directing its motivating energy.

How, then, can the literary theorist find the means for his subject to thrive in its competition with the other arts, despite its lacking the requisite medium that has been central to the development of the aesthetics of the arts in the past two centuries? We can answer by looking first at the inadequacy of language as a medium and then by seeing what the literary artist can do about that inadequacy in order to make language serve him as a medium after all. Language presents difficulties to the poet as artist both for what it does not have that plastic media have and for what it has that plastic media do not have. On the one side, as we have observed, words, as conventional signifiers, have no body, no material substance; they have meaning, but no being. This lack of body leads to the other side of their difference from clay or stone and from paint-and-canvas, which have being without meaning (at least no meaning until they are fashioned into art): words are already fully formed elements in common use, with agreed-upon meanings, before they are picked up for *his* use by the poet. An aesthetic medium is usually regarded as a neutral element open to being manipulated by the artist into *his* meaning. But such is not the case with words which, instead of presenting the material resistance of other media, come already fully laden with relatively stable meanings. (Now, it is certainly true that the media of the plastic arts are not totally neutral: there are tendencies for certain colors or intensities of color, or certain shapes, to produce common responses in viewers. And the artist must accept and work within such given a priori limitations. Within some conventions there are also iconographic givens for the artist to accept before he begins his work. Still, such tendencies are surely vague and permissive when compared to the precise and arbitrary fixities of given verbal meanings and the worlds into which they open as we read our sentences, whether in the newspaper or in a poem.)

I come back to the other difficulty attributed to words as medium within this tradition: that the price of being assigned fixed, prior meanings is their being deprived of any material reality, of body. The only thing we can do with a painting hanging on the wall of a museum is to look at it—to try to look at it as a painting, bringing all our aesthetic habits of perception to the task. So the only use the painting can be put to is determined by our response to what the artist has done in his creation of it. As I have written elsewhere, we do not attempt to eat the oranges off a still-life canvas, knowing them to be only illusions within a painterly tradition, but many readers of poems do try to make practical use of the words in their prepoetic state, wrongly treating them as if they were the usual words and constituted declarative sentences in another sort of discourse; treating words—that is—as if they were *not* functioning as an aesthetic medium. This is why teachers of literature often have difficulty teaching uninitiated students—who insist they already know how to read—how to read poems. It is because these students presumably "know how to read" that they have so much to unlearn before they can read language as an aesthetic medium. The teacher of art appreciation should have many fewer complications in initiating his students—and even fewer when he is dealing with nonrepresentational paintings, in which there are less fixed, pre-aesthetic forms to distract the novice. For the individual painting is, as its place in the museum testifies, a thing in its own right, a valued and valuable something—there composed of materials, of stuff, which as a medium is unambiguous. But it takes considerable effort and skill on the part of the poet, as well as a knowing receptivity on the part of the reader, to allow the poem to take on a similar "feel."

At his best, though, the poet seeks to remedy the a priori deficiencies of language as an aesthetic medium by undoing its prior meanings and by conferring something like a bodily substance upon it, however his action violates the way in which language is used to functioning. As Sigurd Burckhardt puts it, the poet must "drive a wedge between words and their meanings" to keep us drawn to the words themselves as things, "and thereby inhibit our all-too-ready flight from them to the things they point to."[1] It is a making-strange of language, what Russian formalists used to call "defamiliarization" or what Michael Riffaterre calls "ungrammaticality."[2] The fact that critics like Burckhardt or Riffaterre work so effectively with puns and ambiguities (in which, as Burckhardt put it, "many meanings can have *one word*"—p. 32) is a likely consequence of this effort to see words in poetry as taking on material substance. For the poet to transform phonetic coincidence into semantic inevitability is for him to rivet our attention upon the words themselves as sensory entities, converting them into a proper medium, in spite of themselves.

So one striking manifestation of language considered as a proper aesthetic medium is the manipulation of the sounds of words as sensory matter. Here would seem to be one justification for the apparently perverse willingness of so many poets for so long to restrict themselves within severe patterns of meter and rhyme well after the passing of the oral tradition that could claim to need such stimulants. Surely such phonic patterns serve as an extreme gesture to the poets' need to "drive a wedge between words and their meanings," to call attention to words as sensory entities. Words are thus transformed into manipulable elements, displaying an "aesthetic surface" like that of the plastic media, thus emphasizing their sensory character, calling our attention to their substance as self-sufficient things instead of to their transparency as would-be pointers. Words thus manipulated demand that we treat them as an aesthetic medium and not as we do in routine discourse: that we attend them rather than going through them once we have deciphered their code; each formal group of them wants to be seen centripetally rather than centrifugally, as a filled and present center and not as one that has been emptied out and turned into an absence. We pretty nearly can heft them and, consequently, come to pay tribute to their innate powers that overwhelm the distance and the arbitrary relation between signifier and signified that governs the normal use of language. Far from arbitrary, they persuade us of their corporeal indispensability.

Elite literary works, then, despite the ordinary words and sentences that appear to make them up, permit us that "illusion" of presence—of here-and-nowness—though it is accompanied by the self-reference that reminds us of the illusionary state. As Ernst Gombrich has led us to speculate, this illusion is not dissimilar to that imposed upon us by the self-consciously make-believe presence we come upon in the plastic arts. On these grounds literary theorists have found a way to allow their

---

1. *Shakespearean Meanings* (Princeton: Princeton University Press, 1968), p. 24.
2. *Semiotics of Poetry* (Bloomington: Indiana University Press, 1978), passim.

art to partake of the elite character of terminal presence that the post-Kantian aesthetic and our culture have provided for the painting or the sculpture. Whether this illusionary presence achieves its duplicitous character through the manipulations of language, of narrative sequence, or of other representational strategies, the reader is to be encouraged to double the realities he creates or responds to in the literary work. And these are not very different, after all, from the ambiguous realities we attribute to the representational painting or the sculpture, once we understand it to be an illusion in Gombrich's sense.

The history of this aesthetic tradition, with the obvious advantages in it (and in our culture's preferences) enjoyed by the material arts that occupy space, would seem to give the poet—in comparison to the plastic artist—the more difficult task and cast him in a disadvantaged role as, like other artists, he fights to achieve presence for his created object. Surely, we can think of the poem as an object, analogous to paintings or sculptures, only by a metaphorical stretch of the imagination. And the fact that the poet must undo the way language operates in order to make it operate his way, as a medium, seems to double his difficulties—especially since he cannot, even in the end, count on an audience that is prepared to undo their own nonpoetic reading habits to cultivate the poem's totality. Nevertheless, it can be argued that the successful poet can make the most of these handicaps, converting the deficiencies of language as a medium into unique advantages. We have worried here about the ambiguities of language as a medium: the word is an empty signifier, part of a prearranged, conventional code that the poet inherits, and yet at the same time it is remade by the poet who forces us to discover and concentrate upon a fullness that he forces within it. On another level, the poet's fiction reminds us of the world it imitates, and it creates a free-standing, make-believe world of its own. So the poem as language may seem to have a dual character, being seen at once as a canonized text and as just more textuality, at once words as shaped into a palpable form of art and as playing an undistinguished role in the network of discourse. This duality should not be broken up into disjunctive choices: either a spatialized, closed world of metaphorical delusion or the open flow of time that is to set the delusion straight. Instead it is to be seen as two illusionary ways in which poetic texts seem, at the same time, to force us to see them as functioning, the metaphorical world at once constructed and deconstructed. Both verbal functions are to be sustained by the poem, and by us reading it, at the same time. But these very ambiguities open special opportunities for the literary work of art, allowing it to embrace a now-you-see-it, now-you-don't duplicity which gives it a richness and complexity which the arts that exploit less ambiguous media would find hard to match. What I am suggesting is that the literary arts, being forced to find their aesthetic justification on grounds which assimilate them to the material and spatial arts, can make those grounds peculiarly their own, indeed can make the word the most effective of media by straining it to exceed its conventional properties.

Clearly, this aesthetic tradition rests on the notion that poetry begins where what it assumes to be normal discourse leaves off, that it thrives on deviations from normal discourse. The criticism sponsored by this tradition finds its literary values in the patterns created by clusters of such deviations, and—subsequently—by the illusionary enclosures permitted by them. The attribution of value is dependent upon the integrity of the system of deviations—the total realization of the potential purposiveness locked within them and the exclusion of those meanings imposed by untransformed elements outside that system. Under this scheme, the very act of interpretation—an act that seeks to determine what turns this verbal sequence into a proper poem—thereby becomes, at the same stroke, an act of evaluation.[3] The more complete the poem (or the reader's ingenuity) permits the interpretation to become, the greater its value. But the deviationist basis of this aesthetic—like the elite object constructed upon it—as I suggested at the start, is being seriously undermined by the deconstructive efforts of recent theoretical fashions. For, besides those I have observed earlier who would undo the elite status of art by merging it into an indivisible realm of political-economic motives, other recent theorists would deny the separatist aesthetic claim made on behalf of literary objects by merging them into an indivisible, seamless web of textuality whose semiotic operations contain all writing equally. In these poststructuralist days there is severe resistance to any claim based on distinctions in kind within the field of forces made up of signifiers, resistance—that is—to the practice of breaking off and privileging the segments of language we call poems as if they had something special in them. Yet the post-Kantian aesthetic must satisfy just this need to seek discontinuities within textuality, at least for the momentary purpose of our aesthetic experience at the hands of the poem, so that it must resort to the deviationist principle in order to distinguish poems from other texts.

---

3. See my earlier (1967) essay, "Literary Analysis and Evaluation—and the Ambidextrous Critic," in *Poetic Presence and Illusion* (Baltimore: Johns Hopkins University Press, 1979), pp. 303–22. Much of the essay concentrates on the tendency to incorporate an implicit evaluation within the very act of interpretation.

The argument for the deviationist poetics must assume that there *is* a normal, a neutral discourse. But recent theorists have persuasively argued that all writing, engaging the dynamic forces of textuality (and, it follows, of intertextuality), partakes of those features that deviationism would reserve for literature in the narrow sense. If, for example, figuration itself is as ubiquitous as discourse, either there are no poems or all writings are poems; but there are no privileged fragments of textuality that alone are elevated into being called poems and specially evaluated as such.

The delusion that there is a normal discourse has been effectively demythified of late—whether by Stanley Fish or Hayden White or by many of those like Paul de Man who follow the lines of Continental poststructuralism, each of them on different grounds, though they are alike in being persuasive. If all texts originate only in other texts out of common tropes and narrative structures, they are similarly figured and similarly fictional. The tropological nature of all language gives to each text a "swerve" in the direction of its peculiar figuration that leaves no neutral linguistic place for language to swerve *from*. Consequently, there is no "normal" discourse from which poetic language can deviate, no neutral sequence of words on which we have not already imposed narrative and tropological shape. In effect, all language is deviation, except that there is no norm. Thus there is no neutral reference, so that we all speak in fictions, whatever truths we deludedly think we mouth. We have gone beyond Molière's Monsieur Jourdain who was surprised (and impressed) to learn that he had been speaking prose all his life; for in this view we have indeed, like all our fellows, been speaking—and writing—poetry, fictions that we had been taking for sober referentiality. Where all are poems, there need be no special gift of poem-making. Any line we attempt to draw between poetry and nonpoetry is mythical as all discourse is similarly gathered under the blanket of *écriture*.

This undiscriminating approach to textuality intends to deprive the traditional aesthetic of its grounds by precluding the peculiarly aesthetic object, so that there is actually no specially endowed entity about which an appropriate claim to value can be made, all such value being no more than a phantom projection out of our self-mystifying sense of loss. If, as we have seen from the start, aesthetic evaluation required a special sort of function and—consequently—a special sort of object to perform it, then the denial of a normal discourse, and of the poem as a systematic deviation from it, precludes the attribution of aesthetic value. But our everyday habit of evaluating and of responding to works as if value could be ascribed to them leads me to retain some commitment to a deviationist aesthetic and to the doctrine of a normal (or undeviated-from) discourse on which it rests. But how can this practice be justified, in view of the common recent arguments against it?

I find no difficulty with the admission that the concept of a normal discourse *is* mythical, though it is a myth we must tentatively indulge if we are to account for the effects that poetry in the Western canon is capable of producing in those of us who come to it with the trained habit of aesthetic response. Can recent arguments for a seamless *écriture* altogether wipe out our commonsense assumptions of the distinction between those texts which are predicated on the claim (even if it is a self-deluded one) that they are telling us about a "reality" outside language—that they are more or less "true"—and those which are self-consciously cultivated fictions? We do approach made-up stories about imagined people differently from discourse that claims to say things directly to us about the world; and we do so, in part, in deference to what we assume the writer means to do with us and to us. Yet the sophisticated claim about the similar metaphoric fictionality of all discourse would lead us to deny any such commonsense distinction as naïve.

I would urge our commonsense awareness of yet a second distinction, this one between discourse which seems anxious to sacrifice itself in order to transmit extralinguistic notions available in several possible verbal sequences or languages, and discourse which seems to generate its meaning out of the very internalized play of its verbal medium, so that its meaning is untranslatably locked in "these words in this order." Recent theorists may well argue that there is no synonymity in *any* discourse, thus reinforcing the antagonism against a claim for a poetic discourse that would create its nature through its unique untranslatability; but shall we not distinguish between the grappling with language to generate meanings as special as the very words, and the lazier, stereotyped thing most of us do most of the time? It is refreshing to recall that the one earlier and most universally recognized contribution of the old New Criticism was its power to distinguish the originally creative use of language from the general storehouse of stock expressions that appear, in borrowed form, in discourse. To call the latter "creative," whatever the epistemological likelihoods in the mind of man as language-user, is to engage in a basic misuse of the language of creativity. (I thus acknowledge my belief that, even in my desire to say something original here, I am essentially discovering—picking up as best I can to satisfy my minimal verbal requirements at each step—the language I am using. I am not, in any way that suggests what the poet does, creating my language in the sense of making it new, even if everything I am saying turns out, alas, to be a fiction reducible to a shaping metaphor.

I argue, then, that most trained readers of poetry feel an acute difference between discourse characterized by a self-generating play of words that maximally exploits all that is potentially in them, exploding them into its meaning, and the loosely instrumental "use" of words selected from the bag of almost equal candidates for service which our culture places at our disposal to carry—one or another of them in its minimal way—a predetermined extralinguistic meaning. Hence my earlier emphasis on the literary medium. Of course, this difference is a matter of degree rather than of kind, so that boundary cases will have to exist and be debated about—and perhaps with almost every case a potential boundary case. Yet the theoretical distinction is a crucial and felt one for so many readers that there is likely to be considerable agreement about poetic and prosaic extremes. Between extremes of verbal manipulations tending toward and away from synonymity (and all that synonymity implies about the verbal satisfactions of maximal or minimal requirements), there may well be difficult and confusing examples of discourse that may appear to some to ask to be read one way and to others another way. And these often turn out to be the not-quite-philosophical, not-altogether-literary texts at the center of much recent theoretical discussion. But, far from proving the nonexistence of poetry as a relatively separate entity demanding special interpretive methods, such texts (as they have recently been treated by the new rhetoricians) may rather have been seen as broadening the applicability of literary methods, thereby enlarging the peculiarly literary domain of literature to include self-consciously reflexive writers whose fictions include the illusion that they are nonfictional.

So all discourse may indeed be a metaphorically derived fiction at its source, and its language may indeed be creative of its own reality, which perhaps never escapes the bounds of textuality. But, in the face of such epistemological concessions as I make here, I still suggest the phenomenological distinctions that the differentiated structures of our verbal experiences present to us and to our culture, which in turn has made differentiated uses of them according to their various forms.

The self-consciously developed fictional illusion of discourse to which we respond as aesthetic creates in its turn the illusion that there is a normal discourse from which it deviates. (Of course, we must grant that by this time there is nothing either shocking or blameworthy in our creating—among all the fictions we create—the fiction that there *is* a normal discourse or the fiction that, except in poetic discourse, there is a synonymity among words—provided we are always willing to broaden the domain of the poetic.) As we contemplate and seek to define what *can* happen in that fused linguistic "corporeality" which poetic discourse sponsors the illusion of attaining, our habit of finding (or making) binary oppositions may be pressed to invent another class of discourse, a prosaic sort that helps us mark by opposition the magical behavior we feel we have witnessed and have been partner to in poetry. And we come up on the other side with the ruthless instrumentality of a neutral, normal discourse that is self-deceived in its intention to be self-effacingly referential. We need to entertain the notion of such a discourse to mark the norm from which aesthetic deviations, and its structures, can be measured. The structuralist insistence that the signifier cannot have more than an arbitrary relation to its supposed signified is perhaps the strongest way of putting this claim of universal synonymity—a claim that is supposed to allow me here, for example, to grab onto any word that satisfies my minimal requirements, from moment to moment, requirements of the field of linguistic forces developing before me.

The invention of binary opposition as a structuralist principle can thus win the post-Kantian theorist's assent through his own need to have such a principle as one from which the uniquely monistic principle of poetic discourse can deviate, and with apparently magical results. As a reader, his need to operate in a special way upon all that goes on in a poem forces him to retain the opposition between "normal" and "deviationist" models of discourse as *his* binary fiction. It is the enabling fiction of *his* discourse. So let us grant that some fictional obfuscation, with its rhetorical swerving, takes place outside the realm of literary fictions, but let us allow some remnant of the free play of fictional reflexivity to be left to the literary intent. Aesthetic foregrounding may well go on outside poems, but do we not condescend to our writers in all the disciplines when we ignore, or deprecate, the several responses that the body of their works appears to be soliciting from different readers?

I am arguing for a continuing place for *literary* criticism even now, and for the role of aesthetic evaluation in it, despite the heavy qualifications produced by the multiple awarenesses on which I have been dwelling. But, it must be clear, the basis for claims of value cannot be narrowly formalistic once we recognize the duplicitous character of the illusion of fictional, figurative closure. The special character and special value left to the poem, as it is singled out from the general network of textuality, may well be related to its special ordering power over the chaotic materials of inner experience. And this formal power, as we have seen, is revealed in the apparent closure for which the poem strives as it seeks to come to terms with itself. Formalism implies a disorderliness in reality which requires art, as a formal construct, to improve upon it and rein it in, so that value based on form must assume these *dis*values in reality. Yet all the doubts I have been introducing into formalist assumptions here must force us to hold them tentatively, if we still dare hold them at all. The self-consciously illusionary nature of poetic discourse, as of poetic form, reminds us of the resistant world that it struggles to domesticate through the binding closure of its fiction: it reminds us, that is, of all that it can*not* do, of the differences between the conditions of aesthetic play and the existential conditions that persist, undissolved by illusion.

From Aristotle onward, theorists have associated poetic value with the work's paradoxical capacity both to reflect the materials of reality and to contain them within its own ordering transformations. These two conflicting needs—the need to include recalcitrant elements that threaten to explode any unity and the need to tame them within the limits that an arbitrary unity would permit—must manage to coexist. One threatens to keep the process as open as life's untamed variety and one would keep the system closed: one the shotgun and one the arrow. These tendencies are reflected in the duplicitous functions of the language, with the intertextual ties that open out to the language field constantly challenged by the self-generating closure of a filled microsystem. As I have said, this doubleness has been alive in our most exciting theorists since Aristotle. Aristotle may have called for poetry to accommodate history's accidents within poetry's forms, but only while retaining the element of surprise, deriving from life's unpredictabilities, as a constant companion to the trim probabilities of art. As we move through Renaissance theorists like Mazzoni, neoclassical theorists like Johnson, romantic theorists like Coleridge, and modernist theorists like T. S. Eliot and Cleanth Brooks, we find in each some version—however altered—of the plea for the poet to open himself as widely as possible to the heterogeneous, in experience or language, provided he seeks to domesticate it. What the reader would be given by such a poet is the illusion of a self-sealing enclosure that yet reveals its awareness of the world—as well as of the world of language—which it excludes. It may give us as its world an ordered microcosmic reflection of our own—*multum in parvo*—but only while allowing us to remind ourselves of the *much* that still persists beyond its *small*, bounded world. Form may appear to have cultivated its diversionary antagonist—and to have swallowed it, thereby converting the most resistant elements of antiformal experience into its teleology. But what remains central is both the resistant opposition and the poet's metaphorical capacity to reconcile its elements, so that the early-nineteenth-century motto, "unity in variety," can emphasize equally, though paradoxically, its two antithetical nouns.

Such a theoretical emphasis culminates in a critique of form that values it in relation to the antiformal obstacles it has overcome, in relation, that is, to the aesthetically real and resistant elements it converts into materials for aesthetic transformation. These criteria lead to a notion of strenuous beauty, what Bernard Bosanquet called "difficult beauty," dynamically expansive in its subduing its antagonists by absorbing them.[4] Thus we could distinguish great art from merely perfect art (based on the narrowly formal doctrine of perfection), thereby solving an age-old problem in evaluation: for a procedure of evaluation based on a theory of "difficult beauty" would move beyond narrow formalism to a judgment based on the difficulty of the resistances that form has absorbed without surrendering its ultimately unifying function.

Such an all-encompassing organicism, however, must be balanced with an equal illusionism that permits us to strip it away. The poem may be too devoted to its illusionary totality, so that it insists on our taking it, in its wholeness, as a completed, self-sustaining vision—in effect, as all there is. But though its fictional and figurational closure claims a wholeness whose capacity is strained, but not broken through, by the incompatibles it must accommodate without disharmony, the poem's illusionary self-consciousness reminds us of those other conditions (beyond its own) under which what is incompatible remains incompatible, whatever the illusion of harmony fostered by the form that we interpret the poem as struggling to achieve. Our aesthetic habit leads us to view fictional illusion as asking us to play within an ultimate language, though its illusionary status in effect points beyond to the experiential realm that resists being embraced by that play, that asserts only its arbitrariness and contingency. And the poems we value most are very likely those that give us that fullest range of enclosure—*and* of escape from enclosure.

As cultural anthropologists such as every humanist ought to be, we must, I believe, take seriously the aesthetic need for closure, a hunger for form and for verbal presence that accounts for the human quest for poetry, the quest for what I have called an ultimate language. The persistent impulse both on the poet's part to close the form he creates

---

4. This notion of "difficult beauty" figures importantly in Bosanquet's *Three Lectures on Aesthetic* (London: Macmillan, 1915).

and on our part to close the form we perceive accounts for the internal purposiveness that, for Kant, characterizes the aesthetic mode. Presumably, it is this need to make or to find closure that has led us from the first to mythmaking and leads still to the privileging of the objects that deconstructionists would demystify. We look for a structural apocalypse, which imposes the spatial imagination on the radical temporality of pure sequence, shaping linear time into the circularity of fiction. And it is our reading of the manipulations of the verbal medium that permits it.

Led by the figural persuasiveness of the verbal system before us, we seek to close it off into an ultimate language, an eschatological intrusion upon language as we know it. But this apocalypse is self-induced, subject to the momentary conditions of the aesthetic experience and—because of that momentary nature—alive to the whimpering world, of deeds and words, that goes before and after the bang, and gives it the lie. To return to my original concern with the problematic of literary evaluation, I can argue—in retreat—that the act of privileging is anthropologically, if not ontologically, justified. However tentative and skeptical and self-induced it may be, the verbal apocalypse is constantly being sought, so that it is hardly strange that upon those objects which help us produce it we bestow the privilege of value—because for most of us this is as much of apocalypse as we can know.

An E. H. Gombrich Retrospective:
The Ambiguities of
Representation and Illusion

The immediate occasion, or should I say justification, of this retrospective is E. H. Gombrich's most recent volume, *The Image and the Eye.*[1] Its subtitle, *Further Studies in the Psychology of Pictorial Representation*, refers us back to his landmark volume, *Art and Illusion* (1959), which bore the subtitle, *A Study in the Psychology of Pictorial Representation*. So the present volume suggests his return to those problems, which he never really left, and permits us the sense that he is completing the tracing of his theoretical circle. It is to be seen, however, whether he has come full circle or has, instead, returned to a different place from where he began in 1956, when he delivered the Mellon lectures which became *Art and Illusion*.

It is difficult to overestimate the impact, beginning in the 1960s, which Gombrich's discussion of visual representation made on a good number of theorists who were part of an entire generation of thinking about art, and—even more—about literary art. For literary theory and criticism were at least as affected by his work as were theory and criticism in the plastic arts. That work radically undermined the terms that had controlled discussions of how art represented "reality"—or, rather, how viewers or members of the audience perceived that representation and related it to their versions of "reality." And, for those

---

1. (Oxford: Phaidon Press, 1982, and Ithaca: Cornell University Press, 1982).

who accompanied or followed him—from Rosalie Colie to Wolfgang Iser—Gombrich helped transform for good the meaning of a long revered term like *imitation* as it could be applied to both the visual and verbal arts. I believe he must, then, be seen as responsible for some of the most provocative turns that art theory, literary theory, and aesthetics have taken in the last two decades.

However, in much of his work since the early 1960s, Gombrich has appeared more and more anxious to dissociate himself from those who have considered his earlier books and essays as leading to the theoretical innovations that have claimed support from them. In the present volume, the statements that put distance between himself and such followers seem utterly unambiguous. And against the charge that his work has become more conservative with the passing years, I suspect Gombrich would argue that any claim of difference between, say, *Art and Illusion* and *The Image and the Eye* is a result of an original misreading, that the present work is only more explicitly defending a traditional position which was quietly there all along, though supposedly friendly theorists wrongly saw him as subverting it in the earlier work. Thus Gombrich is now self-consciously committed to undoing what he sees as our errors of reading rather than his own errors of writing.

Since I have actively participated in recent theorizing that sees itself as, in part, Gombrichian, I shall—in responding to Gombrich's writings and to his disavowals—presume to be the spokesman for such theorists. Yet, I mean, of course, to be speaking for myself as I worry about how faithful my interpretations have been to his ideas. It is a self-stirring experience—just short of awesome—for me to write, I hope searchingly and even conclusively, about a single author's vast body of writings that have so markedly shaped the directions I have taken in my own work. For such an undertaking calls for more candor than I enjoy summoning up: candor in looking back, at some distance, at a series of writings by another which I have appropriated as my own, and candor in assessing my own sins of misappropriation in the process of making another's work serve mine. To what extent have Gombrich's books and essays influenced me, then, and to what extent have I influenced my reading of them in order to allow them to provide the influence that my own theoretical search required? Especially since Harold Bloom's work of the past decade, it would seem that the question of influence has become thus self-consciously complicated for all of us who wish to be candid about it.

So it may be more accurate to qualify the title of this essay by calling it a "personal retrospective." In what follows I intend to trace the history of my own encounters with Gombrich's remarkable work and my growing concern, under the impact of his successive books, about the conflict between what I wanted him to be saying and what he himself has been telling us he prefers to have said. Yet I have suggested that this question—whether Gombrich has been interpreted or misinterpreted—is not one to be restricted to me among those who have been influenced by him. To the extent that it does concern his influence on literary and art criticism generally, to the extent that his influence may be shown, in the end, to rest on an interpretation of Gombrich which he would prefer to reject, this retrospective may prove to be more than personal after all, so that I hope that it will raise important issues for theory at large.

I remember my most recent meeting with Gombrich, in the summer of 1975, when I was working at the Warburg Institute, that splendid London repository, the gentle esoteric empire overseen by him. We spoke of our dear friend, the late Rosalie Colie, the brilliant Renaissance scholar who, a dozen years before, had first introduced me to the contributions that Gombrich's work could be seen as making to criticism in the literary as well as the plastic arts. And I was surprised as I sensed in him some dismay at the uses being made of his work by some of those whose attitude toward the roles of convention and reality in visual and verbal representation was largely shaped by reference to his essays and books. I felt some unease at his complaints since I had just completed the manuscript of my *Theory of Criticism*, which, as it developed its argument, depended heavily on what I thought to be Gombrichian notions, modeled largely on Colie's interpretation of them.

His complaints that day came to focus on the distinguished philosopher, Nelson Goodman, and his influential work in aesthetics, *Languages of Art* (1968). In that book Goodman sees Gombrich as instrumental to the notion in recent theory that to the viewer of art "reality" is shaped by his or her way of seeing, which is already under the control of the conventions imposed by a culture. Goodman starts from Gombrich's insistence "that there is no innocent eye."

> The case for the relativity of vision and of representation has been so conclusively stated elsewhere that I am relieved of the need to argue it at any length here. Gombrich, in particular, has amassed overwhelming evidence to show how the way we see and depict depends upon and varies with experience, practice, interests, and attitudes.[2]

---

2. Nelson Goodman, *Languages of Art: An Approach to a Theory of Symbols* (Indianapolis: Bobbs-Merrill, 1968), pp. 7, 10.

It was this way of reading the early Gombrich (through *Art and Illusion* and *Meditations on a Hobby Horse*) that supported theorists who would reject the theory of imitation, indeed who would turn it on its head. Ever since David Hume, critical philosophers have been reminding us of our tendency to attribute to nature itself what is true only of our language and the visions permitted by that language. It was an early version of the deconstructive move. Gombrich helped bring this awareness to art critics who had been used to assuming that the representational visual arts reflected a universally available nature rather than—as after Gombrich we saw—the anticipated representations projected by our visual conventions. As Karl Popper (who had a strong philosophic influence on Gombrich) supplied epistemology with an alternative to naïve induction by substituting our controlling expectations for a realm of neutral sense data that we each apprehend and collect into universals, so Gombrich supplied aesthetics with an alternative to the notion that there is a neutral and prior "object of imitation" (Aristotle's phrase) to which the artist's representation must be referred. Although this antimimetic notion is hardly original with him and already had a lengthy history in theorizing about art, Gombrich brought to it a theory of perception and his brilliance as a phrasemaker that made it especially available to current theory, and particularly literary theory, which was just beginning to confront problems of semiotics.

His striking reformulations of traditional doctrines of representation are underlined by his lucidly provocative word-pairings: "making comes before matching," form and function (suggesting that form follows function), norm and form (suggesting that norm controls our perception of form), and stimulation and simulation (suggesting that stimulation can occur independently of simulation, the first provoking the second).[3] These are the elements in Gombrich that led to Goodman's references to his work as a precedent for his own, references that in turn led to Gombrich's concerns about what Goodman and others were doing in his name. These were the concerns I recall his expressing

---

3. These word-pairings can be found in the following places: *making* and *matching* throughout *Art and Illusion* (London: Phaidon, 1960), especially pp. 24, 99; *form* and *function* in "Meditations on a Hobby Horse or the Roots of Artistic Form," in *Meditations on a Hobby Horse and Other Essays on the Theory of Art* (London: Phaidon, 1963), pp. 1–11; *norm* and *form* in "Norm and Form: The Stylistic Categories of Art History and Their Origins in Renaissance Ideals," in *Norm and Form: Studies in the Art of the Renaissance* (London: Phaidon, 1966), pp. 81–98; *stimulation* and *simulation* in "Illusion and Art," in *Illusion in Nature and Art*, ed. R. L. Gregory and E. H. Gombrich (London: Gerald Duckworth, 1973), especially pp. 199–202.

in his conversation with me, as he has consistently and with increasing resistance been expressing them after the publication of *Meditations on a Hobby Horse* (1963), which seems still in the spirit of *Art and Illusion*.[4]

But I should like to return to the suggestions in the early Gombrich which were picked up and turned into contributions to an untraditional aesthetic. The major shift from traditional aesthetics which I described earlier—from representation as imitation to representation as the viewer's constructive response to stimuli—leads to a number of other shifts worth mentioning here.

One is the denial of the antique distinction in aesthetics between natural and conventional signs, that is, between signs which look like their referents and arbitrary signs related to their referents only by convention: in short, between pictures and words. For all representation—even that apparently depending on its resemblance to external reality—comes to be similarly viewed as responding to the perceptual and cultural norms brought to it—in short, to be similarly viewed as conventional signs. And these norms, through usage, establish an authority that does not depend upon fidelity to what (in a neutral, naturalistic sense) is being represented. All signs must be read, not—as with the natural-conventional sign distinction—some signs seen and some read. Even in his early discussions of trompe l'oeil paintings (and Gombrich returns to these, dealing with them from Zeuxis on, in book after book up through the present volume), he is primarily concerned with the role of expectations and the manipulation of the artistic medium in creating the deception rather than with the perfection of resemblance that would justify the mistake by a human viewer. (His emphasis reverts to the latter of these, we will see, in later writings.)

In undermining the notion that objects can be simply duplicated in art, Gombrich comes to see visual representations as going beyond space and invading the realm of time. In emphasizing the beholder's share, he frees us to read beyond the static disposition of shapes given by the painting as we force it to respond to our narrative expectations of sequence. I am delighted that the present volume finally reprints the

---

4. This apparent chronological sequence for the books (1959 and 1963) is misleading since the crucial title essay of the second volume, "Meditations on a Hobby Horse," which furnishes much ammunition for Gombrich's untraditional followers, first appeared in 1951, well before *Art and Illusion*. The difficulty in using Gombrich's succession of books to trace his development is generally complicated by the fact that in many of them the essays collected may date from many years earlier than the publication date of the book in which they appear. Indeed, the present volume, published in 1982, includes as its earliest essay one that dates from 1964, with the final essay in the collection the latest, 1981 (though it was delivered as a lecture in 1978).

important essay, "Moment and Movement in Art" (originally published as early as 1964), in which this temporalizing of art is forcefully argued. It is one of Gombrich's essays that endeared him to literary people by closing the gap between painting and literature which theorists like Lessing had insisted on keeping open.

The move from simple spatial duplication had another major consequence: the shift from the work's reliable reference (to "objects") to its self-reference (its reference to its own status as art and not reality) a favorite notion among Gombrichians. Indeed, many of Rosalie Colie's most perceptive readings of poems and of still-life paintings arise from insights to which her claims of self-reference have opened the way. She derives her brilliant work on still life from Gombrich's hints about the *vanitas* motif in the Protestant ethic on which the Dutch contributions to the still-life tradition rest.[5] The vision in the painting of the vanities, the trivia of the bourgeois world seen as trivia—transient items of artifice fixed in a permanent artifact—creates a paradoxical experience in which art, as an object, reminds the viewer of its own limitations as the container of all that would contradict its very ontology. Thus even an attempt at a representation as realistic as the Dutch refers to its own illusionary character—as illusionary as those falsely valued things it seeks to depict. And in the sustained paradox of transience and fixity it reinforces the need—seen in essays like "Moment and Movement in Art," just discussed—to see the temporal implications within art's frozen space.

We see self-reference also at work, perhaps more spectacularly, in Gombrich's discussions of "impossible paintings" and the "visual deadlock" into which they lead the viewer.[6] Whether treating the rare examples of this sort by Hogarth or the customary playfulness of Escher, Gombrich shows these works—with their flagrant violations of perspective—as instances of representation insisting on its merely illusionary nature, the two-dimensional plane teasing and thwarting our perceptual habit that seeks to see it in depth, as fulfillments of what is possible in three-dimensional reality.

Indeed, there is a sense in which every painting, even the most naturalistic, presents itself, in a more subtle and less self-announced

---

5. Gombrich, "Tradition and Expression in Western Still Life," in *Meditations on a Hobby Horse*, pp. 95–105, especially p. 104; and Rosalie L. Colie, "Still Life: Paradoxes of Being," in *Paradoxia Epidemica: The Renaissance Tradition of Paradox* (Princeton: Princeton University Press, 1966), pp. 273–99, especially pp. 298–99.

6. His extended discussion appears in "Illusion and Visual Deadlock," *Meditations on a Hobby Horse*, pp. 151–59, especially p. 157. See also the discussion of Hogarth and Escher in *Art and Illusion*, pp. 205–11.

way, as an impossible picture. Gombrich repeatedly dwells on the inevitable illusionary failings of the two-dimensional plane, on the fact that the represented objects and space relations among them will not change (as they do in reality) as we move about in front of the picture: eyes will follow us, though they always are looking dead ahead; hidden objects or sides of objects will not appear when we seek to look around the obstacle between us to find them; nor can we look around corners. And we cannot make objects grow or decrease in size relationships to other objects by bringing them forward in space or pushing them back: Gombrich rarely tires of reminding us of the fixed and absolute small-ness of that pole presumably far off in the picture in relation to that enormous foregrounded pole, whatever the illusion that the two are the same size. And the viewer may well retain a double awareness—both the illusion of the real world and the self-conscious knowledge that it *is* a representation which has worked its medium into cues that are to fool us into believing the illusion: in short, that it *is* an impossible picture.[7] As for explicitly impossible pictures, like Hogarth's or Escher's, they only force us to reflect upon what even the most apparently possible picture is doing to us—and to its ostensible "object." In this mood, Gombrich permits himself to be more sympathetic to the art of his time than he usually has been. Indeed, his hostility to that art has grown with his increasing attachment to the Western naturalistic tradition as *the* superior way to produce illusion (presumably less self-critical) in us.

Strangely, the very grounds on which these several untraditional claims were advanced are the ones Gombrich came to reject. He reg-ularly condemns these tendencies as versions of "conventionalism," which he sees as a manifestly absurd relativism. Yet, it was his writings that seemed to point those whom he criticizes toward what he sees as their excesses. Surely, Gombrich argues, it must be obvious that all visual codes cannot claim an equal, if different, verisimilitude for the representations they sanction. Surely, he would go on, we must ac-knowledge that the sense of visual reality developed by the tradition of Western perspective is more immediately persuasive of its authenticity than that of alternative visual traditions—say, the Egyptian or the medieval. Gombrich has for some years now been pressing upon our visual theories the habits established by psychologies of perception

---

7. In "Illusion and Visual Deadlock" Gombrich opens the way to all paintings as impossible pictures by admitting there is a "hidden ambiguity in all representations of solid objects in the flat" (p. 157). By 1973, in "Illusion and Art" (see note 3 above) he confesses himself "not quite happy" with that notion (p. 236), but by pp. 239–41 of that essay he seems to be swinging back to it.

(transcultural psychologies, mainly on the model of Gestalt) at the expense of the varying anthropological codes (although, of course, he betrays an ethnocentric parochialism that permits the Western tradition to become the psychological model for all). But it was Gombrich's own introduction of us to variant cultural codes, each shaping its peculiar reality by enculturating the eye, that helped lead us to give so central a role to convention, and consequently to consider the Egyptian's visual code as having neither more nor less claim to representing reality than one closer to our own tradition.

I remember the excitement, the thrill of discovery, that accompanied my opening and beginning to read—and look at—*Art and Illusion*. What first caught my eye—on the page facing the first chapter—was that cunning *New Yorker* cartoon by Alain, in which a drawing class made up of stereotyped (indeed almost identical) ancient Egyptian males (that is, those modeled on the represented male figures left us by ancient Egyptian art) are sketching a nude female model who stands in profile before them, her feet, hands, and head poised in the stance we know so well from Egyptian paintings. Some of the students are drawing the inevitable figure, while others hold out one stiffened arm, thumb raised, crayon in hand, aiming at her as a tribute to their desire faithfully to capture the "reality" (that is, the model) before them—though, of course, she appears as the stylized, flattened representation rather than the creature herself. And the book's opening words exploit the implications of what the chapter title refers to as "the riddle of style" and the way in which it imposes upon the viewer's psychology—his capacity to name what he sees and to see what he names. But besides emphasizing the influence of pictorial conventions (as established by art) upon how we see, Gombrich—now turning to perceptual psychology—uses the rabbit-or-duck drawing to remind us of the role played by our configurational expectations in determining what we see.

So from the start I was introduced to the two encoding and decoding powers—a culture's conventions about how things are represented and the viewer's perceptual habits which sometimes combine forces and sometimes appear to be in conflict in Gombrich's work. From these early pages I felt myself freed from the mimetic bias that often limits commentary on older art (and prevents commentary on recent art), felt myself initiated into the realm of visual semiotics, constructed in accordance with a post-Kantian awareness of the constitutive role of symbols. In effect, I felt myself licensed to move toward the "conventionalism" (all signs as conventional and no signs any longer "natural") that Gombrich was to condemn, licensed to give way to what Gombrich has called "the 'Egyptian' in us." I saw that, in doing so, I would be measuring art by semiotic codes in a way that would bring it closer to our measures for literature. And literary people may well have seized upon Gombrich the more eagerly because what he did for the visual arts seemed to be applicable, *mutatis mutandis*, to their activities.

I saw also that this escape from imitation into a series of equally authentic visual codes offered a way to move from older traditional art to the best art of our time as alternative constructions of configurations for our reading pictures. Indeed, might it be this potential opening to modern art in its experimental forms that led Gombrich increasingly to turn against these tendencies in his early work as he became more defensive of the Western naturalistic tradition? In spite of those daring early moments that got us all going, it does seem to be his constant conviction that this tradition, with its perfection of perspective devices, solved the problem of representation in a way that permits the viewer to see immediately (that is, without semiotic mediation)—to see without having to read. In effect, it affirms once more the distinction between natural and conventional signs and the mode of response appropriate to each.

Just after Goodman credits Gombrich's role in establishing the grounds on which "conventionalism" can thrive, he laments his failure to carry through when it comes to perspective, which Gombrich sees not as a convention but as a way of representing the world as it appears to us, with laws that "are supposed to provide absolute standards of fidelity that override differences in style of seeing and picturing."[8] And Gombrich's response, in the essay he wrote for the Goodman Festschrift, welcomes that adversary role and from then on quite deliberately conducts his campaign against "relativism in representation,"[9] though it seems to return him to imitation, against which much of the force of *Art and Illusion* and *Meditations on a Hobby Horse* seemed to be directed. I wonder whether it was the Goodman volume that alerted Gombrich with special clarity to the consequences of some of his work, consequences that he dared not recognize and preferred to deny.

Yet it must be acknowledged that there were hold-out moments in *Art and Illusion* that, in retrospect, can be seen as warning us against the conclusions many of us rushed to make. And they do, in the main,

---

8. Goodman, *Languages of Art*, p. 10.

9. Gombrich, "The 'What' and the 'How': Perspective Representation and the Phenomenal World," in *Logic and Art: Essays in Honor of Nelson Goodman*, ed. Richard Rudner and Israel Scheffler (Indianapolis: Bobbs-Merrill, 1972), pp. 129–49. The quotation appears as the essay's final words on p. 149.

concern the supremacy of the naturalistic tradition of perspective, with a consequent denial of conventionalism—much as Goodman has observed—though only at the cost of contradicting what most of us have taken as the main thrust of that book. Though Gombrich in that work admits to arguing that "all seeing is interpreting" and has "often stressed the conventional element in many modes of representation," he finally defends the greater truth ("closer rendering") of our superior representational codes.[10] It is true also that, in later writings, Gombrich at moments feels he must apologize for certain lapses in *Art and Illusion* which are in need of expanded explanation, if not of downright correction, lest they be seen as leading him toward conventionalism.[11] But it is also true that he can produce passages in that earlier work which testify to vestiges of the traditional notion of representation that perhaps should have warned against some of the uses we made of that work.

Despite what many of us have made of *Art and Illusion*, even the earliest Gombrich based his iconographic studies on the distinction between natural-sign representation and conventional-sign representation. (Here is further evidence that Gombrich the historian of Western art is at odds with tendencies in Gombrich the theorist, with the historian taming the theory into conformity with his needs as the years pass; and his major need is to account for the emergence of Western naturalism as *the* way to solve the problem of visual representation.) The earliest version of "Icones Symbolicae" appeared in 1948[12] and rested upon the difference between the Renaissance artist's iconic attempt to reproduce his divine object and his pictographic attempt to allegorize it. It was a difference between using pictures as natural signs that seek to represent the sacred directly and using conventional pictorial signs—in accordance with a semiotic code—which could be translated into messages about the sacred. Indeed, in the latter case any attempt at producing an icon of the divine was to be avoided by an ethic that opposed idol-worship. Thus the use of symbolic animals, furthest

---

10. These quotations all appear in *Art and Illusion*, p. 252, where he seeks to find grounds to claim that, despite his primary purpose of emphasizing "making" rather than "matching" in this book, Constable's painting of Wivenhoe Park—for example—can come "closer" than others to giving us a faithful rendering of the reality it seeks to represent: ". . . this interpretation will tell us a good many facts about that country-seat in 1816 which we would have gathered if we had stood by Constable's side."

11. Among a number of places in works of the past decade and a half, see especially the present volume, *The Image and the Eye*, pp. 30, 279, and 282.

12. The original version of "Icones Symbolicae" appeared in the *Journal of the Warburg and Courtauld Institutes* in 1948. For its expanded form, see Gombrich's *Symbolic Images: Studies in the Art of the Renaissance* (London: Phaidon, 1972), pp. 123–95.

from divinity, is encouraged—"the apophatic way of mysterious monstrosity"—as the iconic representation of like by like is rejected for the safer pictographic and encoded representation of like by unlike.[13]

But, as Gombrich the historian later traces the history of visual representation in the West, he sees the movement from medieval to Renaissance art as the progressive discovery of those techniques related to cues that produce third-dimensionality, techniques that permit our experience of art to move from reading a pictographic code to seeing an illusionary replica of nature.

> There are styles in art which are essentially map-like. They offer us an enumeration of what—for want of a better word—I still would like to call "conceptual images," pictographs which tell a story or give an inventory of stage props. Many a mediaeval picture of the sea would fall into this category. To read it may not differ much from reading a poem about the sea. But the historian of art also knows that at a given moment such diagrammatic pictures were rejected as inadequate, precisely because they fell so far short of the claims that had been made for the power of painting to create an illusion.[14]

Thus the development of Western naturalism in the high Renaissance is for him not the development of another code but a gradual movement to an absolutely true (that is, more "correct") representation, one that requires fewer codes for us to see it. Throughout his work since the mid-sixties and with increasing explicitness, he defends that art which provides us with immediate cues for seeing rather than with codes for interpreting. The ideal end of such a development would seem to be the disappearance of codes altogether, so that all visual representation—once suggested by him to be impossible pictures—can reach toward becoming a trompe l'oeil.[15]

It is instructive to note that, in his continuing return to the trompe l'oeil, usually beginning by referring to Zeuxis, he has significantly changed its function for his theorizing. Earlier it was forced to justify his celebration of art as a self-conscious fabrication; but it is now

---

13. "Icones Symbolicae," *Symbolic Images*, p. 152.

14. "Illusion and Art" (see note 3), p. 228.

15. This is very much the Gombrich described by Svetlana Alpers—indeed the only Gombrich she allows for—in "Interpretation without Representation, or, the Viewing of *Las Meninas*," *Representations* 1 (1983): 35–36: "Gombrich concludes by defining a perfect representation as indistinguishable to our eyes from nature." It would make "pictures disappear." So strong are Gombrich's commitments to the traditional defense of Western representation as naturalistic that even as perceptive a commentator as Alpers is deceived into seeing his position as more single-minded than it is, and thus easy for her to disagree with. The need to complicate this more recent, and I think limited, view of Gombrich is a major reason for my undertaking this essay.

brought to bear as evidence of the deceiving powers of representational resemblance. Instead of focusing on the illusionary devices that seek to trick us, he nows dwells upon the successful effects of the deception itself. In the present volume he even supports his commitment to the possibilities of absolute verisimilitude by pointing to an example of visual deception in the animal world, nature's trompe l'oeil, as if it were relevant to the realm of human artifice.[16] He has come a long way from his use of this most extreme example of imitation to support—a fortiori—an argument for artistic self-reference.[17] This change in attitude toward the trompe l'oeil is a reflection of the difference in his use of *illusion* since his book which made that word famous: always related to human vision, it seems to have shifted gradually from being defined by its relation to our enculturated visual code to being defined by the immediacy of its relation to "nature," a neutral reality available to the "innocent eye." Although, happily, Gombrich's perceptual interests force moments of return, there are also moments in which his *illusion* wanders dangerously close to *delusion*, with dulling consequences for his aesthetic.

I cannot leave this subject without complicating more than I have this movement from early to late Gombrich, especially in his use of *illusion* itself. As a most revealing example of his retaining the original Gombrichian perspective I have attributed to him, I must refer to the concluding discussion in his essay, "Illusion and Art" (1973), which I have treated here as a major document demonstrating his movement into anticonventionalist theoretical conservatism. After basing much of his argument on the distinction between pictorial representations and map signs (see my previous quotation from this essay, just above), he grants he must "concede a point to the 'conventionalists' who compare the

---

16. "Image and Code: Scope and Limits of Conventionalism in Pictorial Representation," in *The Image and the Eye*, especially p. 286. There is also a curious discussion of nature's use of camouflage, which "deceives a great range of predators including ourselves," on pp. 24–25 of this volume (in the essay, "Visual Discovery through Art").

17. Yet earlier in this volume Gombrich does seem to return to his earlier interest in trompe l'oeil as that which is cunningly made rather than that which fools the human or animal eye without reference to its artfulness: "Where art is concerned the surprise of 'trompe l'oeil' can be part of the pleasure; the pleasure does not lie in discovering that what we took to be a real dead duck is merely a painted one—this surely would be the cause of disappointment rather than of enjoyment—it lies in our continued feeling of incredulity that the visual effect of plumes, of gleam or softness has been achieved on a flat hard panel by a skilled hand using a brush dipped in paint." Here we are again close to the consciousness of art that leads to self-reference in the artwork. For this quotation, see "Mirror and Map: Theories of Pictorial Representation," in *The Image and the Eye*, pp. 180–81.

inspection of paintings with the reading of any other notation" (p. 238). And he turns to his "central problem, the double perception of paintings, the one demanding concentration within the frame, and the other a different sequence that takes in the wall and the surround" (p. 239). The balance between these requires us not to be *only* "deluded" "with illusions which remain uncorrected" (p. 241) by our self-consciousness. And the essay closes by trying vainly to "do justice to the complex interplay between reflex and reflection, involvement and detachment that we so inadequately sum up in the term 'illusion'" (p. 242). Here, this late, is all the self-referential interest one could ask for, accompanied by a sense of *illusion* far more complicated (and closer to his earlier use of the term) than what others of his works in retreat would allow. (Surely this *illusion* is hardly in accord with his simpler use of that word in my previous quotation.) Someone of my own theoretical leanings, of course, welcomes this statement warmly, but only while worrying about its capacity to survive Gombrich's own opposition elsewhere. Though one might wish Gombrich would make a firmer choice between positions, it is always refreshing to find a thinker candid enough to indulge the danger of contradiction rather than deny himself his own most searching observations.

"I always like to remind extreme relativists or conventionalists of this whole area of observations to show that the images of nature, at any rate, are not conventional signs, like the words of human language, but show a real visual resemblance, not only to our eyes or our culture but also to birds or beasts."[18] This distinction between two kinds of representation and the privileging of one of them restores precisely what Gombrich's early work—with its interest in all art as code—seemed bent on denying. For him now to see Western naturalism as just another—and different—code would be for him to indulge in just that relativism and conventionalism with which he is charging Goodman and others. His hierarchy within the history of representation, however, must end by returning us to imitation theory after all and thus undoing what those following the lead of his earlier work have done.[19] We have seen that, in his more recent discussions of Egyptian repre-

---

18. *The Image and the Eye*, p. 286.

19. I find it unhappily ironic that a critic like Gerald Graff, embattled against me and others because he insists on poetry's unproblematic referential capacities, can call upon Gombrich's work—and not altogether unjustly—to support his claims against us. It is for me unhappily ironic because it was Gombrich whose work played an influential role in the subverting of the referential by recent theorists like me.

Critical Positions: Self-definition and Other Definitions

sentation, in contrast to Western, he has more and more come to see the former—like the medieval—as requiring code-reading and the latter as requiring only the capacity to see, and to recognize. The opening essay of the present volume, "Visual Discovery through Art," though published as far back as 1965, already introduces a word-pairing considerably less daring than others I have cited: *recall* and *recognition*. Unlike the earlier notion, suggested from Gombrich's commentary on the Alain cartoon onward, that our visual codes are the consequence of our artists' representational forms, Gombrich is now content to say, "The painter, like the caricaturist, can teach us a new code of recognition, he cannot teach us to 'see.' "[20]

It is an irony that, having begun with the Alain cartoon and his own commentary to remind us of "the 'Egyptian' in us," who recurs and is appealed to through much of his work, Gombrich now wants us, as viewers of paintings, to down that non-Westerner.[21] If, as I did at the start, we consider the present volume as completing a circle begun with *Art and Illusion*, it is a confirmation to see Gombrich end with the Egyptian difference as he began with it. But we hardly recognize his attitude toward it, so that we feel he has brought us to a place other than the Gombrichian home we used to think we knew. These are his closing words:

> . . . the Egyptian who looked at a picture of a hunting party in the lotus swamps might early have had his memories and imagination stirred, much as it may happen to us when we read a verbal description of such a party; but Western art would not have developed the

---

20. "Visual Discovery through Art," in *The Image and the Eye*, p. 29. This disavowal differs from his strong claim in *Art and Illusion* that art has the power to "teach us to see." "As Oscar Wilde said, there was no fog in London before Whistler painted it." "Those who have experienced the thrill of such visual discoveries have generally expresed their gratitude in the words that only art has taught them to *see*" (his italics). These statements appear on p. 275.

21. I earlier suggested that Gombrich's commitment to the transcendent authority of the Western representational ideal can be viewed, though only by a conventionalist, as his yielding to an ethnocentric parochialism. He goes so far in this direction, even at moments in *Art and Illusion*, that he seems to see himself as Constable's companion, standing "by Constable's side" viewing Wivenhoe Park and seeing exactly what the English master painted (p. 252). The united fellowship of his vision and Constable's, made one by the transparency of the painting, confirms Gombrich's theoretical retreat that privileges—by identifying—a single mode of seeing and painting, Western and often English. If so, then his rejection of "the Egyptian in us" for the universally immediate reality of English naturalism may provide another example of Western-style "orientalism," that imperialism of spirit which Edward Said diagnosed and condemned in his book of that title.

special tricks of naturalism if it had not been found that the incorporation in the image of all the features which serve us in real life for the discovery and testing of meaning enabled the artist to do with fewer and fewer conventions. This, I know, is the traditional view. I believe it to be correct.[22]

Have we always misunderstood, as we sought to make Gombrich a revolutionary theorist, or at least a precursor of revolutionary theorists to follow? But it is hard not to believe that *Art and Illusion* and *Meditations on a Hobby Horse* were deliberately provocative books, despite the hold-out elements Gombrich could later point out in them, just as later books—and especially the present one—have been deliberately in recoil from the original tendencies, despite the still-lingering moments of theoretical excitement they retain. Instead, then, is it, as I have suggested, that Gombrich—especially after 1964—retreated from the consequences of his own earlier claims—at least his most provocative claims, even if these were mixed from the first with more traditional and cautious ones? Our answer must be an ambiguous one in that it must confront evidence of both possibilities in both earlier and later essays, whatever the dominant leanings of each.

One thing is certain about this final quotation: Those to whom his early work was an eye-opener will find these words disappointing. But they are unequivocal. It was to the great benefit of art theory in our time—and of Gombrich's position in it—that he did not originally make so forthright, and unrevolutionary, a pronouncement.

A Rebuttal: Optics and Aesthetic Perception

I am troubled by the temper of E. H. Gombrich's response[23] to my "Retrospective" and by his preferring not to sense the profound admiration—indeed the homage—intended by my essay both for his contributions to recent theory and for their influence upon its recent developments. But I am more troubled by the confusions his remarks may cause in the interpretation of his own work as well as in the judgment of mine. There are important issues at stake, I feel, especially as regards the relation between scientific and aesthetic inquiry.

The very irritated tone of his reaction helps make what I see as my major point: his work has contained a conflict between two Gom-

---

22. *The Image and the Eye*, p. 297.

23. The previous pages, my "retrospective," provoked (in the same issue of *Critical Inquiry*) an antagonistic answer by Gombrich, "Representation and Misrepresentation," *Critical Inquiry* 11 (1984): 195–201. In what follows, my rebuttal to his remarks, I believe I indicate his main arguments. The exchange between us ended with this follow-up essay.

brichs—one the skeptical humanist and the other the positive scientist—and with the passing years the second has increasingly sought to obliterate signs of the first, becoming increasingly impatient with any attempt to revive those signs or remind us of their existence. On the other side, since the line of literary criticism with which I associate myself has drawn strength from the first Gombrich, this development in his work and his attitudes has caused some disappointment.

In my original essay I tried to distinguish in Gombrich's work between what he does with visual codes that are subject to the psychology of perception and what he does with visual codes that are subject to a culture's conventions about how things are represented in art, these latter also providing the norms for how that culture forms its "reality." Thus I saw his interest in the viewer's visual habits as responding to two sorts of decoding powers, one related to the science of optics and one related to cultural conditioning by created artifacts. His extraordinary contributions to art history—with its description of the ways in which different historical moments taught us to interpret their products, and through them their world—reflect the second of these codes, as his theoretical explorations in perceptual psychology reflect the first. In short, I found a potential conflict in Gombrich between his concern with how we see and his concern with how we see *art*. I observed times when he emphasizes the oneness of these concerns by reducing the second to the first, and times (more of them in his earlier work) when he is sensitive to a significant difference between the two. In his response to my essay he is clearly anxious to deny the scientific standing, and hence the value, of the second concern. For my part, I worried about whether the scientific description of our general perceptual activity as adaptive animals is adequate to our responses, as members of a human community, to its created artifacts. He in turn charged me with being one of those guilty of an "aesthetic misreading" of his work.

His assault on my "aesthetic misreading" reveals his present lack of concern with the question of the perception of art as requiring special avenues of inquiry and hence special assumptions, different from scientific ones, about the nature of "reality." Twice in two paragraphs he chides aesthetic misreaders like me for not recognizing that his "argument" is "not about art." His concern, instead, has been "to establish the study of the visual image as a scientific enterprise," in which "proven facts" will be substituted for "subjectivity and convention." And his subject of "images," he makes clear, refers to all that our eyes seek to focus upon, not merely to images as artistic representations. If what he now claims has always been the case, then we have misread indeed. And our inclination to be influenced by him as a major art historian and theorist, one who alerted us to the role of visual artistic conventions in establishing a culture's momentary sense of its "reality," has been misdirected.

Gombrich's scientific commitment to the "proven facts" about how we see leads him to the security of a realist epistemology, completely opposed to the now-detested "subjectivity" that he sees as the necessary companion of "conventionalism." Following J. J. Gibson, he is convinced that certain representational strategies more than others "do justice to the workings of our visual system" because they show us "the invariants of our environment . . . independent of any viewing point." Here is a neutral, objective, transcultural reality indeed. Thus the Egyptian version of "arrested monocular vision" is "an artificial abstraction which cannot do justice to the workings of our visual system" and therefore must give way to those representational strategies that do produce a greater accuracy ("Representation and Misrepresentation," p. 200). For it is "the appearance of nature"—apparently the same for all of us at all times—which the discovery and the development of perspective manage to "trap" for our seeing, which searches out these images in art as they do in nature. Nature itself has no problem since it gives us its *things* to be seen, but art must resort to its "roundabout strategy" if the appearance of nature is to be similarly apprehended in a two-dimensional representation. Surely, Gombrich must conclude, we can scientifically measure the "different degrees of accuracy" (his phrase) allowed to our perceptual response by each variety of representational strategy. And the score given the kind of painting epitomized by Constable, in competition with the Egyptian, must of course be very high indeed. Presumably, the ancient Egyptian viewer and the nineteenth-century Englishman would have to admit this quantitative judgment equally.

Gombrich uncompromisingly insists upon his present ontological confidence in that neutral, (apparently) scientifically verifiable reality that is out there for our visual system to discover and for the art of representation, with its increasingly accurate strategies, to help it discover. There is equal confidence in our capacity to rule "objectively" on the degree of success with which various representational strategies permit our visual system to apprehend the representations as if they were indeed the things themselves. No wonder, then, that Gombrich must pay special tribute to Gibson's insistence that perspective is not a "mere convention," just one among many, but rather a major corrective step on the road to an accurate representation unachievable by its rivals. A single perceivable reality calls for closer rather than less close approximations to it, and for strategies more rather than less in accord with the visual system that seeks to apprehend it. Conventions, then, are not to be judged as merely different from one another, each productive of its own "reality" (with the quotation marks a crucial qualification upon "reality"), all of them separate but equal. Such relativity—or, worse, subjectivity—must give way before a single gradient in accordance with which we can measure the "different degrees of accuracy" that each strategy permits. Separate-but-equal gives way to closer-or-farther, with one privileged possibility at the highest end of our aspirations. There can be no question, then, that we must score Constable as much, much higher than the Egyptian insofar as we are interested in "one particular learning process" by which the representation of nature is made to approximate "the appearance of nature." Where objectives other than this appeal to "naturalism" are invoked, there aesthetics may at last enter for its quite different considerations, but only because art will have withdrawn from its exclusively optical and hence illusionary functions; but then, with art no longer dependent exclusively on the general nature of how we see, Gombrich the perceptual psychologist will, presumably, no longer be centrally interested.

Yet, as I pointed out in my original essay, I have found Gombrich most perceptive and persuasive when he has observed that our viewing of art, *unlike* our viewing of nature, is, at its best, aware of its activity and of the unreal—merely artificial—nature of the representational object on its horizon. The "complex interplay between reflex and reflection" is caused by "the double perception" of paintings, both "within the frame" and as part of "the wall and the surround" ("Illusion and Art," pp. 239–42). Such a description of the act of viewing art clearly and crucially differentiates it from the act of viewing real things, and in a way that urges a distinction between the general role of optics in seeing the world and the conventional rules of aesthetic perception in seeing works of art. To the extent that Gombrich has devoted himself to the latter, he is unjust to himself in characterizing his argument as being "not about art." Because in dealing with works of art he is dealing with humanly made objects rather than with the found objects in nature, he at times allows into his consideration those ambiguities in the artifact-as-made that dislocate it as a representation from the natural object it presumably represents. Indeed, the more apparently representational the artifact is, the more complex is the ambiguity prompted both by our "double perception" and by the object's self-referential fictionality. One of the least arguable points of consensus in current theory is the notion that representation is a problematic act rather than a transparent image, and Gombrich's was one of the voices used to achieve that consensus. To the extent that one is in agreement with this point, no discussion of aesthetic perception can advance very far if it restricts itself to the concerns of general optics. For the eye is enculturated and always in the state of lost innocence.

No one would deny that the apparent *matching*, as well as the *making*, is in the representation-as-seen; but it was Gombrich who—though now, it appears, unwillingly—taught us that a culture's sense of *matching* is derived, ex post facto, out of the visionary habits induced in viewers by the representations it has *made*. Now this lesson was found, rightly or wrongly, in Gombrich the skeptical humanist, the Gombrich whom I found at the beginning of this rebuttal to be in conflict with Gombrich the positive scientist, the writer of the reply to my essay. This latter Gombrich would totally deny the humanist's attempt to replace the single, neutrally available reality of positive science with the several "realities" constituted by the visual norms of a culture, reflected in or even determined by its art: ontological monism is not to be replaced by anthropological pluralism. Further, in his fight against conventionalism, this Gombrich must deny that he was ever humanistic in this sense.

In my essay I sought continually to acknowledge the extent to which even the early Gombrich tried to avoid the temptations of conventionalism, just as I sought to point out moments, even in the later work, in which traces of such conventionalist tendencies persist. But I did claim a general drift toward a scientifically objective monism from an early ambivalence; of which one side interested critics like me to the exclusion of the other side. In actually raising the question about whether we might have been misrepresenting him to ourselves (for reasons arising from our own enculturated preferences which have displaced our own innocence in reading *him*), I was trying to generate enough candor to produce a fair representation even of a possible misrepresentation. In his response Gombrich concedes the "agony" of my attempt to be judicious and—even this late—concedes also that he may have been less single-minded in earlier works than he has become, or at least that he may have been an occasional backslider: "I am quite ready to plead guilty of having learned something about visual perception since I wrote *Art and Illusion*" and have become "a little more circumspect in my estimate of the 'subjectivity of vision'" ("Representation and Misrepresentation," p. 197).

It is surely unfair to suggest that I found fault with Gombrich for thinking highly of Constable or that I have anything less than admiration for his knowledge of and response to Egyptian art. I did not—would not—complain about his appreciation of so splendid an artist as Constable; I complained only about his suggestion that Constable's "reality" is an absolute improvement, indeed the ultimate progress, in representing reality, beyond earlier representational visual codes. Nor would I presume to question Gombrich's authority to teach us about Egyptian art; I only lament his judgment concerning the greater inaccuracy of the Egyptians' visual system of representation. Gombrich, then, is right to note the absence of "the scientific temper" in me, as he defines that temper, but he is—I hope—less right in lamenting it. I believe he is too easily led to intimidate us with the word *science*. The scientist, like the philosopher, in us has too often had—and should seek to curb—the habit of uncritically attributing to nature, as a universally and equally accessible object of disinterested contemplation, that which is the product of our institutional orientation and the forces that shape it. It is for this reason that I sought to segregate for praise the Gombrich I saw as the humanist concerned with how our constructions help constitute what we see as our "reality" from the Gombrich whose "scientific temper" insists on only the one reality against which we can make corrections in those illusionary constructions that are supposed to guide our eyes to match what we normally see. The central word here is "corrections," the adjusting of the representation to the one true standard in normal visual experience, the closing of the gap between scientifically established phenomenal reality as a something-there-to-be-seen and the actual image seen. In the spirit of Popper, previous errors are to be eliminated.

The "scientific temper" that Gombrich privileges is one that drops the quotation marks from around *reality* by making it a single entity independent of our viewing habits and our cultural and aesthetic perspectives. It establishes an absolute ontological presumption and a privilege among ways of seeing as well as among the "realities" seen, permitting only the reality without quotation marks, the reality established by science, which—however—is to say *our* science and *its* assumptions. This science and its "reality" seem to me too much like the science and the "reality" of the Royal Society in its earliest days (and I put quotation marks around this "reality" lest I give the game away to one parochial view of science and scientific truth). That science and that "reality" turned out to be less universal than had been thought. To remove the quotation marks and to make it everyone's reality is to give total authority to a particular scientific paradigm, despite the greater caution and modesty urged by philosophers of science like Thomas Kuhn. It is "reality" within quotation marks that culture creates and serves (or creates in order to serve) both with its less absolutist version of science and with the normative structures of its art. It is this "reality" also which, in its several versions, is served by the skeptical humanist which I saw in the early Gombrich, while it is that universal reality (without quotation marks) which the positive scientist sets forth and which the later Gombrich, nowhere more forthrightly than in his response to my essay, defends at all costs.

It is my own humanistic bias that leads me to be concerned when artistic representation is subordinated to so-called scientific accuracy or to a theory of optics. I prefer art, as a testament to freedom, to create the forms of its "reality" from within aesthetic norms, instead of depending upon a reality imposed upon it by the authoritarian claims of a monolithic positivism masquerading as all the science there is. Humanists, I should expect, would be primarily devoted to the anthropological project that studies how, at various historical moments, the enculturated human being makes his constructs and constructs his "truths," rather than seeking to approach the one truth, the ultimate scientific answer beyond human control. Especially when the guiding science is *our* science, in tune with and growing out of *our* climate of pressures, do we risk the error of confusing nature with our institutional version of nature. Through the act of making, the human being becomes the formative agent, no longer subjugated to "natural" forms (now seen by the humanist as no more than "conventional" forms and hence his forms). For us to give full license to "the Egyptian in us" is for us to give full license to the humanist in us, not at the expense of Constable but in a lively and equal, and a continuing and expanding, competition with him. I continue to believe in the centrality of the humanistic enterprise, as I have defined it, and, in spite of Gombrich's recent preferences to the contrary, I continue to believe in the monumentality of his contributions to it, thanks to the persistent humanist in him.

However we address "the question of presence" to-
day, there is at least no question about my own presence on this
occasion. Indeed, in view of the position I maintain in contemporary
theory, it would be inconsistent for me not to present myself, instead of
remaining absent, only a ghostly trace inadequately made present
(re-presented) in the words we have heard. So here I am, however
inadequate myself, but a transcendental signified nonetheless—except
that, of course, it is not I but my critical works, my inscribed words,
that are at issue; and we know that signifieds can consist only of other
words and not extraverbal beings. Still, here I am.[1]

I now understand, from the inside and deep down, Northrop Frye's

---

1.   These comments were originally delivered at an MLA session of the Division of
Literary Criticism devoted to "The Question of Presence: The Criticism of Murray
Krieger." They constituted my response to papers on my work delivered by Vincent
Leitch and Mark Rose. Even as I originally wrote these opening words for my oral
performance upon the occasion of the MLA meeting, I anticipated how they would mock
me when I was later to read them (as you do now) as having been written some time ago.
For that very moment during which, when speaking them myself, I was asserting my
presence in them, is now well past, with only their ghostly reminder of their now-absent
author and his belated occasion left to contradict this cocky assertion of his presence.
What more impressive testimony could I muster of the illusionary nature of the assurances given us by *parole* as it fades into *écriture*? But illusion, after all, is what my poetics is
all about.

opening words of lamentation, years ago, when responding to a group of essays I organized about him for the English Institute: "Reading critiques of oneself is normally a distressing pastime, ranking even below the rereading of one's own works." This is true for me now, despite the narcissism induced by the occasion and my feeling flattered by the attention being given my work—so flattered that I'll try to resist whatever crankiness is induced by the distress Frye spoke of, and not spend this small time with specific complaints or happier reactions to the commentaries we have just heard.

I will content myself with saying what is to be expected: that I prefer Mark Rose's representation of my position to Vincent Leitch's. I might say Leitch's "misrepresentation," but how could he—with his version of the deconstructionist view of language—distinguish representation from misrepresentation and claim that his is the one rather than the other? But let be. I was saying that I prefer Rose's version of Krieger over Leitch's because Leitch is less ready to see the continuing doubleness of my claim for an illusionary presence than is Rose, who—I think accurately—suggests that I formulate "the relationship between presence and absence in such a way that neither term is allowed to dominate the other; neither is allowed to become a final resting place." Leitch rather insists that I am less evenhanded, that—while I acknowledge the illusionary, "as if" character of poetic presence—I privilege that presence and only grudgingly concede the negative reality that stands outside its pretensions and undercuts them.

So, unlike Rose, who emphasizes an unyielding system of polar tension in my work, Leitch sees only my one-sided fidelity to a hidden god masquerading as a Manichaeism in order to protect itself from the deconstructionist's attack. He sees me fostering one side, secretly suppressing the other, while claiming an unstable duplicity (which seems to have persuaded at least Rose of its authenticity). But I would join Rose in insisting that it is, for me, not a matter of compromise between presence and absence, in which I urge one while being forced to permit the negative participation of the other. It is, rather, a sustained tensional polarity: both sides, each defined by the other, always paradoxically there, at once sustaining and negating one another.

That brings me, by way of answer, to the plea of my title today, "Both Sides Now," as I turn from this brief general response to these two commentaries on my work to make my own statement in their wake.

So, coming out of that plea for readers to resist identifying me with the ontology of a verbal presence uncritically proclaimed by the New Criticism—the plea to retain my claim for a doubleness without "resting place"—let me begin again: "Both Sides Now." This time my text is the dissemination of another text: my title is taken from the title of a popular song of a number of years ago by the singer-composer Joni Mitchell. With your indulgence I recall the opening lines to reinforce my borrowing:

> Rows and flows of angel hair
> And ice cream castles in the air
> And feather canyons everywhere
> I've looked at clouds that way.
>
> But now they only block the sun
> They rain and snow on everyone
> So many things I would have done
> But clouds got in my way.
>
> I've looked at clouds from both sides now
> From up and down, and still somehow
> It's cloud illusions I recall.
> I really don't know clouds . . . at all.

What seems to be a choice between the airy freedom of metaphor and the inescapable blockage of earthy reality turns out to be only a choice between two ways of seeing, two illusions, with reality something other than her language can say or she can know.

In my work I have persistently emphasized both sides now, and both at once—both now—as I have pressed my own notion of illusion. The notion is perhaps best represented in the emblem created by Joan Krieger for my recent book, *Poetic Presence and Illusion*. In it two identical and opposed mythical creatures, in multiple images, are

This creature fabricated multiplies itself, but moves not; sees itself, or sees not; exists twice, and is not.

— Joan Krieger

invariably twinned in their mutual relations: they look, open-eyed, at one another or are turned, eyes closed, away; and they are together, too, in sharing the blackness of type or the black-enclosed outlines of blank space.

In that book I seek to tie this twinned mutuality to the behavior of the participants in the Prisoner's Dilemma game traced in its infinite variations by contemporary social scientists. In the game model, each of two partners in crime, being interrogated separately, is dependent on—but cut off from—the other's testimony. Each must decide either to cooperate with the police by turning against the other out of fear of the other's confession or to remain a faithful confederate in hopes that his partner remains equally true to him. So the choice between plea-bargaining or holding out with a claim of innocence is tied to the interpretation by either of the partner's likely choice, which is similarly dependent on a reading of *his*.

Each of the partners, then, must define himself through his speculative interpretation of the other as he moves through a process of at once differentiating his own interest and being forced to identify it with the other's interest. He is both a separate individual and a twin, one who can serve his individuality only by discovering another's precisely like his own. His sense of himself as real is riveted to his illusionary sense of the other, and yet he is aware that in the companion interrogation cell it is all being reversed, that the other turns his back to turn the first criminal into a similar illusion that confounds separateness and identity. Like the creatures in the emblem I described earlier, they see each other, or see not. Or should I view them as a single, divided creature rather than as two, doubly bound creatures and say (as the riddle on the frontispiece of my book does) that it "sees itself, or sees not"? This is just the archetypal duplicity long recorded about what it is to be identical twins, born of one egg. So, projected out of this model, presence can be defined only by its illusionary double, by its own vision of its illusionary other, at once absorbed into the self and rejected as an other.

For the prisoner trapped in his dilemma, in the silence of his isolated cell confronting himself and his mate (confronting himself *as* his mate), the question of which is the signifier and which the signified in his interpretive problem is one that shifts on him as he ponders it. I press this semiotic doubleness or controlled instability to characterize the relation between the two elements of poetic metaphor, conceived in the broadest sense; or, indeed, to characterize the relation between presence and illusion themselves, which I find similarly twinned. As with the prisoners, or the creatures in the emblem, the signifier and the signified—like the tenor and the vehicle in metaphor—*both* look at each other in mutual mimesis, and turn away in separateness—though in this act, too, they remain twinned and mimetic.

But I do not believe that the apparent paradox of presence and illusion, as it arises out of the way in which poems have functioned within our cultural tradition, is as difficult or obscure or irrational as Vincent Leitch suggests. As we examine the complex of our responses to the literary fiction, we find in it, I suggest, just such an apparently contradictory combination of presence and the awareness of illusionary emptiness or unsubstantiality, of identity and distinctness, of self-enclosure and openness. Further, I suggest that we are less than satisfied when we do not find it. Far from rare or obscure, it is a rather commonplace response. It is what happens when, as an audience, we must come to terms with the actors and their actions on the stage—are they to be viewed as dramatic characters? or as lifelike (if not real) people and happenings being "imitated"? Our concern with their fate as if it were real, together with our role in constituting the illusion that helps it keep its distance from us, creates the strangely duplicitous terms for our aesthetic contemplation. Given our complicity, once we are in the theater, with dramatic illusion, surely the "reality" we bestow upon them is of a radically paradoxical sort: the flesh-and-blood actor and the actual things we witness him doing, the character and his doings in the text which we say the actor represents (or counterfeits), and the supposedly substantial person and deed—in the world, shall we say?—which the text is presumably telling us *about*. The actor, live but make-believe, is related to the textual character, and the textual character related to the presumed lifelike person behind him, in a way that compounds realities and their illusionary would-be equivalents. In either case the first is to be taken as a representation of the second, as a signifier of a transcendental signified: we need this mythic assumption to allow the drama to do its work.

And how can we have any but an ambiguous ontological sense of what is unfolding before us? What is the reality of a King Lear, who suffers and dies every night (though perhaps played each time by the same actor) and yet is still there because his death is not as ours is to be, even though we must also think of his death as absolute (like ours) if we are to take the dramatic illusion seriously, as we do. We suffer for him while knowing our reality must not intrude upon his. These several simultaneous realities to which we respond, at once reflective of our reality, and somehow free of it, at once tied to the world and locked in a discontinuous realm of make-believe, obviously have paradoxical relations to one another. And yet our age-old habit of aesthetic attentiveness on such occasions has no difficulty sustaining the multiple and conflicting awarenesses, affirming the presence of what is before us without altogether succumbing to it. Thus it is also affirming presence only as illusion, which is to admit that it's not—in another sense—present at all.

There is, among these potential "realities" we sense, no firm ground on which to stand in order to privilege any one of them and from which to deny competing claims since, as in the Prisoner's Dilemma, all claims about relations between reality and illusion can be reversed, and are reversed, as we oscillate between one perspective and its opposite, or somehow, paradoxically, manage to hold both at once. Drama, with its peculiar conjunctions of reality and make-believe, works to remind us of the unstable relation between presence and illusion in all signifier-signified relations—especially within the fictional realm. Drama also leaves us with thematic implications about the illusionary, role-playing nature (the "dramatistics") of all symbols of our presumed realities or, conversely, the apparently realistic consequences of our illusionary realms of make-believe. So, with each stage both affirming and denying its own "real" reality or having it denied by another stage, we move into the infinite regress of illusions within illusions, or presence within presences—as the distinction between presence and illusion blurs before us. And we can move out from drama to discover our similar responses to the other poetic genres, as we observe the power given words to close together *as if* holding a presence within them: indeed, we can observe this about words or any other formal element that is pressed into service as a medium of aesthetic presentation in the struggle to bring to presentation what otherwise seemed to function as no more than self-effacing materials of *re*presentation.

It is this tension of polarities that are overlapping or even interchanging which leads me to reject the charge that I privilege one side over the other, or that I accept one side, however unhappily, as reality; which leads me, instead, to insist on "Both Sides Now"—always now. So I argue for an illusion of presence that, because it can refer—if to nothing else—to its own fictional status, can point to its own empty, insubstantial character—in short, to its character *as* illusion. This affirmation of a self-questioning presence can be similarly made on behalf of an identity (as opposed to difference) and a closure (as opposed to openness) that also question and undercut their own natures. It is self-reference that permits us to ascribe a self-conscious fictionality to the poem which can open us to that from which it may be seen as seeking to cut us off. It is the extrasystematic thrust that authorizes the system and yet denies it authority. The poem, as art—mere artifice—betrays a consciousness about its fictional self that reminds us of the illusionary nature of the aesthetic "reality" which seeks to enclose us. By negative implication, this reminder implicitly points to the world that the poem explicitly excludes in order to affirm its own closure. The world may be reduced to the stage in front of us, but so long as we are aware that it is only the stage in front of us, the world outside threatens to break in. Thus the work of art, as its own metaphorical substitution for the world of experience beyond, is a metaphor that at once affirms its own integrity and yet, by negative implication, denies itself, secretly acknowledging that it is but an artful evasion of the world. This claim to duplicity permits the work to celebrate its own ways and the ways of its language unencumbered, using the negative residue of its language to point us to the language of the world it self-consciously evades.

Of course, both the affirmation of closure and the self-reference that leads us to find the opening in it are consequences of our habits of perception as readers trained in the Western literary canon. The poem is seen as a single entity created through the complicity of the reader who, sharing the author's habit of seeking closure, allows the work—even as he does his share in creating it—to lead him toward the act of sealing it off within the aesthetic or fictional frame that his perceptual training leads him to impose. The metaphorical habits he has learned—from childhood, from religion, from previous traffic with the arts—lead him to seek an eschatology, an end to history, in the work as he seeks through it to bring chronological time to a stop, to find a utopia of fully realized ends.

Such has been the human use of myth—the quest for the myths we need—in the Western aesthetic since Aristotle formulated the distinction between history and poetry as each relates in its different way to time and to beginnings, middles, and ends. In thus emphasizing the poem as a will-o'-the-wisp—as both an object and not—I have meant to reintroduce the temporal element, the element of process and of human experience, into our understanding of the literary work as it is created by the poet and created complicitously by us out of what he gives us. Because I want to see the work as functioning within the metaphorical apocalypse we allow it to create for us even while it remains a piece of language running back into the past and forward into the future (which is all it would be were it *not* for us as aesthetically conscious readers), I am necessarily tempted to look for evidence of a self-conscious duplicity in the work as I come upon it and as I, in effect, ask it to do these things.

The pressure for closure is strong enough in the Western tradition. Our propensity to find (or project) closure may largely account for the role of the story—like that of the picture frame or the proscenium arch—in the history of our culture. The tendency of our narrative structures reveals a responsiveness to what Frank Kermode has called our "sense of an ending." The satisfying ending is one that fulfills internally aroused expectations, that realizes immanent purposes. From Aristotle's concept of denouement to the formal finality called for by Kant, and in the formalistic tradition that is indebted to both, we find the imposition of a mythic ending, a structural apocalypse, which cuts off fiction from empirical happenings. As we have seen, it intrudes the spatial imagination on the radical temporality of pure sequence, shaping time into the separateness of fiction. Linear sequence is suspended, transformed into circularity.

But there is something in literature that also keeps it open to the world, to language at large, and to the reader. As we contemplate the verbal object through our culturally imposed habits of perceiving what is presented to us as aesthetic, we must deal with the two-sided nature of its words, now that they have been, in spite of their normal tendencies, shaped into a poetic medium: they try to work their way into a self-sufficient presence, and yet they remain transient and empty signifiers. This is the paradoxical nature of language as aesthetic medium, and both sides must be exploited. Language is able to create itself into a self-justified fiction, but, because it is also no more than language—just words after all—it is able to display a self-consciousness about its illusionary character. Language seems in our best poetry to be both full of itself and empty, both totally here as itself and pointing elsewhere, away from itself. It permits its reader at once to cherish its creation as a closed system, one that comes to terms with itself, and to recognize its necessarily incomplete nature in its dependence on us as its readers, on its literary precursors, on the general language system—the way of the word—and on the way of the world.

Not that I am claiming these special characteristics to be *in* literary works so much as they are products of our aesthetic habits of perception—when dealing with such works—which seek to find them there. And our aesthetic habit of dealing with fiction leads us to respond to its self-consciousness about the occasion that sponsors it. In other words, the literary work persuades us of itself as a special object even as we retain an awareness of the rather extraordinary activity we are performing in contributing to our own persuasion. It is not fetishism when we recognize the tentative conditions that encourage the closure we celebrate, and when we accept the openness that surrounds the moment of our commitment to what we treat as the closed object—and, in effect, authenticates it.

But I do not suggest that through these workings the aesthetic becomes a game of now you see it, now you don't. Rather, I see the work as touching and unlocking in us the anthropological quest for that which marks and defines every moment of a culture's way of seeing, as well as its inner skepticism that undoes its visionary reality with a supposedly "real" reality which is no less illusionary. The making and unmaking of our metaphors, our mythic equations, in experience as in art only reveal the primacy of the operation of the aesthetic in us all—and perhaps explain the extent to which our drive for art is accompanied by a cognitive itch which even the experience of art itself never quite eases, so that the need to experience more art happily remains.

Since the ascendancy of structuralism more than a decade ago, critics in this country have had to come to terms with the Saussurean notion of verbal signs as arbitrary and as based upon the principle of differentiation. Thus what used to seem to be the simple matter of representation in language—the presence of a fixed signified in the signifier—is converted into a problematic. Signifiers come to be seen as operating in a dynamic field of differentiation and have only arbitrary relations with their presumed signifieds. A culture's confidence in the identity and inevitability of its verbal meanings, rather than its confronting their differentiation and arbitrariness, only testifies to its self-mystifications as it falls prey to the metaphysical habit of logocentrism. The wistful imposition of identity, accompanied by the ontological claim of presence, is now to be undone by a shrewder philosophy of language that reminds us of the field of absence upon which the system of differences play. Hence we have the rejection of metaphor for metonymy.

I grant that the conception of metaphor, with its illusion of identity, may well be a secular conversion of the religious myth of transubstantiation, so that we may wish to reduce it at once to nostalgic mystification. And we may then see it operating whenever we spatialize verbal relations in order to bring linguistic temporality to a stop in an attempt to redeem time. By confessing the illusionary nature of this metaphorical operation we help perform on ourselves, I am suggesting a sophisticated view of a language that knows of its metonymic condition and yet generates among its elements an internal play that appears to create a metaphorical identity existing in the teeth of the principle of difference. It is an identity that knows and has come through the world of difference, a metaphor that has known metonymy, a spatial vision that sustains itself only through the acknowledgment that all may finally be nothing but time. If it functions as what I have elsewhere called a "miracle," it is because it proclaims itself as miracle only while acknowledging that it cannot occur. Yet the differential principle, in its eventual questioning of the representational character of words, reminds us that a world of language founded on difference is not a residual reality, but is only an alternative illusion, however *un*miraculous.

Nothing that deconstruction reveals about the mystifications that sponsor claims to verbal presence should distract us altogether from an interest in how poems have functioned and can function within their cultural tradition, whatever the motives buried in nostalgia or political power that we can find beneath that function. And the metaphorical visions enclosed in the poem open us to ways of cultural seeing that have their anthropological validity, whatever the language myths that guided them. So long as poems have served their culture as if they had an objective aesthetic character, their function must be accounted for, though we may find that, through self-reference, the best of them carry their own criticism of the mythic assumptions that sustain that function. The myth of presence, of transcendental signifieds immanent in words, that operates as an assumption in all a culture's language uses, is self-consciously indulged in poetry by a language freely allowed to go it on its own.

Mark Rose, subjecting my criticism to a perceptive narratological analysis, finds it to be a version of the quest romance. In a recent essay[2] I myself suggest a utopian dimension when I admit that the drive for aesthetic closure expresses the dream of a microcosm of satisfied ends. The dream of unity, of formal repetitions that are seen as the temporal equivalent of juxtapositions, that convert the temporal into the spatial through the miracle of simultaneity—this dream persists, reinforced by every aesthetic illusion which we help create and to which we succumb. We cultivate the mode of identity, the realm of metaphor, within an aesthetic frame that acknowledges its character as momentary construct and thereby its frailty as illusion. But it allows us a glimpse of our own capacity for vision before the bifurcations of language have struck. The dream of unity may be entertained tentatively and is hardly to be granted cognitive power, except for the secret life-without-language or life-before-language which it suggests, the very life which the language of difference precludes (as the poem-as-dream knows and shows us it knows). In poetry we grasp at the momentary possibility that this can be a life-*in*-language. This would be a utopia indeed, one well worth the quest.

Let me suggest that I pursue my quest on horseback—in Tristram Shandy's sense, on "hobbyhorseback." In Sterne's novel, which is a

---

2. "The Arts and The Idea of Progress," ch. 2, above. I refer here to the final section of that essay.

Critical Positions: Self-definition and Other Definitions

superb example of my theme of "Both Sides Now," it is each character's hobbyhorse that carries him into his transformed realm, a private world of figuration which encloses his verbal reality, his hobbyhorsical reality. The hobbyhorse is just the creature to carry each of us off into these tropistic privacies. But in Sterne the hobbyhorse is no less a horse than is an actual horse, whether Uncle Toby's or Trim's or Death's, which is treated just as metaphorically, as itself a hobbyhorse. Again we have not an illusion set against reality, but competing varieties of illusion, of hobbyhorses. Mine has been carrying me for more than a couple of decades now, growing—or aging—and with age spreading, though retaining a firm sense of its nature. It is a friendly creature, one, like Tristram's, which I cannot altogether forsake.

> What a rate have I gone on at, curvetting and frisking it away, two up and two down for four volumes together [actually rather more], without looking once behind, or even on one side of me, to see whom I trod upon!—I'll tread upon no one,—quoth I to myself when I mounted—I'll take a good rattling gallop, but I'll not hurt the poorest jack-ass upon the road—So off I set—up one lane—down another, through this turn-pike—over that, as if the arch-jockey of jockeys had got behind me. (vol. 4, chap. 20)

After such a ride, shall I dismount? What other horse would you have me ride? For there's not a pedestrian among us.

III Reconsideration of Special Texts for Special Reasons

Presentation and Representation
in the Renaissance Lyric:
The Net of Words
and the Escape of the Gods

I begin by trying to convey some idea of the exhilaration I feel as I respond to the dynamics within the linguistic forces set and maintained in motion by the English Renaissance lyric at its best. Let me suggest two rather different, if not opposed, modes of verbal behavior.

Here is the first movement I seek to follow: A word seems about to turn into another word. It is very exciting to watch it happen. But how can the transformation occur? Here is the word in the process of overrunning its bounds, destroying its own sense of territorial integrity along with its neighbor's. It is undoing the very notion of "property," whether we relate the word *property* to that which defines an entity or to that which defines a possession, so that it is defying the operational procedures of logic and law—and those of language itself as well. For property is the elementary basis for the differential principle underlying the operation of language, which in turn underlies the operations of both logic and law.

Still, in the face of such impressive resistance, the word seems to pursue its errant career, if we know how to watch it perform. At which moment does a word stop being its own sealed self and begin to merge with its neighbor? Can a system of conventionally accepted meanings continue to function if any of them turns unstable and thus slides into fluidity? All these difficulties are exacerbated if the differences between the terms being transformed into identity are—more than merely different—wholly contradictory: if they are nothing less than binary oppositions that are forced into a fusion. Often, it is through the exploited coincidence of the arbitrary phonetic properties of words that such fusion is apparently achieved. (It would take another paper to deal with the complicated process by which the act of silent hearing is incorporated into the reading habits of the educated reader when confronted by a poem.) Because words, however different in meaning, sound alike—or almost alike—they are forced, as we hear by watching, to become alike. Often the becoming alike occurs in the coupling act of rhyming or—more extremely—of punning. But often the poet slips from word to word and from sound to sound in a continuing parade of subtle echoes.

We find this extraordinary poetic tactic in many English Renaissance poems. We can begin with an obvious example. In Ralegh's "Poesy to Prove Affection Is Not Love" ("Conceit, begotten by the eyes / Is quickly born and quickly dies"), the poet deals with the death-in-life affection, the "conceit" that "within the Mother's *womb* / hath his beginning and his *tomb*." This collapsing of the womb-tomb opposition into a womb that is also and at the same moment a tomb becomes an enabling act for the poem's complex claim.

Or a more subtle example. In Ralegh's "Nymph's Reply" to Marlowe's "Passionate Shepherd," in the line "Time drives the flock from *field* to *fold*," we find a simplicity that should not hide its density. The single alteration of the vowel from "field" to "fold" carries with it the equation within the course of nature's seasons as well as within man's life: from open freedom to coffinlike enclosure, under the driving hand of time, the second ("fold") already implicit (inscribed) in the first ("field")—in its very letters. And, a bit later, the line, "Is fancy's spring, but sorrow's fall"—following "A honey-tongue, a heart of gall"—uses its chiastic pattern of alliteration ("fancy's" and "fall" on the outside, "spring" and "sorrows" on the inside) to hold its oppositions and yet convert them into the sameness of echo.

Let me cite one last quotation from Ralegh, this one at a desperately and conclusively late moment in the magnificent "Nature, that washed her hands in milk." Having created an elegantly balanced ideal mistress at the behest of love, nature must suffer her delicately wrought creature to be undone by time, which "Turns snow and silk and milk to dust." The sequence of alliteration and internal rhyme leads to the crumbling of language into a negative, universal equation. Nature earlier turned away from earth, using snow and silk instead, as she propagated the moist by excluding the dry, but the moistness of snow and silk and milk ends with the alliterative equivalent of the *d*rying which is a *d*ying: ends, like earth, in *d*ust with the collapse of all distinctions. (Pages could be written on the destructive power that Ralegh—in more poems than this one—imposes on the alliterative extension of words beginning with the letter "d.")

Shakespeare everywhere reminds us of the transformational power of words, their appearing to defy their own distinctness by overlapping and changing places with one another. As he suggests in Sonnet 105, "One thing expressing, leaves out difference." The sonnets are full of examples. I'll cite just a few, choosing almost at random. I have dealt with some of these, often at length, in other places, so that it should be enough for me to do barely more than mention them here.[1]

There is the obvious collapse of the line between truth and falsity, as well as the multiplication of the meanings of those words *true* and *false*, in the lines from Sonnet 72, "O, lest your *true love* may seem *false* in this, / That you for *love* speak well of me *untrue*." Or there is the collapse of the line between opposition and advocacy in Sonnet 35: "For to thy *sensual* fault I bring in *sense*— / Thy *adverse* party is thy *advocate*." In Sonnets 6 and 9 we find a verbal play that muddies distinctions among use, interest, waste, and abuse: "That *use* is not forbidden *usury*" (Sonnet 6, line 5), and later, "But beauty's waste hath in the world an end, / And kept *unused*, the *user* so destroys it" (Sonnet 9, lines 11–12). In Sonnet 71, the calculating world of material self-interest, in its concern to feed the body, is quickly identified with the feeding *off* the body by those most materialistic inheritors of the grave: " . . . that I am fled / From this *vile world*, with *vilest worms* to dwell." The vileness of the world is totally realized only in the superlatively consistent activity of the vilest worms, which correct the spelling (*world* to *worms*) and extend vileness to the ultimate degree.

Opposites are turned into one another even more extremely in the fully realized pun, in which two words—violently at odds with one another—share a single phonetic entity. Thus, in Sonnet 87, "Farewell! thou art too dear for my possessing," "dear" must embrace and identify that which is dear in the marketplace with that which is dear in our unworldly affections. The mixed argument that follows springs from both sides of this doubleness of "dear." We find in a good number of sonnets a similar use of puns to bring together into a phonetic identity meanings that are normally differentiated or even opposed—for exam-

---

1. See *A Window to Criticism: Shakespeare's Sonnets and Modern Poetics* (Princeton: Princeton University Press, 1964), parts 2 and 3, and "The Innocent Insinuations of Wit: The Strategy of Language in Shakespeare's *Sonnets*," in *The Play and Place of Criticism* (Baltimore: Johns Hopkins Press, 1967), pp. 19–36.

ple, in "state" in Sonnet 124 ("If my dear love were but the child of state"), and in "refigured" in Sonnet 6 ("Then let not winter's ragged hand deface"): "Ten times thyself were happier than thou art, / If ten of thine ten times refigured thee." The device of having one word turn into another, under the pressure of the poem's dynamics, is only exaggerated in the pun that forces at least two words to be one another at the same time.

Words seem to undermine themselves and the way they are supposed to function, as if they insist on reminding us that their meanings, with oppositions flowing into one another, must be as inconstant as the experience they would record. Most of my examples, from the inconstant "conceit" of Ralegh onward, have related the inconstancy of these words (despite their pretense to be fixed entities) to the inconstancy of time, so that words as fixed entities would be an inaccurate representation of experience under the fickleness of time. The purely poetic device cannot escape having thematic consequences—indeed must be seen as the consequence itself of a thematic cause. Indeed the thematic and the poetic are circularly related, like the chicken and the egg. The words, as a conceit, may seem to be a fixed or static formula of meaning, but Sonnet 15, furnishing me my final example of the movement from one word into another, indicates how unfixed the verbal formula becomes after all: it refers to "the *conceit* of this *inconstant* stay" (line 9), forcing the conceit itself to collapse into inconstancy.

But I mentioned at the start that I would point out two rather different, if not opposed, modes of verbal behavior, and so far I have spoken of one only. Now for the second. Instead of our watching as meanings come together in violation of the law of differentiation or even binary opposition, we may find what seems to be the reverse operation occurring. As we watch, a word finds itself at odds with itself, falls out with itself, indeed negates itself, in effect cancelling itself out; it undoes the integrity of words upon which the operation of language depends. A stunning example occurs in Shakespeare's 116 ("Let me not to the marriage of true minds"): " . . . love is not love / Which alters when it alteration finds / Or bends with the remover to remove." The negative repetition ("love" to "not love") is indeed a self-denial of language, a self-cancellation. Language in effect wipes itself out as everything is made relative, contingent, arbitrary. The poet must protest a language that operates this way, though this seems to be the inevitable consequence of the function of language.

A similar expunging of the word occurs in Thomas Campion's song, "Thou art not fair," when the poet threatens the beloved to take away her nature (that is, change his mind about her) if she is less than

constant: " . . . thou shalt prove / That *beauty* is *no beauty* without love."
Or Ben Jonson's "Slow, slow, fresh fount," in which time forces the
acknowledgment, "*Our* beauties are *not ours.*" If, in the first poetic
manipulation of language which I have described, differences collapse
into apparent identity in a way that violates the notion of verbal boundaries and property, in this second operation we find the most immediate
linguistic entity losing identity, falling itself into difference—now at a
distance from itself, so that there is no single, undifferentiated verbal
self.

Perhaps the most striking example of this second device is found in
The Phoenix and Turtle in the climactic cry of reason, which, in its
admiring acknowledgment of the impossible union it has witnessed, in
effect denies its own name: "Love hath reason, reason none, / If what
parts can so remain." The miraculous destruction of number in love is a
violation of the operation of reason, and love's very existence changes
what reason must be as it changes the way in which language can
work—in effect, by insisting that, in the way we usually understand it,
language cannot work at all.

But this final example should indicate to us that our two seemingly
opposed modes of poetic devices are themselves in the end identical and
mutually reenforcing. The line "Love hath reason, reason none"
emphasizes both the falling apart of a verbal entity ("reason none") and
the growing together of opposed entities ("love hath reason"). Despite
my separating these two devices, it should have been clear throughout
that there is a similar, if reverse, duplicity operating in both, a duplicity
that forces our observation to see every movement of words toward
identity as accompanied by an equally urgent movement in them
toward differentiation, each from itself as well as from every other. It is
precisely this need to hold both awarenesses at once—the identifying
and the differentiating—that makes these movements we have been
observing so exciting in their stretching of the resources of linguistic
operation.

Probably no example can serve more forcefully to reflect this duplicity than those lines I have already quoted from Ralegh's "Nymph's
Reply": "A honey tongue, a heart of gall, / Is fancy's spring, but
sorrow's fall." The mingling of the move to identity with the move to
differentiation among fancy and fall, spring and sorrow, or rather
spring and fall, fancy and sorrow (echoing the cross-relations within
the parallels of the preceding line) is only the more forceful when we
remind ourselves that these lines are preceded by the lines, "The flowers
do fade, and *wanton* fields / To *wayward* winter reckoning yields." The
unpredictability and indiscriminacy of unlimited fertility turn into the

unpredictability and indiscriminacy of unlimited death, the "wanton" into the "wayward," words that overlap as much as they are distinguished, as they are applied to "fields" and the alliterated "winter." Hence, in "honey," "heart," "tongue," "gall," or "fancy," "fall," "sorrow," "spring," the interlacings of parallelism and chiasmus, of meaning and sound, join opposition to dissolution.

These duplicitous manipulations of words, as they are made either to move outward to interanimate one another or to move inward to cut off from themselves—or to manage somehow to do both at once—arise from the poet's struggle to win from language a representational power that he does not trust words normally to provide. By exploiting the sensory side of words—their sound, which is their only material aspect—the poet tries to invoke the illusion of their presence: he uses the sensible to transform the intelligible. It is his way to overcome our impression of verbal absence—inspired by an exclusive interest in the merely intelligible aspect of words—our impression of words whose object is elsewhere as they mean, often vainly, to point to it. Thus their auditory character, normally most arbitrary in that it has no relation to their meaning, seems—by means of devices like those I have suggested—to turn words substantive, in effect allows them to take on the illusion of body. So, apparently acknowledging normal language to be a verbal parade of arbitrary meanings, of empty, bodiless counters, the poet seeks to turn the arbitrary into the necessary and the functional—into the materially present. It is as if he uses the sound of words as the most extreme symbol of their arbitrary character, forcing those apparently insignificant phonetic elements to prove the poem's power to break through arbitrariness to substantive inevitability, to transform our awareness of words' absent, though intelligible objects to their own material, fully sensible presence.

I can point—as I have elsewhere[2]—to Sir Philip Sidney's Sonnet 35 ("What may words say, or what may words not say"), which I might refer to as his semiotic sonnet in that it deals explicitly with the problem of representation and the futile contribution made by our usual words to solving it. The poet is worried that even our noblest words—names of our most glorious abstractions—can have no meaning because the living reality of Stella forces them to contradict and hence negate themselves. In the sonnet we find example after example of the second of the two devices I described earlier, the self-denial by words of their

---

2. In *Poetic Presence and Illusion* (Baltimore: Johns Hopkins University Press, 1979), pp. 16–17.

own entityhood ("Love is not love . . ." or "Love hath reason, reason none"):

> What may words say, or what may words not say,
> Where truth itself must speak like flattery?
> Within what bounds can one his liking stay,
> Where Nature doth with infinite agree?
>   What Nestor's counsel can my flames ally,
> Since Reason's self doth blow the coal in me?
> And ah what hope, that hope should once see day,
> Where Cupid is sworn page to Chastity?

How can words have meaning if Stella's very being forces truth to speak like flattery, forces nature to be one with infinity, forces reason to be the sponsor of desire, forces Cupid to be "sworn page" to chastity? And then the climactic inversion: instead of a person growing rich through achieving fame, ". . . Fame / Doth even grow rich, naming my Stella's name." The invocation of the one true name, the one word in the language that encloses its own essential value, is the only act that authenticates language, gives it a reality. Fame can grow rich in the act of naming Stella's name; and the poem itself guarantees the claim by at that moment naming Stella's actual name, Rich, following it with her mythical name, Stella. (Is the double name the reason for the poet's repeating the word *name*—"naming my Stella's name"?) So fame has aggrandized itself, it becomes "rich," in effect it becomes Stella. The one way for other verbal names (truth, nature, reason, chastity, fame) to have substance is for them to share the substantive magic of the one true name, the name that *is* its meaning (thanks to a fortuitous pun). Otherwise words are without substance, empty. And the sonnet's conclusion follows: it is she who teaches wit what perfection is, and it is she who raises praise to the level of being itself praised in the moment of being praised herself: "Not thou by praise, but praise in thee is raised: / It is a praise to praise, when thou art praised." Once Stella herself has entered the poem by way of her name to en-rich fame, she is able, similarly, to convert the incapacities of words ("wit," "praise") to a new power, though she licenses them only for the single act of serving her own reality, her being finally bestowing meaning upon them.

The poet has in this sonnet indulged—and in this sonnet sequence freely indulges—the magical act of invoking Stella's name to convert all other names, those unmagical nouns that fill both our language and our empty poetic conventions, from nonsense to meaning, a living meaning attached to her living being. In sonnet after sonnet we find the magic word *Stella* incanted and then watch the transformations that follow from that incantation. From the first sonnet in the sequence (and the first sonnet itself is a splendid example), the poet is struggling with a halting, recalcitrant, and inoperative language that will not do the job of representation, and resolves his struggle by breaking through to the substantive image of Stella, a reality carried in the image and usually invoked by the name, the latter being the one signifier that suffers no separation from its signified. Stella, her being as well as her name, must be made by the poet to invade the unreal net of words—and to invest it with substance. In this one case, the nominal reality becomes the fleshly reality, a language that enables this poetry to speak as man otherwise cannot. Thus, in Sonnet 74 ("I never drank of Aganippe well"), the poet, a "layman" forsaken by the antique, figurative muses and unfit "for sacred rites," has his mouth inspired by the mouth of Stella, a fleshly muse who gives speech through oral embrace: "My lips are sweet, inspired with Stella's kiss." The introduction of Stella's kiss, in the final couplet, is an invocation of a present and literal muse indeed. The poet's invocation is an act that puts the sonnet in the present tense, and since her name alone is substantive, she is to enter the poem with her name.

It is as if the poet has discovered the built-in futility of our usual attempt at verbal representation. That futility is carried in the prefix, the *re* of *re*present. Words are empty and belated counters because it is their nature to seek to refer to what is elsewhere and has occurred earlier. Any pretension by them to present reality is frustrated by the *re*, which requires that what they would represent—what has already presented itself in person—has had its presence, its presentness, elsewhere and earlier. But the poet would dabble in verbal magic, calling upon a sacred name that would overcome belatedness and introduce a living, bodily hereness that would make language more than properly representational; that would make it nothing less than presentational.

What, in Sidney's enraptured fiction, makes Stella's name so special in its powers, at once exempted from the empty inconstancies of words and able to re-endow language with a vital function? The name is to remind us that the language around it has long been deactivated, even as it creates for us a new dispensation under which words can be reactivated, given substance, *her* substance, once again. But what permits the name to function in this remarkable way? Clearly, as in much Renaissance lyric poetry that reaches ambitiously toward presence, what is paramount is the analogy to Christian paradox, with its insistence on the participatory magic by which spirit partakes of, and becomes one with, body. Unlike the now-absent gods that once inhabited verbal abstractions often represented by the gods in classical mythology (truth, reason, love, etc.), Stella *is* her name and constantly remains so, just as that name actively intrudes upon and participates in these poems both as name, with its heavenly trappings, and as the physically present lady herself.

In Sonnet 28 ("You that with allegory's curious frame"), the poet rejects the use of allegorical structures and references in favor of the plain and literal statement, in favor of "pure simplicity." Though he speaks extravagance enough in the poem, it is—because he speaks of Stella, because he speaks the name *Stella* and speaks under its aegis—to be taken as literal simplicity. Thus, "When I say Stella, I do mean the same / Princess of Beauty . . ." And the conclusion: "But know that I in pure simplicity, / Breathe out the flames which burn within my heart, / Love only reading unto me this art." That direct speech should be so apparently metaphorical and simplicity so apparently extravagant is attributable—as in other sonnets—to Stella and the poet's invocation of her rather than to any empty appeal to "allegory's curious frame." But, guided by her powers, the speech remains direct and simple, whatever it may seem; for it is literal speech. After all, the invoked name, Stella, like the lady herself, is at once her name and an *apparently* allegorical reference to the star (thus qualifying her poet-lover as an Astrophil, or star-lover). But, the sonnet is insisting, this too is no allegory; it is simply what she is (and what, consequently, she makes him). Again he would have her participate in and become consubstantial with these meanings (as he did with the abstractions in Sonnet 35), claiming a new dispensation for language, not unlike the typological identities being claimed for a semiotic controlled by the Christian paradox.

But, with Stella enacting the role of his goddess, why not this claim? It *is* an outrageous joke for the poet to deny using allegory at the very moment he is speaking her apparently allegorical name ("When I say, Stella, I do mean . . ." and mean nothing more; but what he says he means is more than enough—"princess of beauty" and the rest). Still, his very point is that all that he says is what, simply and literally, she *is*. Whatever he has given away is won back through her; whatever he has given away in language is won back through her name. It all pours into her and out of her—*as* her name. And, as this new dispensation for language, that name is the only language he speaks—and really the only word, since all other words are to be read—or rather reread—in light of it. No wonder, then, that, as he tells us in Sonnet 19, no matter what he tries to write, "My very ink turns straight to Stella's name." And Stella, with all that name means and is, is captured in the poem and, once in it, reconstructs its meaning and its action.

On the other side, in the cynical poem by Fulke Greville, one of Sidney's close contemporaries (Ralegh was another), "Away with these self-loving lads," there are the following lines:

My songs they be of Cynthia's praise,
I wear her rings on holy-days,
On every tree I write her name,
And every day I read the same.
   Where Honor, Cupid's rival, is
   There miracles are seen of his.
If Cynthia crave her ring of me,
I blot her name out of the tree.

Where there is inconstancy, a failure to overcome the ways of the world under the sway of time, there no name is sacred; a name cannot replenish the emptiness or undo the arbitrariness of language but only shares in both. Names, like all words, come and go, are written and subsequently erased, are interchangeable. Honor is the rival of Cupid and, so long as Honor holds out, justifies the miracle of the lady's name written and each day ritualistically adored. But the eventual victory of Cupid and inconstancy leads to erasure and substitution.

One can look upon such apparently light, if bitter, love poems as serious attempts to treat man's desire as the extreme emblem of the earthly, of the absolutely arbitrary, with the interchange of names representative of the interchangeability of words within a failed and impotent language. Sidney himself is in some sonnets expressing failure, aware of the failure of his magic, of his attempt to invoke the sacred name and, with it, Stella's presence. Nowhere is the invocation of the name more explicit, or the failure—and Stella's continued absence—more starkly acknowledged than in Sonnet 106:

O absent presence Stella is not here;
False flattering hope, that with so fair a face,
Bare me in hand, that in this orphan place,
Stella, I say my Stella, should appear.

The lack of response leaves the poet, his world, and his language, untransformed as, in the balance of the sonnet, he comes close to (but resists) the temptations of Greville's fickle world of change.

It is the poet's double awareness that concerns me here: he knows, as a result of his impatience with language's representational—to say nothing of its presentational—failures, that he must indulge the pious attempt to use the poem to invoke and contain its object, its goddess; but he knows also the illusory nature of his attempt, the recalcitrance of language, together with its refusal, after all, really to give way. So he knows also the transcendence of the gods, their abandonment of the world and of the world of language. But he continues to try and to cultivate his (sometimes ironic) poetic illusions.

The sonneteer's invocation of the poem's object, bringing her into the poem as an active presence through the use of verbal devices like those I have examined, returns me to a theme that has been central to all my writings on Renaissance poetry—and especially on the English Petrarchan sonnet: the phonetic struggle for an illusion of presence which we find in it reflects the poet's effort to force into the network of language the elusive object which words—his words of love—have not been able to capture. Here is what I have referred to as the poet's quest for a representational power or—more extremely—a directly presentational power which he finds words normally lack. The referent—as the beloved, the poet's goddess, his Platonic heaven—insists on remaining transcendental to the poet's words that would enclose her in order to transform her state from one of absence to one of presence. After all, the fictional given of the Petrarchan sonnet is precisely that which demands such an effort on the part of the poet-lover. He writes his poem out of his lack, his want, of his beloved, who is—and threatens to remain—at a distance from him, like the absent god from the supplicant. But, as we have seen with Sidney, in his poem the poet can do more than complain of this absence, though complain he surely does; he can seek to use the poem to close the breach between his sacred object and himself, to make her responsive and hence present by having her enter the poem by way of her invoked name. So the poem can be as much an entreaty as a lamentation, as much an act—and a call to action in return—as a sorrowful recitation.

What the poet is trying to bring about—whatever his skepticism about the chances for his literal success—is a miracle of linguistic presence as much as a miracle of quasi-religious presence. His task, and the breakthrough he hopes to accomplish, partake of the realm of semiology as well as that of love's theology. The beloved goddess, who is absent from him and who is beseeched by his poem, must be brought bodily into it by having her name break through the emptiness of words to fill them with itself and—through name-magic—with herself. As Sidney's Sonnet 35 ("What may words say, or what may words not say") has shown us, it is the language process itself, with all its un-magical incapacities, which must be reconstituted in the act of naming the beloved. To the extent that the poem would succeed, it must transform the naming process of language in order to retain the present goddess trapped within it. Thus, as I earlier pointed out, in Sonnet 74 ("I never drank of Aganippe well"), we see the actual kiss of Stella's lips by the poet's lips replace the empty allusions to the muses with the actual consequences of physical presence.

So the absent goddess sought by the Petrarchan poet is one among the absent signifieds to which the normally dualistic process of language testifies. It is for this reason that I have claimed the poet's trial to be at once semiological and theological, if—indeed—love's theology is not being reduced to a problem in semiology. The world of references stands outside the network of words which seeks in vain to capture it. As the Petrarchan poet conceives the problem, chief within that world, the all-dominating transcendental signified among a host of transcendental signifieds, is the beloved-as-goddess. If the poet can work the magical breakthrough into presence for her, the others will follow within a remade language process.

I see the poet, then, as setting himself the objective of capturing the absent god (or goddess) within a verbal network which he knows cannot hold him (or her). The poet works his magic, changes lamentation to invocation, sometimes claims success; but we see him start the next poem anew as if the task has to be performed all over again. This is a Sisyphus-like concession to the failure of his word-magic to produce more than a momentary illusion of a breakthrough to presence. The absent goddess and the world of being which she dominates are out there still, still resisting capture by his words, whatever he may momentarily have appeared to bring about with his phonetic word-play and the invocations that it permits.

The path I have been traveling has led us back to my title, which is my theme: "Presentation and Representation: The Net of Words and the Escape of the Gods." My reference there was to the language of Ben Jonson's "Why I Write Not of Love," which I have discussed at greater length on another occasion.[3]

> Some act of Love's bound to rehearse,
> I thought to bind him in my verse;
> Which when he felt, Away, quoth he,
> Can poets hope to fetter me?
> It is enough they once did get
> Mars and my mother in their net;
> I wear not these my wings in vain.
> With which he fled me, and again
> Into my rhymes could ne'er be got

---

3. See *Theory of Criticism: A Tradition and Its System* (Baltimore: Johns Hopkins University Press, 1976), pp. 234–37.

By any art. Then wonder not
That since, my numbers are so cold,
When Love is fled, and I grow old.

The poet has set himself the task of binding Cupid in his verse, and Cupid is equally determined to evade capture. And, of course, momentarily the poet does have him—indeed has him as a speaking character. The god reminds the poet of Homer's earlier capture, in *his* net of words, of Venus and Mars in their lovemaking. It is significant that Cupid is attributing the act of binding to the poet rather than to the irate Hephaestus, who in the narrative forges the net (of metal and not of words) to display the lovers. The responsibility, so far as Cupid is concerned, is Homer's: Cupid is looking beyond the narrative cause in the jealous god to the ultimate metapoetic cause in the poet. He is looking, then, to the net of words which, for Cupid's purposes on the present occasion, is more substantive and threatening than the net forged within the frame of the story. Cupid's escape from the present poet follows, and the poet's verse must do without the erotic god.

But the god is referred to in the poem not as Cupid but as Love. And what makes the poem work so brilliantly is the gradual movement—anticipated in the poem's title ("Why I Write Not of Love")—which allows *Love* also to take on all the roles of *love* as it functions in the poet's life. When the god Love is fled, so is love, leaving an old, cold poet, with his verses emptied of the god—and of desire. If he does not have Love (the god) in his verse, he cannot have love, consequently cannot write of love. Presentation must accompany representation. The language of myth is given life by being made participatory, as literary allusion and living immediacy are made one. Isn't this very much the unified doubleness we saw in Stella as she functioned in her several ways in Sidney's Sonnet 28, with its denial of allegory? Stella's function as star, goddess, and beloved is similar to Cupid's function as erotic god and the poet's desire. The god is both the mythological creature and the existential force which the mythic name represents, so that she or he forces herself or himself into presence and beyond allegory, beyond *re*presentation.

Still, despite the entry into experience by myth, as the poet describes it the mythic god himself struggles against the poet to maintain his absence, to remain transcendental to the words, to keep them from filling themselves with divine presence. So once again, as with Sidney's Sonnet 35, Jonson's poem is concerned with its subject and theme by virtue of its being concerned with semiotics, with what its words—or what words in general as signs—can mean and can enclose, as well as with what escapes words to remain unreachably outside discourse, to remain the gods and transcendent.

In his well-known song, "Drink to me only with thine eyes," Jonson explicitly raises the question of the divinity of the object of desire, prefers her fleshly humanity, and then—if only ironically—suggests the divine consequences of her earthy powers. Early in the poem, the rhyming words, "wine," "divine," and "thine" carry the contrast and permit the inversion.

> Or leave a kiss but in the cup,
> And I'll not look for wine.
> The thirst that from the soul doth rise
> Doth ask a drink divine;
> But might I of Jove's nectar sup,
> I would not change for thine.

The lady's kiss is preferred as a substitute for the sacrament of wine, the "drink divine," as the speaker seems—in an anti-Petrarchan vein—to insist upon her as an antithesis to divinity. It is this un-divine nature which is for him precisely the source of her power. But, in the second half of the song, the speaker attributes the transubstantiating power to the lady's effect on the flowers which, if we are to believe him (he says, "I swear"), can be nothing less than miraculously divine, even though that effect is restricted to the world of sense (how the flowers smell).

> I sent thee late a rosy wreath,
> Not so much honoring thee,
> As giving it a hope that there
> It could not withered be.
> But thou thereon didst only breathe,
> And sent'st it back to me,
> Since when it grows and smells, I swear,
> Not of itself, but thee.

The poem is utterly good-humored about its insistence upon the ungodly sensual appeal of the lady: it halfheartedly seeks to make her his goddess by virtue of that appeal, and, having found the words which—through a rhyming exchange—could effect her transformation, it relaxes its pressure in order to keep itself within the realm of the sublimity of human limitations. In the contrast and exchange between the wine and the kiss, I am reminded of Sidney's "I never drank of Aganippe well" (Sonnet 74), in which the kiss functions as the earthly substitute for the muse—literal inspiration (mouth to mouth) for empty figurative inspiration. The bodily world of sense is accepted through the exalted metaphors of myth, though those metaphors now appear in their literal nakedness, as deconstructed equivalents of transcendental signifieds brought inside human language for the purpose of functioning in a thoroughly human experience. The poet's lofty language, for all its reductions, does not fail, because his application of it, accompanied by a wink, is restricted to a world from which transcendence has been excluded. The creatures and the actions he has constructed are verbal only, since he implicitly acknowledges the incapacity of his words to do more, though we may—for the occasion—rest in the satisfactions and momentary persuasions of the fusions and transformations his language seems to have worked upon us.

I return to Ralegh's "Nature, that washed her hands in milk" for a final observation about the attempt of a poem to construct an artful object of idolatry within its verbal bounds, and its confessed failure to do so. But, I must insist, if it is thematically about failure, it is a failure that only supports the poem's confidence in its own artifice, which is to say, in its own illusionary success.

> Nature, that washed her hands in milk,
>   And had forgot to dry them,
> Instead of earth took snow and silk,
>   At love's request to try them,
> If she a mistress could compose
> To please love's fancy out of those.
>
> Her eyes he would should be of light,
>   A violet breath, and lips of jelly;
> Her hair not black, nor overbright,
>   And of the softest down her belly;
> As for her inside he 'ld have it
> Only of wantonness and wit.
>
> At love's entreaty such a one
>   Nature made, but with her beauty
> She hath framed a heart of stone;
>   So as love, by ill destiny,
> Must die for her whom nature gave him,
> Because her darling would not save him.
>
> But time (which nature doth despise
>   And rudely gives her love the lie,
> Makes hope a fool, and sorrow wise)
>   His hands do neither wash nor dry;
> But being made of steel and rust,
> Turns snow and silk and milk to dust.

Presentation and Representation in the Renaissance Lyric

The light, the belly, lips, and breath,
　　He dims, discolors, and destroys;
With those he feeds but fills not death,
　　Which sometimes were the food of joys.
Yea, time doth dull each lively wit,
And dries all wantonness with it.

Oh, cruel time! which takes in trust
　　Our youth, our joys, and all we have,
And pays us but with age and dust;
　　Who in the dark and silent grave
When we have wandered all our ways
Shuts up the story of our days.

This poem may serve as an allegory of what I have tried to describe in this essay—and, pace Sidney's sonneteer, critics may resort to allegory and its transparencies even if poets should not. Speaking about this poem, I commented earlier on the rejection of earth for the moist-smooth-whiteness of milk and snow and silk as materials to be used in nature's attempt—in response to "love's request"—to "compose" an ideal mistress for the pleasure of "love's fancy." But this mistress, which nature—with whatever self-contradiction—has composed artificially, is a perfect Petrarchan creation since with her beauty nature has given her an unnatural "heart of stone" (unnatural though conventional—that is, thoroughly in accord with Petrarchan convention). The consequences for love and his ideal mistress are controlled within a "real" world which runs in accordance with enmity and its spite. Nature's cold creature kills love, for whom she was created, and time—nature's enemy—in turn destroys nature's prized creation: "His hands do neither wash nor dry; / But being made of steel and rust, / Turns snow and silk and milk to dust." Even worse, time's destructive action is not even a special damnation, specially enjoyed, contrived for a most precious creation slated for extinction. It is no uniquely prized victory. Instead, the action is, like time itself, automatic in its application: he feeds her specially created parts to death indiscriminately, like any of nature's less endowed creatures, so that death is fed but hardly filled by her.

The light, the belly, lips, and breath,
He dims, discolors, and destroys;
With those he feeds but fills not death,
Which sometimes were the food of joys.
Yea, time doth dull each lively wit,
And dries all wantonness with it.

The poem preciously and delicately composes nature's creature, an absolute poetic creation supposedly responsive to love's poetically conventional desires. That her "heart of stone" is unresponsive to love's actual needs is in accord with the convention that dictates her creation and is a result of nature's forgoing of earth for more delicate, if cool, materials. As a creature of artifice, there is no earth in her, and so no earthiness in her response to love. But the creature, this superb work of art, is reduced—with all of earth—to dust (and I recall my observation about Ralegh's deadly use of the alliterated "d," each instance of which I have italicized in the above quotation). The extravagant metaphor invented by nature to constitute the creature, with all its substitutions of milk and snow and silk for earth, collapses; it dissipates, with the rest of us, into a negative residue. With the metaphoric attempt thus shown to be only a fragile illusion, no more than an aesthetic construct, time takes the stage to give us the sense of an ending that converts the deconstruction it has traced into a narrative that finds formal closure. The metaphor may have failed to sustain itself, since the creature is no more than earth after all, but the illusion it permitted before its deflation is one of the most glorious of the stories that, at the end, time closes off. Which is why the poet has chronicled it.

By the final stanza the characters have been eliminated, one by one: love, the mistress, and—by implication—nature itself. Only time is left at the end to tell the story by ending all stories, supplying the closure for all our stories:

Oh, cruel time! which takes in trust
Our youth, our joys, and all we have,
And pays us but with age and dust;
Who in the dark and silent grave
When we have wandered all our ways
Shuts up the story of our days.

"Shuts up the story of our days": an echo of "Time drives the flock from field to fold" in "The Nymph's Reply," it sees the flock of all of us shut up by time in the "fold," the universal coffin.[4] In effect, then, time brings even itself to a close in that, though still standing onstage, beyond the last line even it must cease to exist. For the closure, the shutting up the story of our days, is absolute. Ultimately—which is to say beyond the last line—it is only the final negating character, death,

---

4. I remind the reader also of Ralegh's similar use of "fold" in the concluding line of "Like truthless dreams": "Whom care forewarns, ere age and winter cold, / To haste me hence to find my fortune's fold."

time's agent, that remains. Only death remains—together, of course, with the words of the poem ("the story") which seems to have eliminated everyone but itself, now emptied of all it has created narratively and metaphorically, though insistent upon its own verbal presence as testament of what is lost.

I have tried here to center our concern upon English Renaissance poets wrestling with the problem of verbal representation. They see that it is the nature of signifieds—gods and beloveds among less glorious ones—to continue to be transcendental, as it is the struggle of poets to use their specially wrought net of words to capture them and to keep them trapped within discourse. All things that come before the poet's present belated discourse—whether in language or outside it—stand like elusive gods outside it and its attempt to name them. In Sidney's Stella, Jonson's Love, and Ralegh's creature, we have seen various methods by which the poet both closes and reopens the gap between transcendence and participation, between standoff and breakthrough— in other words, between failed representation and satisfying presentation.

Renaissance poets seemed capable of giving themselves a secular mission that was to demystify language as language operates outside the theological realm. When they were most self-conscious, which was not infrequently, they were aware of the deceptive tendency of all language to deify its would-be objects. Their own obligation was to expose this deception and confess the abandonment of language by the gods. But at the same time they had, themselves, to undertake to create a language that could truly tame the gods and bring them inside. So the poet had to acknowledge what language normally cannot do, what words may not say. He had to manipulate them, in hopes of turning them into *his* words, magic words, so that, in spite of their usual incapacities, he could enrich them, endow them with the power to speak after all, the power that attested to a present signified, a captured god within.

But the transcendent god is never caught, after all, however well the verbal net seems to be forged. The poet has sought to open up that net in order to seize and return with its would-be signifieds; to open it up and then, as with "the story of our days," to shut it down. He tries to display them and succeeds in giving us an awareness of the semiotic exhilaration that would accompany such an entrapment. He may even give us a momentary sense that he has them and that we have caught a glimpse of them. But a higher linguistic reality is there, too, one that the poet uses to remind us of his sleight of hand, as he shuts up his own story, packs up his verbal magic, and walks off, leaving our gods intact and far away, as we return to our babbling. Fortunately, however, we may still be rescued from time to time; for the poems remain, a permanent presence, ready to perform.

A Humanity in the Humanities:
Literature among the Discourses

" 'What is truth?' said jesting Pilate, and would not stay for an answer." The story of education in the humanities is the story of those who stayed for an answer; the story of those who, in their search for truth, honored it as did Sir Francis Bacon, who opened his essay, "Of Truth," with the sentence I have just quoted. In that essay, however, Bacon reveals that his devotion is to a truth conceived too simply and singly and absolutely. It is because he had unquestioning confidence in the firm singleness of that truth and its accessibility to us that he rejected a more skeptical outlook. Thus his irritation with Pontius Pilate's contemptuous suggestion that truth is indefinable, unknowable. Next to such an austere and fixed sense of truth as Bacon's, even the poet's imaginative flights are found not altogether trustworthy by him in that essay. This attitude should perhaps not surprise us when we think of Bacon's devotion to empiricism, the doctrine that truth can be derived wholly from generalizations drawn from the raw data of our sensory experience. From such a perspective the poet as imaginative fiction-maker can be seen as a downright liar; and this is about what Bacon suggests. And those defending the humanities in the spirit of Bacon would be happy to subject poems to the same constraints we impose on the other humanistic discourses, seek-

---

This is an expanded version of my Phi Beta Kappa lecture at the University of California, Irvine, in June 1981.

ing to deny them any special license and to reject the claim that those commenting on poems should proceed—in relating discourse to truth—any differently from commentators on other kinds of texts.

Most defenders of poetry and literary criticism in the history of humanistic study would disagree, assuming special freedoms for poetry and its critics. But at the present moment in the development of critical theory, there is a broad reaction against our conventional acceptance, previously unquestioned by literary people if not by Baconians, of a criticism that is exclusively literary. That acceptance presupposed that there is a collection of privileged texts called *literature* and that we must continue to develop a special group of methods to account for them. Recent "critical theory" might well put this assumption in question as an outmoded idolatry, seeing both "literature" and an exclusively literary criticism as the temporary recourses of social institutions that could make use of such elitist inventions to further their interests. And those of us who over these centuries have succumbed to the authorized seductions of literature as a fine art must now receive the (antiliterary) critical theory that would disabuse us of these mystifications. It is in the teeth of such sobering reductions of the literary that I would defend both literature as a cultural entity that still repays separatist considerations and the criticism of literature as an enterprise that must continue to thrive if we are to realize all that words can do, so that our verbal powers can continue to flourish.

Nevertheless, my argument that would claim a special place for literature, even at this late date and despite strong arguments for a monolithic conception of discourse, requires the humanities to be conceived as a common body of disciplines (the "human sciences") as well as a differentiated sequence of them. It is hardly original for the humanist to observe, if only half-jocularly, that his subject appears to have no singular; that, while he treats the humanities, he cannot speak—as an academic—of a "humanity." Indeed, the singular "humanity" refers not at all to any academic discipline but to the suffering collective (the humanity) that is its subject; and the agent who serves humanity, the "humanitarian," is hardly to be confused with the "humanist," the scholar who serves the humanities, a group of academically defined disciplines. The humanistic scholar is made uncomfortable by this confusion of a moral category with an academic category—and perhaps guilty about his own disinterestedness which his scholarly obligations presumably call for. But, as I said, it often seems significant to him that the humanities, as his subject, seem to be exclusively a plural subject. He then can proceed to suggest, as a corollary, that this linguistic convention (a humanities without humanity) reflects the multiplicity rather than the unity of this assemblage of disciplines—history, philosophy, the several national languages and literatures—and leads to a distrust of the interdisciplinary enterprise as a unifying enterprise. For it leads to a suspicion of any method or any paradigmatic analysis that cuts through all humanistic disciplines (the humanities) by reducing them all to a single principle. If they were one, an implicitly logocentric logic suggests, then we would have a singular term for them. Yet might one not claim just the reverse: that the very fact that there is no singular within the humanities argues for the indivisibility of its plural domain?

I should like to examine the extent to which the humanities are or are not an indissoluble entity, the extent to which we may still think of them either as a single discipline or as a collection of autonomous disciplines—and, if the latter, what the relationship is among those disciplines. Should our study of them be characterized by a single method or by a variety of methods, a variety no less various than what is called for by the diverse subjects gathered together, whether arbitrarily or deservedly gathered together? I will focus here on literature as it relates to the other humanistic disciplines and will limit my discussion of the humanities by treating them exclusively as discourse (or discourses). As documents that are objects of our study—as texts—discourse is, of course, what they are, so that, as critics and theorists of the Continent have been reminding us in recent years, the instrument to examine these disciplines is semiotic, the study of sign-functioning in these varied documents. I ask you to see discourse as the shared symbols that shape their society, in effect to see discourse *as* the society itself. Through discourse society constitutes its visions, its fears, its very definition of itself. Its words create its name for itself, as it were, so that a society in this sense becomes its discourse.

But to treat the various humanistic disciplines exclusively as discourse seems already to have decided on their sameness since they would appear not to be differentiated in the way they function within systems of verbal signs. Or may it be that discourse is not monolithic in its workings? If we are to find any distinctions among the humanistic disciplines, we would have to find radical differences in the ways in which they are encoded by the writer, or are decoded by us; in the way—that is—in which their signifiers and signifieds are to be related to one another. Our usual sense of what discourse is and how it functions would seem to militate against our finding any such differences. It is this semiotic reduction that has produced the monolithic principle of analysis we associate with recent structuralist practice as it has been derived from Continental theory.

Orthodox structuralism treats all linguistic texts as elements in a single anonymous code of writing (*écriture*). It is as if the mind possesses one universally generative grammar. A single set of systematic inter-relationships becomes the key to unlock the universal syntactical powers with which man, as a speaking subject, generates and controls all that his mind, by way of language, touches and organizes. As speaking subject, he is only the "I" of the sentence, generating and controlling its variety of predicates in whatever discipline (in whichever of the "sciences of man") we choose to see that sentence, as a linguistic code, being reflected. What the academy has arbitrarily broken up into its different objects of study has been projected out of this single syntactical process. Thus the several so-called disciplines make up one unified field, as we can translate them into one another—move from one to the other—with each revealing the same disposition of signifying forces. These disciplines, whatever their ostensible subjects, are related to one another by the single principle of homology, all of them being multiple reflections of a monolithic structural principle. All forms of writing, in whatever area, can be similarly viewed as speech acts (*paroles*) that are manifestations of the one, all-controlling language system (*langue*) which contains all *paroles*—all sentences in all disci-plines—potentially within itself. What is being signified in the individ-ual text is a subsidiary matter; that is, the shape of the discourse is controlled by the syntactical relationship among the signifiers them-selves, and it is this fact that guarantees the homology among the several different fields being pursued within a language system. Those of us who are less analytically keen may be misled by the variety among the subject matters (signifieds) of apparently different disciplines and, con-sequently, may fail to perceive the similarities in the signifying struc-tures. Thinking that these discourses are being controlled by their subjects or signifieds, we will tend to overemphasize what they are saying and mythologize their claims to speaking truth because we have not reduced the variant signifieds to the controlling (and monolithic) structure of signifiers.

Writing (*écriture*) becomes, for structuralists and poststructuralists alike, a single blanket term. All distinctions among discourses are collapsed into writing as these theorists seek the single syntactical principle that, homologously from discourse to discourse, accounts for the disposition of elements within each. All instances of discourse, of whatever sort and in whatever field, are treated equally as subject to structuralist analysis or (later) to poststructuralist deconstruction. If the literary man's penchant for mystification leads him to honor some of the texts that concern him with the name of poems and to treat them as sacred objects with self-enclosed systems, his theoretical antagonist would demystify such an act of fetishizing by deconstructing the aesthetic that authorizes it. Even if one would seek to distinguish among the affective varieties of speech acts (as other recent theorists suggest), the poetic usually finds itself leveled into the manipulative capacities of language at large.

If all of language, conceived as a system of signs, is seen as one universal structure, then any writing sample—regardless of apparent subject or intention or method—must be similarly treated for interpretive purposes as part of that single code, with predictable relationships both among its signs and between its signs and the meanings to which they pretend. Further, the operation of the code may be seen to be controlled by hidden subtextual pressures from the surrounding social-political context. Among the texts within that code, no writing sample has privilege over any other, so that none can claim to be a sovereign entity cut off from the rest, even provisionally, as a system unto itself. Even more extremely, the code that determines the workings of written signs may be applied to other symbolic human relations as well (and all relations are seen as symbolic, which is to say "semiotic"), so that all sorts of social situations—in life as in word, in life *as* word—may be treated as texts. Everything is a text, even as—really—nothing is a text, since it would be more accurate to say that everything is an *inter*text. In the midst of such a ubiquity of texts within a single, seamless fabric of textuality, we should indeed be hard put to mark off an area that we could call "literature" or, for that matter, even to claim any isolable verbal artifacts as special objects—literary objects—for study.

So such a blanket notion of speech act and writing (*parole* and *écriture*) does away with any distinctions among the modes of discourse, indeed in principle even the distinction between the piece of literary criticism and the poem that presumably is its object and the reason for its existence: it would deny that criticism serves, as a secondary and derivative act, the primary act of poem-making. Instead, it would see them both, with all their sister disciplines, sharing—as coordinates and equals—the common realm of writing (*écriture* in the broad, all-inclusive sense). For, from this structuralist perspective, there can be no primacy in discourse (or, perhaps, there can be *only* primacy in discourse), and no privilege among its several forms. Consequently, poems are to be treated as speech acts or as written texts essentially like any other.

The structuralist unification of what has been termed the human sciences, with the consequences it holds for considerations of literature, runs counter to the assumption of earlier literary criticism of our century that literature should be treated as a unique mode of discourse, different in kind from others, and that the revelation of its peculiar literariness remains the special task of the critic. Indeed it is very likely this separatist definition of literature, normally associated with Russian formalism and with the American New Criticism of several decades ago, that helped to stimulate American versions of structuralism and poststructuralism as reactions against formalism and the New Criticism and also as their successors in becoming our most fashionable critical doctrines.

As early as the 1920s, Russian formalists developing out of nineteenth-century theory, sought to define literariness or poeticity as the defamiliarizing of words, the making-strange of our normal language. In other words, poems are to begin where other kinds of discourse leave off, creating their own systems by violating the norms of the language (*langue*), those norms adhered to by nonpoetic discourse. This notion formed the basis of literary theories that have been grouped together by their recent enemies as "deviationist," in that each poem is to build itself through its deviations from what we usually expect in the operations of language. Prague School formalism and American New Criticism in their different ways developed deviationist theory into a broad poetic, concentrating on the habit of poetry to "foreground" its medium, manipulating language into violating its own nature by seeming to become a thing in itself, riveting our attention upon its playful aesthetic presence instead of allowing us to pass through it (as we are accustomed to pass through other discourse) to the more important things it is supposed to point us toward. This separation of the poetic from all other discourse was also a privileging of it, an apparent idolatry of specially endowed, elite verbal artifacts. This privilege was extended to its social and visionary function as well. Freed of the incapacities of normal language, poetic language was uniquely endowed with the power to reveal a culture's social and psychological consciousness. Hence the study of poetry, thanks to its privileged position, could become a unique anthropological instrument.

Although such elite literary works may begin as ordinary words and apparently ordinary sentences on the page, properly attuned critics could argue that they can give rise to an "illusion" of presence—of here-and-now-ness—together with the self-reference that follows from an aesthetic consciousness of that illusionary presence: the awareness the work shares with us that this is indeed only artful "imitation" of reality rather than "reality" itself. Of course, though we have seen these critics concentrating on language, they could claim other than purely linguistic ways to achieve the effect of a physical presence in literature.

We become more aware of these ways as we move from lyric poetry to the other major literary genres. As the writer in verse manipulates his medium, creating the illusion that has converted words into things, the novelist seeks the illusion that converts his fictions into apparent histories or biographies (or, if in the first person, into apparent autobiographies or journals). These would-be historical genres shadow the created fiction, at once defining its limits and freeing it from them. Though we retain our awareness of the created illusion, the act of make-believe, the fiction, we also entertain it as an illusion of a real happening, with which we do not confuse it. This is the lingering truth behind the mimetic doctrine in literary criticism. We must be conscious of what the work is not: the fiction must not be permitted to dissolve into that real happening; we must remember that it is merely mimetic, an illusion that knows itself as such, that has its own terminal presence—all this thanks to the author's manipulations which keep us formally rooted in it.

Similarly, the dramatist—simply by the make-believe that is his primary given—creates the illusion that has converted the action of his characters within the space of the stage, into real-life happenings in real places. Yet those actions retain their own peculiar status-in-being or "reality": when we view King Lear, we should see him as more than a character (and mere actor) and less than a person. He lives and loves and hates and dies like all men; but he does so in an immutable pattern with which we cannot interfere by leaping onstage. He is even doing so now, as I speak, if we but choose to review the course of his career in Shakespeare's play that bears his name. He is always there, undergoing the same tortured course because of the inevitability of the aesthetic form that encompasses him. He thus represents the universalized particular that is himself. Such is the power of formal closure against which recent theory inveighs. For the secular world, Lear and other fictions like him (but which could ever be like him?) have the typological force which, for a period imbued with the sacred, the biblical allegories had: the single story of a mortal individual, adrift in normal human history, yet eternalized into a fixed pattern that serves us as an absolute model. As a system of linguistic signs, the play *King Lear* has a presence always capable of being brought before us as yet another *now*, happening yet again, creating for itself a new present.

We see, then, that more than the words themselves can serve as the literary medium, which is to be worked into the illusion of a presence analogous to what can be more immediately achieved in the plastic arts. In the language arts anything will serve as a medium that the author can distort from its usual nonaesthetic way of functioning into the peculiar

Reconsideration of Special Texts for Special Reasons

function that the purposiveness of his work requires. The essence of the medium for him is its capacity to sponsor deviations, under his guidance; and, as he makes these deviations internally purposive within his special construct, he demonstrates his power to convert yet another commonplace aspect of language or its usual references into his aesthetic medium. Whether it is language itself, or the space (real space and stage space) in the drama, or the imagined space in which events and character interact in life and narrative, the literary artist is seen as manipulating these into that strangely duplicitous reality which literary illusions enjoy, allowing us to see them both as mimetic of the world's terms and as unremovably here on their own terms.

All the varied levels of literature can thus be seen as operating to create a dual reality, just as poetic language does, so that we can use the term *poetry* to characterize them all, *mutatis mutandis*. In this operation language outdoes the more single-minded function of the media of the plastic arts. For the deviationist, the poet must undo the way language normally operates in order to make it operate his way, as an aesthetic medium, even though he cannot always count on an audience that is prepared to undo their own nonpoetic (or prepoetic) reading habits to cultivate the poem's verbal totality. Nevertheless, it can be argued that the successful poet can make the most of these handicaps, converting the usual deficiencies of language as a medium into unique advantages. Language in the poet's hands becomes a wonderfully ambiguous medium: the word may be, as recent theory can claim, an empty signifier, part of a prearranged, conventional code the poet inherits, but the deviationist urges that it can be remade by the poet who forces us to discover and concentrate upon a fullness which he forces within it as a sensory-intelligible complex. On another level, beyond the verbal, the poet's fiction reminds us of the world it imitates, *and* it creates a free-standing make-believe world of its own. Both verbal functions and both worlds must be sustained by the poem, and by us reading it, at the same time. But these very ambiguities open special opportunities for the literary work of art, allowing it to embrace a now-you-see-it, now-you-don't duplicity which gives it a richness and complexity that less ambiguous nonverbal arts would find hard to match and nonpoetic discourse would disdain.

Nevertheless, these last years, as I have observed, there have been assaults from several directions on the theoretical deviationism which for some time had been a basic assumption underlying the dominant aesthetic. Poststructuralists mean to deprivilege poems by treating them as just more textuality, avoiding the closing off of texts as elite systems, although they themselves often do just that, paradoxically, by applying to the other varieties of discourse the techniques of analysis we used to reserve for fictions. Finding all discourse to rest on narratological and tropological shapings that divert it from its intended reference, every text is seen similarly to blur toward a literary intent—although critics today prefer the term *rhetorical* to *literary* as less privileging. A number of social theorists have also broadened what used to be attributed to literature to include other discourse as similarly endowed—or rather similarly deluded. What is being denied in either case is the special workings of a kind of language (yes, *kind*) that not long ago we called literary without the uncomfortable proddings of our present insecurity. It is, as I began by saying, this insecurity that has prompted my remarks on this occasion.

In light of structuralist and poststructuralist arguments, there would seem to be good reason to be persuaded of the deceptive nature of sign functioning and the unified character of our apparently varied discourses at given moments in our culture. But I propose that we still worry about whether we wish to include literary discourse within this monolithic construct. Or, on the other hand, do we rather wish to see each literary text as achieving a self-privileging exemption from that construct by manipulating all generic linguistic elements until they are forced to subvert their own functions and do precisely what a structuralist view of language would preclude them from doing: from functioning as a signifier that creates and fills itself with its own signified as it goes and, thus, from setting itself apart from discourse as its own unique, self-made system? Without some such notion, are we capable of accounting for all that our greatest works perform for us? Do we not, further, have to recognize the peculiarly fictional, and even self-consciously fictional—which is to say self-referential—character of our most highly valued literature, even if we wish to grant also to nonliterature a fictionality and reflexivity that less sophisticated readings of would-be "referential" discourse did not used to grant? And are not literary fictions, with their peculiar self-reference, sufficient to separate the work which they characterize from the rest of discourse? If these remarks of mine stubbornly retain an acceptance of the notion of "canon" as a culture's collection of its elite literary objects, they do so with a full awareness of the institutional pressures that can make the notion—and the favorite literary works on which it rests—suspect. Still, locked as I am within that culture and its institutions, I must continue to be responsive to the power I feel in these literary works, a power (my faith assures me) beyond the power of the institutions that would keep them, as our fetishes, before us.

Why? And whence this power? In spite of the deconstructive intent of recent theorists that would hardly exclude the literary from the texts that fall prey to their operation, I believe we can speak the more persuasively on behalf of this power as a result of what these theorists have been urging. We are in a moment when discourses that claim to tell the truth—historical, philosophical, whatever—are being deconstructed into fictions that function rhetorically in the service of various subtextual purposes, whether social-political or psychoanalytical. But at just such a time we may find a special value in those self-conscious fictional constructs which, as poetry, cherish an alien and yet familiar "reality" which makes no claim to truth, to being really real. The poet, Sir Philip Sidney said, "nothing affirms, and therefore never lieth," for "to lie is to affirm that to be true which is false," a fault which few writings outside poetry can consistently avoid. Since, then, of all kinds of discourse only poetry cannot lie, it should be excepted from the deconstruction that reduces other discourse to fictions which do deceive because they function in a way at variance with their ostensible truth claims. So, in a competition with nonpoetry, the defenders of poetry as a discursive kind, a privileged discursive kind, find for these specially organized words an alternative function, an alternative relation to "reality," an alternative to telling the truth about "reality," which is what our common sense tells us we use language *for* and what our deconstructionist urge has been denying. Poetry may make us less impatient with its self-conscious fictionality, its once-upon-a-time character, when we compare it with the unavowed deceptions of its more sober fellow-discourses, now all seen as forms of rhetorical disguise.

What, then, is truth or reality for the poet, who reaches for something beyond his words even though, in his modesty or in his willful freedom, he seeks to avoid being a teller of lies by evading an act of literal affirmation? The poet must, in the words of Nathaniel Hawthorne, "dream strange things, and make them look like truth," though of course without claiming them to be truth. His is an as-if truth, with the frame around his fiction assuring us that it is not seeking to be truth itself. The philosopher and the historian, on the other hand, are normally assumed to be directing their discourse toward truth, however the deconstructor may transform that function in order to reshape the discourse into rhetoric. What more shall we say about the dream-truth to which the poem presumably has access, in contrast to the common daytime truth that escapes the efforts of nonpoetic discourse to catch it?

In an exemplary poem, Sonnet 113, Shakespeare (a contemporary of Bacon, but not—I assure you—to be confused with Bacon) seeks to provide an explicit answer to this question. In the poem two apparent truths of perception struggle with one another: the truth of the everyday world and the truth sponsored by the poet's mind, or—put otherwise—the truth provided by apparent fact and the truth provided by a poet-lover's faith.

> Since I left you, mine eye is in my mind;
> And that which governs me to go about
> Doth part his function and is partly blind,
> Seems seeing, but effectually is out;
> For it no form delivers to the heart
> Of bird, of flow'r, or shape which it doth latch;
> Of his quick objects hath the mind no part,
> Nor his own vision holds what it doth catch;
> For if it see the rud'st or gentlest sight,
> The most sweet favour or deformed'st creature,
> The mountain or the sea, the day or night,
> The crow or dove, it shapes them to your feature.
>   Incapable of more, replete with you,
>   My most true mind thus mak'th mine eye untrue.

The final line ("My most true mind thus mak'th mine eye untrue") couples the two kinds of truth, and they are mutually incompatible. The speaker in the sonnet has yielded up the usual truth of the eye—or rather his eye sees a truth other than what is presumably there to be seen—seen neutrally, that is, as if it were independent of our idiosyncratic vision. The objects of our daily experience are thus being seen by the speaker not as what they are, but as what the mind, filled with love and with the sole object of that love, must have them be. So the eye, though it "seems seeing," "effectually is out," having abandoned its place and retreated to the mind. But it has abandoned its role along with its place. Its truths are no longer those of sight, but those of thought. Yet the eye still "*seems* seeing," still appearing to capture birds and flowers and the rest of common experience. But it now sees those things only by means of—under the aegis of—the vision and love of his beloved.

All objects of sight, however imperfect, are adapted to the perfection of the beloved. In effect, all has been collapsed into love's vision of goodness, a vision suddenly become the poet's sole reality. Hence the variety of the world, and its many differing values as we move through the stages from the worst to the best it has to offer, all are reduced to that single perfection.

For if it [the eye] see the rud'st or gentlest sight,
The most sweet favour or deformed'st creature,
The mountain or the sea, the day or night,
The crow or dove, it shapes them to your feature.

Polarity yields to an identity in the beloved. The world is conceived totally as composed of binary opposites; yet all these oppositions, its good and evil, are merged into one sublimity as all the world's objects are equally shaped to the one set of features. Everything is seen through the one lens that reads the world as if beauty were the only reality. Oppositions like the crow and the dove melt into the oneness of a vision regulated only by love's fidelity. The Manichaean reality, which splits the good and evil of the mixed world we all know, dissolves into the one flawless reality that the speaker's mind permits the speaker's eye to see.

At the same time, the speaker makes it clear that the opposed dualisms still exist in the empirical world, however he may read them. Filled only with the beloved's goodness so that he can see nothing else, the speaker yet acknowledges the untruth of the vision fostered by being "true" to the beloved:

Incapable of more, replete with you,
My most true mind thus mak'th mine eye untrue.

Language itself violates its obligation to have a unity of meaning: in this single line the criteria for what is "true" are shrewdly double, as the poem's words—at odds with themselves—partake of the realm of paradox indulged by the lover's faith. The truth of the eye has been traded, not for error (though it *is* error), but for another truth, the truth of faith. It is not that one is true and the other false absolutely, but that each is true (and the other false) under specified conditions. And the poet who writes the poem recognizes that, as lover, his vision is limited. He sees doubly, both the truth seen by himself as lover and the worldly truth he thereby distorts. Thus the ultimate paradox: since both are truth, neither can be "truth," which is single.

Thus the two truths are in conflict with one another, the warm truth dictated by love's faith against the cold truth seen by the ruthless eye of empiricism. The older notion of truth that we used to call "troth" (or faith) resists the newer truths unmodified by faith in a historical conflict between world views and concepts of value. The choice seems to be between being true to a person and a belief and being true to a dead world, a world of inhuman objects. And the two truths seem incompatible with one another, even though history has seen the word *truth*—in accordance with the scientific spirit of Bacon's "advancement of learning"—pretty well appropriated by literal reality at the expense of faith.

Still, even now, for Shakespeare, the faithful, trothful vision that gilds our experiential world, turning brass into gold, resists yielding to what a grimmer realism (the mundane realism of the Baconian scientist) may insist upon as the only truth. If this gilded version of reality is taken as actual—and not just as illusionary—then, as Shakespeare is to suggest, so long as the self-mystification holds, the lover is a successful alchemist in that he has literally transmuted impure materials into pure gold, elixir of the life of the spirit. His golden vision—a world seen through the idolatrous eyes of love—is thus treated as an alchemical transformation of the world, which has truly, and not just metaphorically, turned all dross into gold. But even if the poet is persuaded of the alchemy, is he not aware, too—in his more skeptical moments—that it is also a deceptive flattery of the world that raises it to values higher than it deserves?

The next sonnet in the sequence, number 114, completes the argument by confronting just this need to decide whether the golden vision is alchemy—and thus a new and miraculous truth—or is mere flattery, and thus a deceptive untruth.

> Or whether doth my mind, being crown'd with you,
> Drink up the monarch's plague, this flattery?
> Or whether shall I say mine eye saith true,
> And that your love taught it this alchemy,
> To make of monsters and things indigest
> Such cherubins as your sweet self resemble,
> Creating every bad a perfect best
> As fast as objects to his beams assemble?
> O, 'tis the first! 'Tis flatt'ry in my seeing,
> And my great mind most kingly drinks it up.
> Mine eye well knows what with his gust is greeing,
> And to his palate doth prepare the cup.
>   If it be poison'd, 'tis the lesser sin
>   That mine eye loves it and doth first begin.

Alchemy or flattery, visionary truth or dangerous delusion? To turn "monsters" into "cherubins," thus creating "every bad [as] a perfect best," would indeed be an act of alchemy, one produced under the influence of a transformed vision of truth such as faith alone allows. Still, the poet concedes that his special vision may be no more than flattery of the world, and hence an inaccurate exaggeration, at least when it is viewed from the world outside faith. So his eye is forced to be the flatterer, feeding flattery's poison to the love-smitten mind in response to its demands. But, the poem ironically concludes, the eye—though a conscious flatterer—is so enamored of the beauteous golden vision it is obediently creating for the mind that it begins to worship that vision itself, taking it as if it were the alchemical reality indeed. In effect, the eye becomes self-deceived before it begins to deceive the mind about the heightened nature of reality. It believes its own vision which it began by creating to sooth the visionary needs of the lovesick mind. Its flattery becomes its truth, all that it is capable of seeing as its reality, at whatever expense to the eye's old naked truth.

Shakespeare, at once pious and skeptical about the poet's and the lover's vision (or rather the vision of the poet *as* lover), acknowledges it as false *if* viewed from the world's cold fish-eye of objectivity, though as mystified vision it is the only truth he has, a truth that he rushes to embrace. The beloved, as the poet's god, cannot countenance anything in the world that falls short of perfection. Through the beloved, love transforms the poet's mind (and the mind's eye) into a sun god which alchemizes all it touches, like the sun turning everything it shines upon into gold (or is it only the appearance of gold?). Thus, we are told, the mind creates "every bad a perfect best / As fast as objects to his beams assemble." This is what Shakespeare in another sonnet (Sonnet 33) has called the "heavenly alchemy" of the sun, the god that transforms our imperfect world, a god empowered by the faith engendered by the perfection of the beloved, his sun god. This vision is so persuasive that it persuades the eyes themselves, despite their normally world-bound character as the prime agent of naked empirical reality. Indeed, for human consciousness the reality we experience always arrives already clothed by us, since the eyes themselves, instead of being the agents of a neutral empiricism, fall prey to the illusion permitted by the lens of the mind, thus reminding us that so-called empiricism is itself a fiction, requiring its own faith, one we can never altogether give up, however persuasive our visionary power.

In these two sonnets (which I am here considering as a single dialectical poem) the eyes have traded their passive, receptive role for an active, transforming role as agents of the visionary mind, though only while the poem reminds us of the illusionary nature of that role. And the verbal play within the poem must capture both the idolatry and the stripping away of this vision, both its mystified moments. In the collisions within its language which permits it both to define oppositions and to collapse them, it is the poem itself which represents as well as enunciates its delicate and ambiguous relation to truth and fiction. In this way it becomes an allegory of its method, but only as it subverts its own conclusions. The poem, then, defines itself as such by acknowledging its fiction as its only truth, unlike other—presumably nonpoetic—discourse, which must have its claim to truth stripped away and revealed as its fiction. Those fictions now seen outside the realm of what we conventionally think of as fiction—presumably nonfictional discourse, discourse that means to tell the truth—are now seen as in conflict with their apparent discursive intention, which insists on its nonfictionality and would argue against any denial of their primary referential objective. It is by our deconstructive conversion of them to the realm of fiction that we free ourselves to operate upon them as if they were what we used to think of exclusively as "literary" discourse. The recent deniers of poetry's specialness do not insist, in the spirit of Bacon, that poetry be as responsible to truth as nonpoetic discourse is, but the reverse: that there is nothing special about poetry's right to pursue its fictionality since all texts are doomed equally to that fate, and none speak truth.

We would be deliberately blind to the best of recent interpretive work if we failed to acknowledge how much poststructuralist rhetorical criticism has done with apparently nonliterary texts—as a result, of course, of what it had denied them: any pretension to truth. Tropological and narratological criticism has yielded impressive results on texts that, in an earlier time, we would not have thought receptive to such analysis. Indeed, many of the most extreme of our newer critics, who are most antiliterary or anti-aesthetic in their theoretical commitments, leave remarkable interpretations of undifferentiated writing that may remind us of the special analytic efforts made on behalf of poetry not long ago. The attention paid to subversive textual elements that undermine any monolithic argumentative line may thus carnivalize a text's dominant authority; and while it may have political consequences for our study of a society, behind the rhetorical analysis there is a literary sensibility that keeps the criticism literary in that it makes an implicit claim for its object as revealing literary characteristics after all. Clearly, even to such contemporary avant-garde movements, it is still literature, self-consciously devoted to such play among its elements, that leads the way for other kinds of texts and the methods by which to read them.

It must be my conclusion, then, that we do well to keep some distance between literature and the other humanistic discourses—even after the structuralist insights that remind us of the generic language structures that hold them together and the poststructuralist insights that break each text apart, though similarly, on the basis of a common semiotic that merges them. Throughout the history of its power (and weakness) in the West, literature has functioned independently of the other discourses, in its own way reflecting the private human consciousness, which is in its turn reflective of a society's inner consciousness. It thus, as a model discourse, has provided primary materials and structures for the other disciplines that make up the humanities. More importantly, it has come to serve as the example, *par excellence*, of how the play of language disrupts and undermines the conventional function of language. So, in its relation to its more directly discursive fellows, literature may indeed come first. It may only be my own self-interest as a literary person that is speaking, but I am convinced that, if there *were* to be a singular in the humanities—if one of them were to claim the right by itself to represent humanity—literature would be that one (though literature here is only the collective term representing a myriad of single works).

I concede that recent discussions of the verbal disciplines remind us that these words of mine constitute an unabashed grabbing for privilege perhaps not altogether justified by theory. Consequently, we must not overdo the idolatry and isolation of the literary object, but should rather make our peace with the humanities as a collective, a plural—and pluralistic—domain of disciplines and languages, perhaps of kinds of consciousness. Still, out of my parochial literary interest, I cannot help but urge that literature, as one of the forms of discourse, is *primus inter pares*, a first among equals. It is just such a paradoxical place that I have sought to establish for it and, through it, for the humanities itself (themselves), so that we may conceive it-and-them as creators as well as receivers of our private and our social experience. Thus, if I may revert to Shakespeare's words, the literary faith can help shape our discourse toward a "truth" that can train our "eye" as well as our "mind." It trains us to keep that truth—or rather those truths—as supple and as varied as our discursive practice itself can, under literature's guidance, learn to be.

13

The Conversion from History to Utopia in Shakespeare's *Sonnets*

It has been some time since I have written extensively on Shakespeare's *Sonnets*, but since those writings of mine in the sixties I have thought again and again of them as my theory of criticism came increasingly to concern itself with the social-historical forms reflected in the peculiar generations of literary discourse. And I have come to think of them differently, or—if not—at least my thought takes on a different emphasis. I'd like to explore these newer directions today.

There are many places in the *Sonnets* in which Shakespeare laments the mercantile values of the world about him and his beloved friend, values that militate against the archaic values that guide and treasure the devotions of personal love. Indeed, the world's become a crass place, challenging our capacity still to love. It is commonly observed in Shakespearean criticism—often reinforced by reference to the History plays—that, like other Renaissance writers, Shakespeare suffered from a wistful nostalgia, in light of which the world about him represented the current lowly moment in a steady decline from a far-off golden past. This mythic narrative seemed to find substantiation in what he saw as the reduction of sacred human relationships to what was permitted by the practical realm: the reduction of absolute and cherished human values to the give-and-take arithmetic of an economics of equivalences.

This essay was delivered at the Shakespeare Days of the *Deutsche Shakespeare Gesell-schaft* of the German Democratic Republic in Weimar in April 1986.

Like his contemporary, Cervantes, Shakespeare mourned the necessary loss of a chivalric fidelity, now overcome by a practicality whose efficiency could achieve its beneficial effects only by a no–nonsense dedication to a quantitative marketplace shrewdness.

I seem to be describing the Bolingbroke who, in his efficient and ruthless devotion to expediency, accepts the historical task of overthrowing Richard II, whose archaic pretensions are both vain and in vain, though always accompanied by a rhetorical splendor. Bolingbroke, as the "new man," usurps the kingship in the name of cause-and-effect practicality, whatever be the consequences for the future of the crown once the succession is thus permanently unsettled. So he initiates a century of blood, of revenge begetting revenge, once the now–outmoded doctrine of divine right is set aside and the forces of might-makes-right are unleashed. Only when Richard III, the final incarnation of the unprincipled principle of assassination and usurpation and more assassination, is himself purged along with the evils he epitomized, can we look toward a new day with the advent of the Tudors, represented by the vague, heroic figure of Henry Tudor, acting the savior and founder of the line that leads to Elizabeth. Of course, into *his* reign Shakespeare—wisely—does not lead us.

So the pattern is set: a noble prehistory, declining in its latter days into a parody of its graces without the substance, is overturned in a victory of the newer worship of expediency. Thus a noble principle turned decadent is succeeded by a vigorous adherence to the *unprincipled*; but beyond this fallen realm there beckons a utopia (united in Henry Tudor "the white rose and the red" in a "harvest of perpetual peace") in which fidelity to principle and the refreshed means of making it succeed hold out their promise—to be fulfilled by the glories of the queen-goddess presently reigning in England.

This pattern of history's decline resurrected in a present saint can be seen—if in less blatantly political a form—in the *Sonnets*. Thus it should not surprise us that in them Shakespeare continually displays his revulsion against the world that surrounds his speaker and his beloved. It is a decadent world that (as his nostalgia sees it) has perverted the true nature of the old into the false ornaments of art's counterfeits presently displayed, so that only the beloved friend remains as testimony to what nature and beauty were before the fall.

> Thus is his cheek the map of days outworn
> When beauty lived and died as flowers do now,
> Before these bastard signs of fair were borne
> Or durst inhabit on a living brow:
> Before the golden tresses of the dead,

The right of sepulchres, were shorn away
To live a second life on second head—
Ere beauty's dead fleece made another gay.
In him those holy antique hours are seen,
Without all ornament, itself and true,
Making no summer of another's green
Robbing no old to dress his beauty new;
    And him as for a map doth Nature store,
    To who false Art what beauty was of yore.

(Sonnet 68)

The friend, then, is the still-living incarnation of an original, true nature no longer available in a world of dead copies. These copies, robbing their ornaments from dead nature to dress themselves up as if alive, only reveal a world already dead before it actually joins the accumulation of history's dead. Yet, strangely, the friend can properly reproduce in himself the nature of prehistory as true and living ("in him those holy antique hours are seen, / Without all ornament, itself and true") without robbery of the dead—as a magical reincarnation: the antique thing itself as again alive, and no mere dead and deadly copy.

Anticipating this movement, Sonnet 67, the first half of this two-sonnet unit, bewails our fallen world as unworthy of the beloved friend's presence, his magical presence that restores ontological reality to mere appearance, as in the days before the fall: "Ah, wherefore with infection should he live / And with his presence grace impiety. . ." Here is a world that worships appearance, eager to turn nature into cosmetic products to create a false beauty since nature's own is beyond it.

Why should false painting imitate his cheek
And steal dead see[m]ing of his living hue?
Why should poor beauty indirectly seek
Roses of Shadow, since his rose is true?
Why should he live, now Nature bankrupt is,
Beggared of Blood to blush through lively veins?

The couplet completes the assault on these fallen days, bad days, in which a bankrupt nature, poverty-ridden, can show only the beloved as a nostalgic reminder, but also as a restoration, of her grandeur: "O him she stores to show what wealth she had / In days long since, before these last so bad."

The word *wealth*, as applied to nature, turns ironic by reminding us of the realm that nature should be free of, by reminding us of the material realm that has turned nature into products to enhance appearance, thereby destroying life in a worship of dead imitations that is characteristic of a reductively commercial value system. Other sonnets reinforce this irony as they play on this unfortunate monetary reduction. Shakespeare repeatedly resorts to the quantitative language of accountancy, the number consciousness of the bank teller primarily concerned about the "bottom line," in order to demonstrate how inadequate a measure this is for the intangible character of human affection. (I almost said "intangible *values*" in a momentary seduction by the hidden metaphors of our own culture's discourse.) In a Platonic spirit Shakespeare insists upon the deceptiveness of those finite appearances that constitute our material world, so that we delude ourselves if we limit the realm of human attachments to the counting of tangible goods. The shopkeeper's world the poet sees around him—the world that a declining history has left to him—would reduce the lover's dream to what the merchant can hold in his hard grasp, and Shakespeare wants to emphasize all that eludes that grasp: simply the entire domain of troth, which must in its fidelity resist being reduced to marketplace truth. What is central here is the rejection of quantity, of number, as a measure of an older faith that transcends it: love "is the star to every wandering bark, / Whose worth's unknown although his height be taken" (Sonnet 116). It is as if Shakespeare is rejecting in advance the empirical realm of Baconian induction by making it part of the shopkeeper's value system.

Among the sonnets that carry forward this attack upon "these last" days that have become "so bad," an extraordinary example is Sonnet 87 ("Farewell, thou art too dear for my possessing"), in which the speaker cries out against—and yet must bitterly accept—the reduction of his love to the exchange value that governs the rules of commerce. From the crucial pun on "dear" in the opening line in which any thought of the "dear" of affection must be subordinated to the "dear" of the merchant, the speaker subjects his love to the tests for equivalence in the marketplace, where it is forced to fail.

> Farewell, thou art too dear for my possessing,
> And like enough thou know'st thy estimate:
> The charter of thy worth gives thee releasing;
> My bonds in thee are all determinate.
> For how do I hold thee but by thy granting,
> And for that riches where is my deserving?
> The cause of this fair gift in me is wanting,
> And so my patent back again is swerving.
> Thyself thou gav'st, thy own worth then not knowing,
> Or me, to whom thou gav'st it, else mistaking;

So thy great gift, upon misprision growing,
Comes home again on better judgment making.
  Thus have I had thee as a dream doth flatter:
  In sleep a king, but waking no such matter.

The speaker is left with the deceiving flattery of his royal dream, far
from the "waking" realm of "matter" that insists upon differentiation—and the distance between him and his beloved.

The world that forces him to surrender is one he condemns even as he
relinquishes his claim to his beloved to the no-nonsense claims of the
countinghouse. This is precisely what he does in Sonnets 71 and 72, a
unit in which he calls for his beloved friend to mourn his death no
longer than the sensory reminder of the funeral bell.

No longer mourn for me when I am dead
Than you shall hear the surly sullen bell
Give warning to the world that I am fled
From this vile world with vilest worms to dwell.
Nay, if you read this line, remember not
The hand that writ it, for I love you so
That I in your sweet thoughts would be forgot
If thinking on me than should make you woe.
O if, I say, you look upon this verse
When I perhaps compounded am with clay,
Do not so much as my poor name rehearse,
But let your love even with my life decay,
  Lest the wise world should look into your moan
  And mock you with me after I am gone.

O, lest the world should task you to recite
What merit liv'd in me that you should love
After my death, dear love, forget me quite,
For you in me can nothing worthy prove;
Unless you would devise some virtuous lie,
To do more for me than mine own desert,
And hang more praise upon deceased I
Than niggard truth would willingly impart:
O, lest your true love may seem false in this,
That you for love speak well of me untrue,
My name be buried where my body is,
And live no more to shame nor me nor you.
  For I am sham'd by that which I bring forth,
  And so should you, to love things nothing worth.

The death of the body and the sound of the bell once ended, so should
be the friend's love ("let your love even with my life decay"). Otherwise

Reconsideration of Special Texts for Special Reasons

"the wise world should look into your moan / And mock you with me after I am gone." It is the world's insistence on honoring no values beyond the sensory that allows the poet, in his bitterness, to call it "the wise world." This is the world which the poet, in his death, is fleeing, because, being "wise," it is "vile" in that very wisdom. And it is a vileness it shares with the "worms," creatures that all through the *Sonnets* are the symbols of that which, by celebrating only the single, biological life, feeds on death. The life entombed within itself, which cannot open to another through love beyond the sensual, is a life already doing the womb's work even before the grave. (See Sonnets 1, 6, 74, and of course 146 for some other places where Shakespeare relates the feeding activity of worms after death to the narrowly pragmatic view of life he is rejecting.) Thus the "wise world," which in the couplet he asks the friend not to offend by mourning him after death, is the "vile world" which he has fled "to dwell" with "vilest worms." In its wisdom that world shares its vileness with the worms in that it feeds on the body of life (by reducing life to body) as the worms feed on the body of death. It is indeed a Bolingbroke of a world, in relation to which the speaker seems to be playing the ineffectual Richard II. Out of loving consideration of the friend, who must live on beyond him, the speaker asks him to conform to the demands of that wise, vile world by cooperating with (instead of fighting against) the activity of the worms: allowing love to decay with life, no longer even naming the speaker.

In Sonnet 72, the sequel, the vile wisdom of the world is seen as demanding an accounting from the friend, who presumably may insist upon loving beyond death even at the risk of being mocked. It is evident that Shakespeare sees vile wisdom operating on this side of the grave in the ungenerous insistense on value received for value given. Here, as elsewhere in the *Sonnets*, love is generous while the world's "truth" is a "niggard" that insists on exact measurement. The friend's memorial acts are in excess of the demonstrable "worth" of the poet. If the friend can "nothing worthy prove" to satisfy "niggard truth," then, serving a higher end than such truth, he will invent "some virtuous lie" that makes him "true" to the love by being "untrue" in the eyes of the world's wormy criterion for truth ("your true love may seem false in this / That you for love speak well of me untrue"). Again, in order to save the friend from this paradox, which would expose him to the scorn of the vile, wise world, the speaker asks the friend to yield to its wisdom, to bury the name with the body, and to accept the quantitative judgment of value, as the speaker repeats the "nothing worth" as the final two words of the poem.

Of course, it is the poem itself that outlives the poet and that, though it has no material value (is "nothing worth"), is often called upon in the Petrarchan tradition to transcend death and bestow a kind of immortality upon the beloved. Yet Shakespeare enjoys treating the tangible reality of the poem as that which yields the transcendent product: he enjoys forcing the terms of material immediacy upon the poem's more-than-material consequences. He wants to use the world's terms to undo its wisdom, its sensory reality to undo its "truth." Sonnet 74, still dwelling on the poet's death, pursues just this strategy.

> But be contented: when that fell arrest
> Without all bail shall carry me away,
> My life hath in this line some interest,
> Which for memorial still with thee shall stay.
> When thou reviewest this, thou dost review
> The very path was consecrate to thee:
> The earth can have but earth, which is his due;
> My spirit is thine, the better part of me:
> So then thou hast but lost the dregs of life,
> The prey of worms my body being dead,
> The coward conquest of a wretch's knife,
> Too base of thee to be remembered.
>   The worth of that is that which it contains,
>   And that is this, and this with thee remains.

Though the speaker is beyond all bail to save his life, yet in his account that life yields "some interest," namely, this very poem being read by the beloved friend which thus itself becomes the memorial. And the poem, the repeated "this" of the poem's present tense, contains the poet's "spirit" (his flesh or "earth" being confined to "earth" as the "prey of worms"). Through this minimum indexical word, the "this" that is captured in the act of being read, a way to attribute "worth" to the poet's life is at last found: "The worth of that is that which it contains, / And that is this, and this with thee remains." Here is "interest" indeed in an accountancy beyond being fathomed by the world's wisdom.

Back in Sonnets 30–31 there was also an attempt to use the language of accountancy, but to indicate its *in*capacities by forcing it to yield a realm that defies number.

> When to the sessions of sweet silent thought
> I summon up remembrance of things past,
> I sign the lack of many a thing I sought,
> And with old woes new wail my dear time's waste:
> Then can I drown an eye, unus'd to flow,
> For precious friends hid in death's dateless night,

And weep afresh love's long since cancell'd woe,
And moan the expense of many a vanish'd sight:
Then can I grieve at grievances foregone,
And heavily from woe to woe tell o'er
The sad account of fore-bemoaned moan,
Which I new pay as if not paid before,
    But if the while I think of thee, dear friend,
    All losses are restor'd and sorrows end.

Thy bosom is endeared with all hearts
Which I by lacking have supposed dead;
And there reigns love and all love's loving parts,
And all those friends which I thought buried.
How many a holy and obsequious tear
Hath dear religious love stolen from mine eye,
As interest of the dead, which now appear
But things remov'd that hidden in thee lie!
Thou art the grave where buried love doth live,
Hung with the trophies of my lovers gone,
Who all their parts of me to thee did give,
That due of many now is thine alone.
    Their images I lov'd I view in thee,
    And thou, all they, hast all the all of me.

The speaker is apparently conducting a legal audit of his personal history, seeking to subject his recollection of lost friends to a profit-and-loss statement as he "tell[s] o'er" the "sad account." He is trying to reduce narration to entities on an accountant's ledger, his memorial telling of the account of human losses becoming debit entries in a teller's account of another kind. The incongruity of this quantitative reduction is revealed by the fact that it will not work: the repetition in words like "woe" and "grievances" and "moan" and "pay" ("woe to woe," "grieve at grievances," "fore-bemoaned moan," "new pay . . . not paid") as he tries in vain to cancel them out indicates that the economy of the accountbook cannot expunge the pain incurred by the loss of those who have been themselves removed. In matters of human affection, one can be removed without ever being expunged. The speaker himself, however hard he tries, cannot play the world's game of allowing the body of love to decay with the body of life, if I may insert the language of Sonnet 71, in which he urges his beloved friend to make the same attempt.

But beginning with the couplet of Sonnet 30 and justified by the intricate argument in 31, the speaker finds a way to recoup his losses through a metaphorical move that is, in effect, a claim to resurrection.

Turning to his present "dear friend," he finds in him the living incarnation of all the friends he has been mourning without end because he "supposed" them dead. From their individual, lamented deaths, each past friend attains new life in the single, consummate identity of the present beloved. All of them are in him—and the word "all" appears seven times in the fourteen lines of Sonnet 31, ending in the climactic equation of them with him in the final line: "And thou, all they, hast all the all of me." The friend becomes the paradoxical "grave where buried Love doth live." Given his life, "all those friends" were mistakenly "thought buried" only, since they "now appear / But things removed that hidden in thee lie." Taking all their past claims upon the speaker as his own, the present beloved friend claims their "due," as he assumes his right to be the "interest" owed them, replacing the tears of sorrow that were never enough to pay the account described in Sonnet 30 and the second quatrain of 31. Again Shakespeare is forcing the language of the wise world's arithmetic to reveal its own inadequacy.

But these sonnets move beyond complaints against the mercantile mind and language. In them metaphor claims the right to produce a miracle that converts history to eschatology and the fallen world to a private utopia. History may well have led society to "these last" days that are "so bad," but a new paragon arises (at least in the poet's eyes) who embodies past excellences without the accompanying flaws, so that he is at once the culmination and the transcendence of history. Obviously here, secularized, is the pattern of the Christian *figura* through which history is redeemed, though here the poet's transformation, through an act of loving perception, is built upon a different theory of value and a different theory of language. The poet's utopia as the dream of a history transfigured is *in* the beloved because of the way in which the poet breaks through the laws of differentiation in life and in language in order to create his vision of him as beloved.

It is these laws of differentiation that are seen as historically conditioned, as the limiting conceptions of a world obsessed by the shopkeeper's notion of value and its language. The marketplace language for worth is a language of measure. It seeks an exchange in which every measure demands an equal measure among the distinct, irrevocably separable entities it would keep in balance. To extend, as Shakespeare does, from language to existence, we are asked to see the fall from a lover's "antique" troth to the merchant's truth as resulting from this worship of differentiation and what follows—singleness, finitude, and the individual, sealed death that accentuates the sensory realm created by a semiotic of quantitative measure. This historical decline is to be

Reconsideration of Special Texts for Special Reasons

rescued for the lover by being resurrected into a language of identity in the person of the beloved, as the religion of love speaks the words that make it the secular equivalent of the Christian mystery.

It is in just this way that we can account for the careful figural language of Sonnet 106, in which the beloved serves his typological function as utopian persona even more explicitly than in Sonnet 31.

> When in the chronicle of wasted time
> I see descriptions of the fairest wights,
> And beauty making beautiful old rhyme
> In praise of ladies dead and lovely knights;
> Then, in the blazon of sweet beauty's best,
> Of hand, of foot, of lip, of eye, of brow,
> I see their antique pen would have express'd
> Even such a beauty as you master now.
> So all their praises are but prophecies
> Of this our time, all you prefiguring,
> And, for they look'd but with divining eyes,
> They had not skill enough your worth to sing:
>   For we, which now behold these present days,
>   Have eyes to wonder, but lack tongues to praise.

We "lack tongues to praise" because (except, perhaps, for the poet-lover) we are doomed to speak in a fallen language. Here this language is resurrected into poetry and history is converted to eschatology as we watch: all the "fairest" personages of the past ("in the chronicle of wasted time") have their "praises" turned into "prophecies" of the present ("Of this our time"), all "prefiguring" the beloved ("all you prefiguring"). The alliterative move from "praises" to "prophecies" to "prefiguring" itself figures the transformation of history's imperfect many into the present, perfect one, and the repeated use of "all" again confirms it, passing the "all" into the "you." The past, viewed through the cool eyes of history as a text, a "chronicle," is the world of single, discrete, differentiated beings, history's isolated facts, its proper nouns. It is now amended (indeed, emended) by the beloved friend, who, viewed through the eyes of love, is a present presence that assumes a multiple, consummate identity, overwhelming all difference. This is the many-into-one relationship between the friend and all of human history that Shakespeare spells out in the opening lines of Sonnet 53:

> What is your substance, whereof are you made,
> That millions of strange shadows on you tend?
> Since every one hath, every one, one shade,
> And you, but one, can every shadow lend.

He goes on to list Adonis and Helen as exemplary foreshadowings that, inversely, appear as but weak imitations of the perfection that has arrived only now with the beloved friend.

The poet-lover, in these and other places, has had to gather up the brass pieces of history and alchemize them into a golden world, to forge the isolated jagged scraps into a sublime oneness. It is "you yourself, being extant," the poet tells his beloved in Sonnet 83, that creates the new dispensation, thanks to its new semiotic. If, finally, this is a rejection of history, it arises out of his rejection of the direction it has taken. For history is seen as being in the service of a loveless semiotics of identity and oneness that, through the magic of a literalized metaphor, would yield forth history's transfiguration and history's end. As we have observed, difference, as the distinctness among worlds, among verbal properties and proprieties, is the appropriate realm of the property-owning, exchange-conscious, greedy bourgeois. The gluttonous feeding of this wormy world can lead to the aggressive imperialism we witness in the continuing struggle for self-aggrandizement in Sonnets 64 and 65. Just one representative quatrain will make my point:

> When I have seen the hungry ocean gain
> Advantage on the kingdom of the shore,
> And the firm soil win of the watery main,
> Increasing store with loss and loss with store . . .

This "interchange of state" (line 9) is indeed the politics of all activities between rival entities (all entities being seen as in rivalry with one another) unless transformed by the "miracle" (Sonnet 65, line 13) that is granted power—a power, paradoxically, that shuns aggression—by the state of love. It seems to be an existential power only insofar as it is sanctioned by the power of the poet's word.

Opposition can be healed, then, only by being dissolved into the single union, human and verbal, that fulfills all and does not know difference, just as in love one does not know other-ness. Further, the union is resolved on the side of beauty and perfection, as realized in the beloved himself and in the poet-lover's feeling for him. In Sonnets 113 and 114 the speaker can perceive the entire visible world of objects only as they are transformed by the persistent vision of the beloved through which they are filtered as they reach his eyes. Hence all oppositions, mountain-sea, day-night, crow-dove, monsters-cherubims, are dissolved into the beloved's perfection: "Creating every bad a perfect best."[1]

---

1. I refer the reader to my discussion of Sonnets 113 and 114 in Chapter 12.

This refusal to countenance difference in the interest of a sublime oneness is precisely what is enunciated in Sonnet 105, Shakespeare's testament, in the form of a secular liturgy, to the object of his love's worship.

> Let not my love be call'd idolatry,
> Nor my beloved as an idol show,
> Since all alike my songs and praises be
> To one, of one, still such, and ever so.
> Kind is my love to-day, to-morrow kind,
> Still constant in a wondrous excellence;
> Therefore my verse, to constancy confin'd,
> One thing expressing, leaves out difference.
> "Fair, kind, and true" is all my argument,
> "Fair, kind, and true" varying to other words;
> And in this change is my invention spent,
> Three themes in one, which wondrous scope affords.
>   "Fair," "kind," and "true," have often liv'd alone,
>   Which three till now never kept seat in one.

The thrice-repeated trinity of adjectives ("fair, kind, and true") unites in a constancy of tribute to the "one," "wondrous" in being "one," object of a proper worship and not of mere idolatry. And the worship, the speaker's poems, are prayerful praises in proper liturgical form: "To one, of one, still such, and ever so." Thus all the differences of his separate poems, like the different requirements for the three adjectives, in the single case of his love (both his beloved and his feeling) converge into becoming the constant one. By "one thing expressing," he happily "leaves out difference," achieving—in the teeth of the world's distinctions—his own private utopia, both a utopian object of love and a utopian principle for language.

Yet, if we have been watching carefully, we should have observed that, in every case of the poet-lover's magical claims about a transformed reality and an end of history's downward path, he has attributed the miracle only to his own perceptions and not to the nature of things. It is all the lover's enraptured perspective only. In Sonnet 31, for example, it is the "images" of his earlier loves that he *sees* in his beloved: "Their images I loved I view in thee." The transformations are in his seeing, not in the way things are in the sensible world—that is, the world of sense—which, alas, he and his love seem incapable of changing. All his visions and his unions are the product of love's psychology though they produce in him the reality, illusionary or not, by which he chooses to see and to live—and, most of all, to speak. Sonnets 113 and 114 deal explicitly with the willful way in which his eyes, dedicated to one sort of truth (troth) at the expense of a literal untruth, serve up the utopian vision for his mind to take as its sole reality. But the poet confesses that the eyes have not changed reality, that they have flattered the world rather than alchemized it.

> Or whether doth my mind, being crown'd with you,
> Drink up the monarch's plague, this flatt'ry?
> Or whether shall I say, mine eye saith true,
> And that your love taught it this alchemy
> . . . .
> O, 'tis the first; 'tis flatt'ry in my seeing . . .

But in the end, in the couplet, it turns out that the eyes, trapped within their vision, have themselves already swallowed the flattery which they have persuaded the mind is alchemy, swallowed it as if it were indeed alchemy. Still, flattery it is—only flattery, and thus a poison accepted cheerfully as the grand illusion it must have. The poet-lover stops short of a total commitment to love's theology by refraining from confusing his psychology with ontology.

The poet-lover's psychology is controlled by his strange system of valuing as a lover and by the way in which it permits him to see and to record what he sees in a language he must create to carry in it so rare a vision: a language of identity for a vision of identity. Turning backward from the ways—moral and verbal—of a declining, loveless human history now dominated by an acquisitive society, he seeks to reinstate the ways of faith, though the semiotic system he borrows from Christianity is applied to the secular realm of private human relations. In the face of a society that has degraded all person-to-person relations to the quantities of material worth, Shakespeare saw no alternative but to retreat to a privatized world of personal love, a private utopia, which could remake for the lover the reality that history had made into public goods. History seemed to make no communal realm of love, a utopian society, available to him. (In saying this I disregard the merest glimpse of this possibility, perhaps inserted by reason of local political pressures, in the advent of Henry Tudor, founder of an ideal dynasty, at the end of *Richard III*.)

Yet there is a dream of a communal utopia, again created by looking back, this time to the pastoral idyll that defines the golden world. We could trace in *As You Like It*, that quintessential romantic comedy, an opposition of systems much like the one I have marked in the *Sonnets*. Under the magical, all-healing spell of the Forest of Arden, all is converted to harmony. Those poisoned by the evil influences of the history-ridden court, with its endless intrigues sponsored only by

Reconsideration of Special Texts for Special Reasons

self-interest, find themselves instant converts to the general harmony. At the end, as we observe the sequence of instant moral conversions, each more unbelievable than the preceding one, and as we watch the enlarging assembly of those to be married, we are simply to surrender to the universal magic that asks only that we remake the world just as we'd like it, as one after another of its members, in a ritual repetition of an identical ceremony, are included in the general concord. Can this concord be transported from Arden back to the court? Jaques—and I suspect Shakespeare—has his doubts, as do we. For the make-believe has its pastoral context that both allows it and limits our belief in it. But all that is beyond the utopian vision created by the play, even if its very extravagance reminds us that Shakespeare has his own skepticism about the relation of that vision to history's world. He means us to listen to his play's title: here is the world of universal conversion of evil to good, the world in which—to paraphrase Sonnet 114—"every bad" is created "a perfect best." Let's freely indulge the land of the heart's desire: let's let love conquer all and leave no one out, however unlikely. Here is the world *As You Like It*. Like it? Who wouldn't?

14

Orpheus *mit Glück:*
The Deceiving Gratific(a)tions
of Presence

I have long been fascinated by the double and paradoxical sense of reality-as-illusion or illusion-as-reality that the drama, more than the other verbal arts, has been able to sustain, thanks to its unique mode of representation as, ostensibly, a moving assemblage of natural signs. Nowhere else in the arts is this apparent relationship between the signs of art and actual experience-as-lived so immediate (actors in time representing characters in time representing persons in time). This specialness of drama allows it to be the ideal example to serve recent discussions of the now-you-have-it, now-you-don't character of art's signs, the concern with absence in the face of apparent presence that has dominated much theoretical debate about the nature of representation. It is in our response to drama that we, as audience, most willingly delude ourselves by indulging the gratifications of presence. But, as my title suggests, such *gratification*, as a conspiracy we enter to mystify ourselves, may be revealed—in a deconstructive moment that is inimical to aesthetic indulgence—as no more than a *gratifiction* (if I may be forgiven the coinage).

Thus the alternation onstage of a beloved's loss and recovery, of present laments over past joys now gone, together with the prospect of finding them anew, has created powerful dramatic structures over the ages in many literatures. In them the primary characteristic of representational duplicity is echoed in the structural, and hence the thematic, significance of the story being acted out. Every such work thus becomes doubly dramatic—or as James Calderwood would say, metadramatic—in that what befalls its characters repeats the very play upon hereness and vacancy, nowness and belatedness, celebration of sensuous immediacy and memorial lament, that characterizes its mode of representation. When we view them this way, we come to value especially highly those dramas that enhance this reflexive relationship between the act and the very medium of the representation. And we come to value especially highly those performances that use every technical means to enhance this mirrorizing effect, because it is both totally aesthetic and totally self-conscious about its illusion-making, so that it stands outside the aesthetic, watching its own aesthetic workings having their effect while that effect is being undone. Or at least I value them this way.

Which brings me to Innsbruck and to Gluck's *Orfeo*, or rather to Orfeo's *Glück*. Thanks to Gluck, Orpheus does indeed have luck. Indeed, in the radical emendation of the story in Gluck's operatic version, Orpheus not only has luck, but finally has Eurydice, too. As in the traditional story, Orpheus has lost Eurydice twice, the second time shortly after having just regained her; but in Gluck's opera—or, more precisely, in Calzabigi's libretto for that opera—there is yet another turn, a final transcendent recovery of her as the human receives an ultimate salvation by the divine.[1] The opera, in imitation of the myth, has the rocking, back-and-forth movement between deprivation and recovery, but here we end with a permanent restoration. It is, I think, a singularly unsatisfying, even irritating, alteration; yet the opera, as drama and music, has many satisfactions. I

---

1. Gluck's librettist, Calzabigi, includes two all-important changes in the Orpheus story. In the classical versions, related primarily by Virgil (*Georgics* 4. 451–558) and Ovid (*Metamorphoses* 1. 1–111; 11. 1–84), as in this one, Orpheus, bereft of Eurydice by her death, uses his continuing lamentations to make his way to the underworld and persuade the gods to return her to life and to him—but they do so only on the condition that he does not look upon her until they have crossed the River Styx. The two changes occur only after he recovers her, one of them controlling their departure from Hades and the other controlling the conclusion of the action. First, in contrast to the Virgil and Ovid versions, in which there is total silence between the lovers during the departure from Hades, Gluck and Calzabigi permit the lovers to talk to one another, so that through her constant complaints Eurydice seeks to persuade Orpheus to look at her: as they are departing the underworld, she berates him for his apparent disregard of her. Moreover, in the Gluck-Calzabigi opera, a version inspired more by Monteverdi and his successors than by Virgil and Ovid, Orpheus is forbidden not only to *look* at Eurydice, but even to *tell* her why he won't. Still, under constant pressure from her, which he has in advance been rendered powerless to relieve satisfactorily, he violates the condition for her release by yielding to her entreaties. At once she dies again, and he returns to his lamentations, now more desperate then ever and threatening suicide. Here, in its second change, the opera follows a major departure from the classical versions: Love (*Amor*) intervenes a second time, Eurydice is restored, and the two lovers end singing with the chorus of happy spirits in the temple of Love.

would like to speculate about the causes of both the irritation and the satisfaction, looking at the common version of the story together with the transformed version that I witnessed in the opera.

I am moved to these speculations by the strikingly original production of the opera which I saw and heard in Innsbruck, Austria, in the spring of 1982. What I witnessed in the attractive modernity of the Tiroler Landestheater was the imaginative Viennese staging created by Werner Michael Esser. The Gluck opera has been performed in many versions since its introduction to audiences in 1762, from which time, in all its versions, it has stood as a revolutionary landmark in the development of opera toward the music drama it became for Wagner. And Gluck's own writings make it clear that he meant to be self-consciously instrumental in pushing that development. There have been performed versions in which significant alterations and substitutions have been made in the original Calzabigi libretto, besides the obvious translations into several languages, and there have been a number of alternative voice combinations, especially the use of two female voices—contralto or mezzo-soprano and soprano—for Orpheus and Eurydice instead of the more obvious male and female, tenor and soprano. It is not my purpose to deal with these varieties here. But what holds true for all versions is the significance of dramatically new operatic forms and the manipulation of the rich potentialities of the Orpheus story which had already attained operatic distinction in the pioneering work of Monteverdi more than a century and a half earlier.

The version I saw claimed essential allegiance to the Calzabigi libretto and in every way enhanced the dramatic impact of Gluck's contributions to operatic form. In opera as a dramatic ritual, the sense of presence, diminished by the stylized representation to a vanishing point, is pushed to utter absurdity. Credibility in the illusion is abandoned from the first moment a singing voice subjects the urgency of its verbal message to the formal control of melody. The designing director who knows this can exaggerate the paradox of his apparently mimetic mission by pressing all the devices at his disposal to enhance our awareness of his, and humanity's, semiotic plight. And this is what I saw Esser as doing. In Esser's staging, Gluck's *Orpheus* was full of its unrealities. It came to me wrapped in veils and evanescences of scenery and costumes and lighting that mingled persons with projected images both literal and abstract. Not only was it an exciting visual experience, but I was persuaded of a continuing functional precision in the set and lighting designers' visions of web and vortex, of shifting mists and screened transparencies in which the appearances and vanishings of actors and action interchangeably played in this world, in the underworld, and in the heavenly realm of *Amor*. By themselves these technologically inspired trappings might have seemed to be the recognizable pretensions of a self-conscious modernist theatricality. Here, however, they seemed brilliantly transformative, serving the needs of the always strange Orphic myth and the yet stranger adaptation of it by Gluck.

The illusionary uncertainty of abstraction, of image, of veiled transparency, emphasized the centrality in the Orpheus story of the frustrating persistence of deprivation and absence—Orpheus's deprivation and Eurydice's absence. In Orpheus's dream of a regained presence, his need to break through a divinely ordained absence, to force the gods to undo their own decrees and to restore Eurydice, that drives forward the legend behind the opera. And it sponsors his lamentations as well—the lamentations of Orpheus, the poetry that moves gods and changes the rules that govern our world and theirs.

In all the variations of the story there are a couple of strange constants that call forth comment. One of the most striking is the persistence of the two-time losing, the repetition of his deprivation, and only shortly after his regaining what had been lost earlier. We must concede that the second of the losses results from Orpheus's own action, so that it is his own fault—though it is, originally Eurydice's fault for imposing her will upon him in an act that mimics Eve's persuasion of Adam to break a divine compact. But her act is at once extenuated, if not altogether absolved of fault, by her ignorance, an ignorance the gods have forced upon her through the injunction they have imposed upon Orpheus not to reveal their conditions. And, while he eventually breaks the god's fatal rule by looking back, under pressure from Eurydice, it never seems to occur to him to stretch the less immediately absolute injunction about telling her of the arrangement by giving her—however indirectly and thus perhaps blamelessly—the slightest hint or warning that might shut her up. There are, after all, two parts to the agreement he has worked out with the gods: he must not tell (what the taboo is) and he must not do (look upon her in her radiant presence). But he does not test the slippery possibilities of language, since, as a result of her abuse of language (though in the name of love) he moves—beyond any placating mediation—to the disobedient act itself.

As with their forebears Adam and Eve, the disobedience of Orpheus and Eurydice seems the less blameworthy because the rules laid down by the gods seem so arbitrary. Why, after Orpheus has suffered his first loss of Eurydice so grievously that his music of lamentation has softened the gods, must their gift of restoration be qualified by the absurdly petty commandment that ends by taking it all away? Why must they withhold—and threaten by that withholding to take back—even as they grant the lover's most fervent desire? Is it that they know his weakness in advance, know that he cannot in the end refrain, and are demonstrating the need for humans to moderate even the strongest passion, to tame it now for an unimpeded satisfaction later? But this is cruelty indeed, to make such sport of him even as they seem so moved to pity by his music that they suspend the most crucial mortal law that separates death from life. Lest their act of divine grace in his behalf be too persuasive of his more-than-mortal powers, the gods impose the arbitrary—indeed bizarre—condition to remind him of who he is, and isn't.

But again, as with Adam and Eve, reason seems to be on Eurydice's side though she would—however unwittingly—bring about her self-destruction by persisting in it. If his love has miraculously achieved her return to him, then whence his reticence, once he has her back, to look at and respond physically to her? The reasonableness of her demands upon him surely exceeds that of the demands of the gods, who, when their bizarre conditions are violated, would take back what they have given. In spite of all this, we strangely accept the conditions imposed and do not question the gods' right to impose them—and to enforce them. We want Orpheus *not* to listen to Eurydice and want her to desist from her querulous demands upon him (yes, we see them as querulous!), so that they can be free of restraints—just beyond the River Styx—and can recover one another. We accept the arbitrary and don't want the lovers to question it any more than we do. For lowly mortals, mere slaves to the gods, to be granted such grace, the relaxing of the iron law of mortality, should lead to blind obedience so that the fruits of grace may be enjoyed. The slave does not make the laws and should welcome the master's sudden—if momentary—suspension of them. And, as I watched that night in Innsbruck, I once again—as I always do when rehearsing the Orpheus story—found myself on the master's side, gratefully welcoming this special—though highly qualified—yielding to the human slave and impatient with that slave for not playing the master's game as it has been ordained to be played. Is it not just like a slave, who has not the sense to retain what he has—through the master's gesture of goodwill—gained? Does he not know who makes the rules and can make them stick, who unsticks one only to stick us to another?

But why should I side with the gods, whose irrational pardon would bridge life and death, earth and underworld, though only when accompanied by an absurd condition that reasserts the gulf between them? Why do I not reject the divine process as unjust and side with the mortals? What is there in the drama that works upon me so that I feel impatience with Orpheus and Eurydice for being all too human and feel too little anger at the irrational arbitrariness of the gods? Though I must concede that Orpheus is a very special mortal, not only because of his incomparable talent but because he is the son of Apollo and Calliope, this proximity to the gods through descent from them only makes the gulf that separates him from them, his power from their power, the more marked and the more painful. And it makes all the stronger my impatience with his failure to comply with that temporary obedience which could win him back his Eurydice for good.

Of course, I am discussing the common elements of the Orpheus story itself, rather than the special shape Gluck (or rather his librettist Calzabigi) gives it. And these authors have reacted not at all as I have been suggesting, so that their version clearly comes down on the lovers' side and will not accept as final the gods' fatal judgment upon their love. (After all, it is always true in fiction-making that even the gods must succumb to the hand—the author's—that manipulates *them*, so that they can manipulate mortals only as far as *their* creator permits. And Gluck-Calzabigi have decided firmly to overrule the dread finality of the gods' decree.) I earlier mentioned the alternating movement in the story of deprivation and recovery: first he has her, then—in the usual mortal way—he loses her, then he has her again (thanks to the special dispensation of the gods who yield to his musical pleadings), and then loses her finally as the gods coldly reassert the law, invoking the contract between them and punishing his disobedience. But in Gluck's opera the alternations have one more swing in them and conclude permanently up rather than down: his musical lamentation proves its power to move the gods yet one further time, and the intervention of *Amor* restores the pair of lovers to eternal bliss in his domain. Indeed, there is an unseemly haste, almost an impatience, not to leave Orpheus unhappy for long, in the process by which we move through the second deprivation to her second revival. Eurydice is left for almost no time at all as Love conquers all by restoring her for good to Orpheus.

This final restoration —or rather this restoration beyond finality, beyond the supposedly final deprivation—severely tears the fabric of the fable, however much we may be moved by the music of the hallelujah chorus directed by Love and the lovers at the end. I have labored here to argue for the aesthetic justness of the usual version of the story that concludes in permanent loss because I wanted to account for the dramatic letdown I feel at the end of Gluck's opera—especially felt in Innsbruck where it seemed untrue to the shape of that performance. It is just wrong, I am convinced, for the two lovers to be reunited by *Amor's* (or, really, Gluck's) arbitrary fiat, the *deus ex machina* that is to send us home exhilarated.

Yet I have tried to be just: I candidly conceded that reason in the case does not belong to the gods, that the condition they impose upon their miraculous gift of a regained life is unreasonable and arbitrary, and that Eurydice's complaints to Orpheus about his turning away from her as he leads her out of Hades are utterly sensible. Surely the gods, even in their concession to him, seem to be teasing Orpheus in the agreement they insist upon his keeping: in effect, "you may not look at her or touch her till later, only talk (though not about the forbidden subject), or we take her back." This after his earlier deprivation—her death— after which he can do no more than talk since she is beyond his look or touch. In Gluck's version of course, after Orpheus's recovery of Euryd- ice, it is she who does the talking, persuading him to the transgressing act as he had earlier persuaded the gods to suspend their own laws. Her words fill the void created by his apparent refusal to respond to the gift of her renewed presence and—because these words persuade him—they lead to her absence once more, when he is again reduced to *his* words of lamentation. Nevertheless, I argue, however irrational and even cruel the gods may be in their apparent relenting, we are persuaded that it is the role and thus the right of the gods—given the nature of their power over humanity—to be arbitrary, especially when they are offering a gift of grace that suspends and reverses what we think of as the ironclad laws of mortality. The game *is* theirs, and must be played by their rules. In their offer to Orpheus of a resurrected and returned Eurydice, they are bestowing an arbitrary privilege, so that he (and we) cannot haggle at their imposing conditions no less arbitrary, even if these conditions end by undoing that gift. It is undone by them only because Orpheus proves himself only a mortal, a man who cannot withstand the perilous in- sistences of his ignorant beloved. And if we feel—a bit angrily—that the gods must have known that he would have to succumb, then this too is a confirmation of their divinity and his mortality, a mortal- ity which—whatever his divine gifts—he failed (and had to fail) to overcome.

I suppose what I am claiming is that it is appropriate dramatically (and narratively, too) that the alternations between having and losing should end with the lovers' paradise finally lost after it has been re- gained, and that it is inappropriate that it should be regained a second and last time. (How many chances can one have at so extraordinary a suspension of the normal process of living and dying?) I am claiming, then, that while the gods' fiat may be arbitrary and beyond human reason, we accept it as the way the story ought to go, and we accept Eurydice's doom; however we sympathize with Orpheus, we will not side with him against the gods when he abandons his final chance by disobeying them in order to obey her. So, for him again to receive her alive because *Amor* (on behalf of Gluck-Calzabigi) wills it that way turns out to be more than we want to be asked to accept. What is logically arbitrary in the traditional myth's less happy ending, then, is dramatically just. I am claiming, in short, that while we can accept the arbitrary fiat of the gods because it is dramatically justified, we cannot accept the further arbitrary fiat of Gluck—even in the name of human justice and mercy—because it is not.

My preference for ending with the loss instead of the regaining requires me to insist upon deprivation and absence as the center of the opera. And I do. So, I believe, does that brilliant staging of the Werner Michael Esser production which I earlier described. The veiled transparencies, the mists, the projected images of webs and vortices, the deceptive use of light and shadow, all emphasize the slippery hold Orpheus has on the visions he thinks of as his reality. It is the absence of Eurydice—her absence in death from Orpheus and from the earth itself—that moves Orpheus and, through him, the opera's action from the opening moment. For much of the opera Eurydice is, for us as for Orpheus, only a name, most arbitrary of our arbitrary signifiers— though, of course, Orpheus must fight to have it more than arbitrary, to turn it substantive, into flesh. He continually calls the name, speaks the name, bemoans the name, accompanied only by his lyre. Thus repeated, the name is all he has, his reiterated testimony to her bodily absence, the absence that calls forth his lament, forerunner to lyric laments by poets to come, all followers of Orpheus. So he seizes upon the name as his mediation.

But of course the name, crucial representative of language, which is the lyric poet's substitute for living presence, cannot satisfy Orpheus, who must have the person herself present, with him. So he would reject mediation and break through language to presence; he uses his language, his name-calling, to persuade the gods to consent to the breakthrough, to allow him to cross over, from earth to underworld, from life to death, and to bring her back, so that her living presence can replace the empty name mouthed in vain so long as it cannot summon the actual person herself. And he wins permission to cross over, to make the passage beyond the living. Yet it would be an ironic exchange in that the live person, relying on a language of absence in the face of death, must go to the underworld—home of the dead—to find the home of the live body he seeks. Still, his crossing over, his passage beyond human limits with divine consent, only presents another limit that shuts him off again, and sends him back to the living with his language—and her name—on his lips again, but with Eurydice herself still left behind, beyond the living and in the underworld, her presence only a memory, a belatedness to be testified to in his mournful language. Orpheus has, inevitably, lost the game but—in his loss—has regained man's need, with absence as his only companion, for language, his need for the calling of names representing absent persons, and thus his need for poetry, the lamentation for absent objects of love and worship which we call, after Orpheus, the lyric.

The Esser staging of the opera plays effectively upon the conjunctions and oppositions among absence, desire, and representation in language and image. After Orpheus is deprived of Eurydice the second time for having turned to look at her before leaving Hades, he sings— alone on stage—the great aria (perhaps the loveliest in the opera), "What shall I do without Eurydice?" Behind him, projected across the backdrop, an enormous image of Eurydice is flashed and held throughout the aria. It is perhaps the one clear, unambiguous projection of an image in the production, its precise outlines in stark contrast to the mistiness or the linear abstractions we have otherwise been given. There the portrait remains, looking at his back and at us as he sings. Eurydice has again been removed from him because he dared try to look at her; but as he sings his want of her, calling the name because he is deprived of the person ("What shall I do without Eurydice?"), the image of that object of desire asserts itself to remind us (and him, if he would but look around at her picture) of her former presence. Of course, the image is presumably a representation of the image that the forlorn lover carries in his mind's eye, the image of the lost love which is further—though less iconically—represented by the empty sound of the (to him) sacred name. But, as we recall that Orpheus was forbidden by the gods to look upon her and that he lost her because of his uncontrollable need (sponsored in part by her) to see her, can we help but note, ironically, that her projected image now filling the backdrop, though with its sensuous emptiness, is there as if beckoning him to look upon it, now that it is too late and the image has only a lifeless referent, as lifeless as itself? Now he may look if he likes, now that it can do no good. The stage itself, like his mind which it represents, seems to cooperate with the gods in teasing him maddeningly. The image of Eurydice on the backdrop reminds us of the futility of his merely looking, since it is only an appearance, the illusion of reality, a mere representation—the visual translation of the name—which he can see. The look must be father to the fleshly touch if he is to achieve the satisfactions that move beyond representation to reality, beyond absence to presence, beyond deprivation to consummation. Because this translation has not been allowed, Orpheus is left only to sing of what he has been denied.

The poem of lament, emerging as song out of the mouth of our archetypal, ancestral poet, turns metapoetic, becomes an allegory of itself.[2] Singing gloriously of his lack, of his without-ness, while her disembodied image fills the spaces of his mind and of the stage we view, Orpheus seals the fate of poetry to be consecrated to the absence of its object and to the lamentation of that absence. Though the signified of his song, the imaged idea of his beloved, is for him unambiguously contained in her name, the signifiers of his discourse testify to their dissatisfaction with any merely intelligible signified, however clear, their dissatisfaction with any signified that is not a sensible living presence—in short, with any signified that does not put the discourse, and the need for discourse, out of business. Discourse—even that perfection of discourse which is poetry—must be an empty testimony of absence so long as signifiers are dependent upon conceptual signifieds that must exclude the substantive reality they would represent. The signifier cannot be filled with substance and remain a signifier; nor can the signifier, however empty, be replaced by reality's heavy substance unless language itself be at an end. It is the name, Eurydice, and even the mental image of her which have not been enough, which drove Orpheus to the underworld to revive the person herself who could dispel any need for language. Prevented by the gods from seizing upon her reality, he was reduced to mere talk again, her talk having newly doomed them both. Now alone, with her picture filling the entire reality of his mind and our stage, he returns to the primitive linguistic function of naming again and again, though repeating her name (preceded by "without") only to deny life to its referent, in an allegory of all human speaking and *poesis*.

One is almost tempted to wonder whether Orpheus secretly anticipated that his yielding to Eurydice's entreaties and his giving her up again to the gods would guarantee his having his poetic subject intact by having the object of his desire not at all; to wonder whether he unconsciously was complicitous with the gods in their making sport of him, so that he might stay in business as a poet, holding his visioned image of Eurydice rather than the person herself, who is kept beyond his grasp forever. And stay in business he does, even to the point that—as the dominant version of the myth goes—after his later dismemberment, his head, though disembodied, continues its plaintive singing. Further, it is

2. No one today can touch on these metapoetic extensions of the Orpheus story without acknowledging the influence of Elizabeth Sewell's *The Orphic Voice* (New Haven: Yale University Press, 1960) and Ihab Hassan's *The Dismemberment of Orpheus: Toward a Postmodern Literature* (New York: Oxford University Press, 1971), as well as his earlier essay, "The Dismemberment of Orpheus: Notes on Form and Antiform in Contemporary Literature," *American Scholar* 32 (Summer 1963): 463–84.

because of his rejection of all sexual pleasures, his insistence on carrying forward, ascetically, the poet's verbal dedication to loss, that he is dismembered. But this Orpheus, however dedicated to his fate and that of poetry, never reckoned with Gluck-Calzabigi, who must—they believe—ultimately save Orpheus and the poetry of love in another way, the very opposite way.

The sequence I have been tracing, from Orpheus's first loss of Eurydice to his lament over his second loss of her, has its force undermined in Gluck's opera, since the opera's transformation of the story disrupts and transcends the game being played between gods and mortals by having Orpheus' second series of lamentations once more produce a living Eurydice, forever at his side, to replace the mourning echo of her name on his lips. Orpheus, threatening suicide or—in other versions of the story—destined to be torn apart by the Maenads, a second time dissuades the usually stern gods from the rules they play by. Perhaps, according to the Gluck-Calzabigi version, his promised end may make the gods fear for the future of poetry in the wake of the impending destruction of its mythic human origin in him. In any case, Orpheus appears to have been saved by Gluck-Calzabigi in an attempt to avoid apocalypse and produce reconciliation, a bridge to cross the abyss. I suggest, on the other side, that it is this second return of Eurydice that may well doom the orphic voice, since poetry, as the ultimate naming power, can be sustained only by the deprivation of presence. Orpheus will have to be a poet no longer in *Amor*'s permanent idyll. By bringing Orpheus and the re-regained Eurydice into the divine realm of *Amor*, the opera passes beyond the human condition as the merely verbal condition, the condition of deprivation which uses language, the language of lament, to testify to the absent object of desire. By passing beyond to the grasping and holding of presence itself, the opera's fable becomes untrue to its own grounding in deprivation and absence, untrue—that is—to its own semiotic self-consciousness.

Yet it is too simple to claim that, even in the Orpheus story itself—as well as in its adapted form in the opera—everything about the lovers must be seen as forms of an unmitigated absence, so that, as entities, they are unambiguously separate from one another. I can make so stern a judgment in favor of the implacable ending that the opera has passed beyond, only while acknowledging the hidden implications in the story that suggest that the lovers are signs reflecting one another as well as signs shut off from one another. We find throughout that the enforced separation of the lovers—at least until that final, questionable swing of the opera—creates a mutual dependence between them, and hence a sense of oneness, that seems the stronger for what the gods have torn asunder. Theirs is a paradoxical union in that it cannot coexist with Eurydice's actual presence. The tradition of love poetry is characterized by this paradoxical simultaneity between the separateness of duality between the lovers and their indissoluble oneness. In exemplary poets like Shakespeare (in the *Sonnets* or *The Phoenix and Turtle*) or Donne, the power of metaphor, as the verbal equivalent of this duplicitous state of the loving couple as both two and one, is derived precisely from this paradoxical simultaneity of difference and identity, although at times we feel the paradox is evaded by keeping the identity between the lovers only an illusion prompted by the desperation of love's psychology. The very notion of the couple—and coupling—carries this double sense of oneness and twoness within it, that incorporation of the other which distrusts itself, sees itself as illusion, so long as the other remains other. And it is just such an awareness of illusion that this staging of the opera enhances with its every visual device. Orpheus is seen continually to be grasping at a slippery reality, a reality forever veiled and thus, for him, beyond the realm of the real after all. Is the final moment of *Amor's* transcendent reality to be trusted any more than the rest? Or is another undoing about to begin in these successive alternations? Gluck may wish us to be more secure than his work—especially in this staging of it—will permit. For every moment of union must be accompanied by the anxiety induced by the unbridgeable separateness of one lover from the other such as the myth, controlled by Pluto's realities, has demonstrated allegorically.

Seen this way, love is an expression of one's need to possess, to possess as one's own, finally to possess as one possesses oneself. This is to press the narcissistic element that leads to loving another as oneself. I mentioned earlier that the casting of voices for this opera has produced various combinations, and that the use of two female voices (soprano and contralto or mezzo-soprano) for Eurydice and Orpheus has been common. (This is close to Gluck's original [1762] version, which provided for a soprano and a castrato alto in the two roles.) This proximity of voices—and even sexual confusion—can help sustain our sense of apparent identity, or at least mutual reflection, between these lovers who are doomed to separation from one another. So I believe that the Innsbruck performance I witnessed would have profited—musically as well as dramatically—from using a contralto or mezzo-soprano instead of a tenor for the role of Orpheus.

The mutual reflection produces an apparent identity that yet is split in two. Not only does this incipient narcissism characterize the paradoxical notion of coupling, especially when conceived within the context of Renaissance paradox, but even more it suggests the miracle of twinning, in which separate destinies emanate from one origin. The doubleness within identical twins fills our literature. As an emblem, I think of the twin-faced Janus, a single entity with its two halves facing in opposite directions and to that extent mutually exclusive: their looking away from one another is the prerequisite to their being joined. And I therefore find it excitingly fitting that the one injunction placed upon Orpheus by the gods—the one that he cannot obey—is that he look away from Eurydice.[3] In looking away from the other, he can see nothing, and all his world fades into absence. For his world is reduced to her as his own reflection. Trapped together in separate isolations, the lovers can only dream of a unity that would break through to the presence of an enlarged identity, but yet must know it as dream, while the absence of the other (still other) persists.

Again the reminder of Adam and Eve beckons. (I mentioned earlier the parallel rationalizations of Eve and Eurydice as each leads her mate to the disobedience that destroys the mortal dream of earthly paradise.)[4] In this first couple—model for couples who follow, but with special applicability, I have claimed, to the opera's Orpheus and Eurydice— there is indeed a oneness of origin, with Eve emerging out of Adam, and yet there is also the polarity that separateness leads to—though a polarity whose other face is mutual dependence. Adam's narcissistic identification of Eve with himself is especially evident in John Milton's Adam as he describes God's molding of Eve ("Man-like, but different sex") out of his rib (*Paradise Lost*, Book 8): "I now see / Bone of my bone, flesh of my flesh, myself / Before me." "I see . . . myself before me," but of course she is herself, turns her own way, and persuades him to the destructive act that undoes their paradisiacal union, introducing them both to mediation and the kind of language—our language—that mediation requires. The woman that Adam sees as part of himself ("of

---

3. In this discussion I am reminded of the ambiguously twinned emblem designed by Joan Krieger for my *Poetic Presence and Illusion* (Baltimore: Johns Hopkins University Press, 1979). In the accompanying riddle the doubled creature represented in the emblem, we are told, "see itself, or sees not." And indeed each paired moment of mutual viewing is matched by a mutual looking away. In "Both Sides Now" (see above, Chapter 10), I pursue the implications of the emblem and my theme of presence and illusion into the domain of Prisoner's Dilemma theory. The parallels to my treatment here of Orpheus and Eurydice show clearly the extent to which my theorizing has invaded this hardly innocent report of my reactions to the Innsbruck performance of this opera.

4. I am aware that, without advancing evidence of influence, I am joining materials of Christian mythology with materials of classical mythology. But of course, they *are* joined in our literary tradition as related *topoi* that help constitute our mythopoeic imagination.

Reconsideration of Special Texts for Special Reasons

man extracted") becomes an illusionary other, not unlike Orpheus's Eurydice, and the identity of their unified presence—of her presence in him—is not recoverable, except in the rare utterances of a poet like Orpheus.

I have suggested that the double vision of the lovers as one and as two is an analogue for the relationship between the two elements of poetic metaphor as identical and as differentiated. In this suggestion John Keats, one of Orpheus's more conspicuous followers, has anticipated me. Keats, commenting in a well-known letter[5] upon the above passage from Milton, sees Eve's creation, in the moment of its being witnessed by the dreaming Adam, as the model for the poetic imagination. For Keats, who was an optimist of the imagination, "The Imagination may be compared to Adam's dream—he awoke and found it truth." In Milton, God, in order to cure the otherwise blessed Adam of his loneliness, his singleness, creates Eve out of Adam as "thy other self." He artfully fashions her while the sleeping Adam in a dream sees the glorious reality he will seek to grasp when he awakens. The dream, in the perfection of its vision, is almost a tease as it ends: "She disappeared, and left me dark; I waked / To find her, or for ever to deplore / Her loss, and other pleasures all abjure." But no need for Adam to become like the abandoned Orpheus. It is almost a tease—a vision accompanied by the withholding of presence—but God at this point will fulfill the promise of consummation. It is only later that vision and reality split apart once more, and where illusion has to thrive on itself, there poetry will find its role.

But Keats seems less responsive to the evanescent character of Adam's dream, to his anxiety about turning it into a reality he can hold, than he is to its magical property of converting itself from vision into "truth." There is an insecurity in Adam's speech, a threat of loss and of his endless deploring of a single life that finds no reflection of itself; but these interest Keats less than does the divine capacity to turn the dream into substance. In a concept of imagination less optimistic than Keats's is here, one that accepts our fallen state and so cannot hope for such transubstantiation through divine intervention, the lover-become-poet still dreams of a beloved—his reflected self which is never altogether other and thus never quite escapes possession—and seeks to make her a reality, though it is alas one to which he dares not quite awaken. At stake are her reality as a sovereign self and his role as a poet.

My complaint, then, is that Gluck-Calzabigi cannot rest until, like Adam's God in Milton, they have Eurydice, as Orpheus's dream,

5. His letter to Benjamin Bailey, dated November 22, 1817.

permanently real and permanently Orpheus's, imposing upon the gods a consummation of presence in an undying garden of Love. For me, the very musical power of the chorus (joined by the lovers and *Amor*) that sings this imposed happy ending underscores, by contrast, and returns me to the *angst* of the isolated voice of Orpheus I have been hearing before. Only the music of the Elysian fields, earlier in the opera, anticipates this finale, but that was music for "blessed spirits" dancing, not for mortals singing. May we believe, perhaps too forgivingly, that this imposed ending—thanks to the very lack of conviction we feel in it—allows us to feel the more strongly the power of deprivation in the original Orpheus story, and in this one before its added reconciliation? That Orpheus story has revealed to us the power—but also the cost—of language and, especially, of language as poetry. Still, it is poetry (as music) that has presented us with the transcendent dream of the opera's final moments, though it is a dream whose realization poetry (as drama) leads us to doubt. So we provide for ourselves the veils and the mists with which this staging of the opera has earlier armed us, and we thrust them between ourselves and the concluding affirmation, making it into the brightest—though not the clearest—of illusions. Yet poetry can make momentary believers of us all, so that the glorious final moments—like the glorious Eurydice herself—convince us, as she did Orpheus, that here is a reality we can grasp, and take home with us, and make our own—at least until absence strikes from the underworld again to inspire in us the lamentation that returns us to our own language-making once more.

15

"A Waking Dream":
The Symbolic
Alternative to Allegory

The war between the poets and the philosophers, out of which Western literary theory began, is with us still. Though it has taken many forms, it is there now, stimulating yet new varieties of dispute. As a war, it continues to partake of the oppositional force of the Platonic dialectic, forcing us to choose which of the two ways we will accept as a path of knowledge, or which of the two we shall reject for having no valid claim to lead us there.

In recent times we have become increasingly aware of that other enemy of the poet since antiquity—the historian. Plato himself saw the poet as substituting his illusions for empirical reality as well as for philosophical truth; indeed, if the phenomenal world of experience was an inadequate imitation of universal truth, still its small particularities required, as a first step toward truth, a fidelity that the distortions of the artist invariably thwarted. Thus, at the level of worldly experience, the poet had to overcome the empirical reality of the historian even before he came up

---

When I originally delivered a version of this paper in Evanston, Illinois, in spring 1981, at a conference celebrating the opening of the School of Criticism and Theory at Northwestern University, it had the benefit of a stimulating, though not altogether friendly, critique by Paul de Man. This is probably what it deserved since it was in large measure aimed at him and his enormous influence on recent discussions of romantic and modern theories and literature. A second critique by M. H. Abrams completed the spectrum of alternative possibilities in recent considerations of this subject. These create extremes for me to try to stand between.

against the rational purity of the philosopher. We know that Plato had good reason to distrust the influence of the poet, whose readers would allow his authority to spill over into history and philosophy. What role could there be for those devoted to describing the experiential world around us or speculating reasonably about the ontological world beyond, if the mythologies of Homer were to serve also as both source of fact and guide to metaphysics and morality? For Aristotle, who had a greater commitment to worldly phenomena, the crucial line of distinction was that drawn between history and poetry, between the world of what is and the world of what (aesthetically) may be in accordance with the laws of probability and necessity.

In these distinctions and antagonisms we find the intense effort, arising out of a growing awareness of science and philosophy, of fact and metaphysic, to come to terms with and to limit the untamed realm of myth. The presumptuous attempt by the mythmaker to be our historian and philosopher can succeed only by precluding those rigorous disciplines that the demythifier among us must take to be history and philosophy. So demythification must proceed, in the name of discursive and rational progress, to reduce the leaps of the poetic imagination—no longer seen as a divinely sanctioned irrationality—to the rejected nostalgia of a romantic primitivism. Myth, like poetry (or *as* poetry), is to be accepted only as a projection of the human imagination—the shape that the imagination imposes on the flow of experience to make it conform to itself. From the perspective of its enemies, myth, in spite of its high-flying pretensions, is seen only as an untruth, a wishful projection out of accord with how things really are. One consequence of this attack on myth is the charge that its imposition of a human shape upon our experience is a deceptive spatialization of elements that are ineluctably temporal. It is charged that spatial form, as an anthropomorphic delusion, characterizes the way our minds work rather than the way the world does. Thus the denial of its authenticity shifts all interest away from the anthropological concern with how we envision our realities to the epistemological concern with what our existential destiny—controlled by the clock and beyond mythifying—really is.

As, through the history of Western thought, our philosophic interest becomes more riveted to our earthly existence, with methods that, accordingly, become more empirical, the emphasis falls more heavily upon the clash between myth and history (than upon that between myth and philosophy), and at the expense of myth. At stake is the concept of time that will govern our sense of experience: will our imagination confront and yield to the stark disappearances of all the moments of our time, or will it transform them into the comforting metaphors of space that allow us to hold onto them? As man seeks—as seek he must—to dominate the history of sensory events, to what extent should he distrust the forms he invents to order the repetitions, the internal relations, which he finds (or creates) among them? If he comes to cherish those fictions that he cannot help but create to order his world, can he not set out, willfully and self-consciously, to create special free-standing fictions that are unfettered celebrations of the fiction-making power itself? He would thus be brought around to a new affirmation of myth, of poetry, of the spatializing power of humanly created forms: the romantic reassertion of his (momentary) power to overwhelm his temporal destiny.

I have put the matter in this melodramatic manner in order to set the scene for the emergence of the romantic doctrine of *symbol*, as it claimed ascendancy over *allegory*, and to do so in a way that set it *up* for the poststructuralist critique that would once more invert our comparative estimates of the two. And I continue my narrative, still emphasizing the spatial and temporal languages, the examination of which will concern me later. The dream that myth had early inspired of subduing—by rereading—the recalcitrance of our historical experiences, of unifying time and the forms of the mind, was threatened with extinction first by rationalist and then by empiricist forces in the seventeenth and the eighteenth centuries. Psychological doctrines that related "sensations" to "ideas" and to one another reminded us of the inevitably sequential nature of human experience and the equally inevitable "belatedness" between our experiencing and our thinking. Language, seen as the words that represented our ideas, was similarly belated—which is to say secondary—in its relation to the mental recollections of sensory presence. As an idea was only the ghostly memory of a sensation—in effect the remnant of a sensation with the object removed—so the way was open for the notion of language as essentially empty, pointing to the past and representing an absence. Language, then, was in a tertiary position with respect to the immediacies of sensation.

Here was an exaggeration of the dualistic character of the signifier looking helplessly across the chasm of time at an unreachable signified. Any attempt at a poetic representation that would accord with this notion of language clearly had to stop at allegory, the modest device that permitted no pretension on the part of the signifier to exceed its self-abnegating function of pointing to an earlier and fuller reality outside itself. It is this cursed principle of anteriority that governs the chain that links events to one another, that links events to the language that seeks to represent them, and that links the elements of that language to one another. It is this principle that humanistic and romantic thinkers of the late eighteenth and the nineteenth centuries saw as beating the human mind into mere passivity, enslaving it into resignation to unelevated temporality. In reaction, the new metaphysic, with its consequent psychology and poetic, insisted from the outset on the unifying power of mind, a form-making power that could break through the temporal separateness among entities, concepts, and words to convert the parade of absences into miracles of copresence. The spatializing magic of human metaphor was again granted privileged status, and myth and poetry were returned to their place of visionary eminence. Where the incapacity of normal language to reach beyond belatedness was recognized, poetry could be given special powers to leap across the breach between word and meaning, achieving an identity between them and thereby establishing a presence and a fullness in the word.

It is no wonder that allegory, as dualistic and thus subservient to the normal incapacities of language, was relegated to an inferior place as a less than poetic device, and that the symbol was newly defined as a monistic alternative that became identical with the poetry-making power. From Goethe's early groping toward a definition of the distinction between symbol and allegory to Coleridge's firmer formulation (by way of Schelling), and to the systematic exposition in the idealism of Croce and the practical analyses of the New Critics, the dichotomy holds fast between the dualistic as the character of all our fallen language (including nonpoetry and allegory) and the monistic magic that poetry as symbol can accomplish.[1] The union in the symbol between subject and object, man and nature, of which Goethe spoke, is extended by Coleridge into the statement that becomes characteristic of claims made for the symbol: that it "always partakes of the reality which it renders intelligible; and while it enunciates the whole, abides itself as a living part in that unity, of which it is the representative."[2] It is, of course, the participatory power of the symbol, partaking fully rather than pointing emptily, that allows it to overcome otherness, thereby distinguishing it from allegory. And "an allegory is but a translation of abstract notions into a picture-language which is itself nothing but an abstraction from objects of the senses; the principal being more worthless even than its phantom proxy, both alike unsubstantial, and the former shapeless to boot" (p. 30).

In the many attempts to enunciate this distinction in a way that valorized the symbol (and poetry associated with it), we consistently

---

1. More than thirty years ago, in my first published essay, I began my own career by treating the symbol-allegory distinction and affirming my affiliation with those arguing for the power of the symbol (among whom I then placed Croce and the New Critics). See "Creative Criticism: A Broader View of Symbolism," *Sewanee Review* 58 (1950): 36–51.

2. *The Statesman's Manual, The Collected Works of Coleridge, Lay Sermons,* ed. R. J. White (London: Routledge & Kegan Paul, 1972), p. 30.

Reconsideration of Special Texts for Special Reasons

find allegory allied to the unexceptional way language functions as a dualistic instrument, while that something special beyond the normal incapacities of language—a power to participate in and thus fuse with its meaning—is reserved for the symbol. Obviously, what is being sought in the symbol is an alternative to the fate of words to be empty, belated counters (Coleridge's phantom proxies) testifying to an absence, whose immediate presence would be beyond language, the instrument of mediation. If the language of these theoretical monists dissatisfies us, as we see it in Goethe or Schelling or Coleridge or Croce, we must acknowledge that there may be no discursive problem more difficult than the attempt to use our dualistic language to describe a monistic way of language-functioning—in other words, than the attempt to use a language that accepts its differential nature to define a language that functions in the breakthrough realm of identity. It is this difficult attempt that habitually seems to lead theorists into evasive mystifications[3] or led Coleridge, for example, to resort to desperate terms like *esemplastic* or *coadunative* as he sought to find a way of making discursively credible the subversive verbal process of fusing many into one.

The difficulty of finding a formula for the unmediated in the language of mediation did not inhibit the continuing efforts of these theorists and their followers. One way or another, since the original attempt to achieve a special definition of symbol within a symbol-allegory dichotomy, this need to describe a manipulation of language that explodes its usual limits has extended this dichotomy to a number of others. The New Critics, concerned with a poetics demanding figurative unity, translate the opposition between symbol and allegory into a more observable opposition between functional metaphor and ornamental analogy. Further, members of this symbolist tradition,[4] confronted by the challenge of structuralism, recognize elements of their pet project on the opposite side of the structuralist's principle of verbal difference (their own commitment to identity) and on the opposite side of the structuralist's interest in metonymy (their own interest in metaphor). So when the poststructuralist attacks the assumptions of

---

3. As in Goethe's finding "true symbolism . . . where the particular represents the more general, not as a dream or a shadow, but as a living momentary revelation of the Inscrutable." This is from his Maxim No. 314. The translation is René Wellek's.

4. In this essay I am using the word *symbolist* to designate the theoretical tradition (or a member of it) that seeks a separate definition of *symbol* and proceeds to claim it to be the defining characteristic of poetry. I mean to use the word here in this broad way, for purposes of shorthand, without intending to relate the word or this group of theorists in any precise way to French symbolists or their doctrine.

verbal presence in Western logocentrism, the symbolist's own theoretical need to find an alternative to the absence that haunts the usual process of signification leads them to embrace that very notion of presence.

As I have framed the problem here in its historical and problematic dimensions, underlying these several sets of oppositions are the alternatives of difference and identity. The dualistic conception of language, the language of rationalist or empiricist, of philosopher or historian, assumes its signifiers to be arbitrary in their relations to their signifieds, and hence utterly distinct from them and from all other signifiers with which they are joined in a system. In poetics the proponents of such a conception find allegory to be an acceptable device, one that does not violate this conception of language. On the other side, the symbolists, who seek in poetry the power of monistic breakthrough beyond the powers of differential discourse, try—however hedged in by their own discursive limits—to define a poetic symbol as a signifier that generates and fills itself with its own signified. The magic of poetry, for them, must begin only where prose leaves off, restoring man to the world around him (or rather making the world around him once again *his*) as if the effects of the Fall had been momentarily undone.

It is not surprising that theoretical movements of recent years have seen this symbolist aesthetic as being no more than an extravagant romantic mystification. With it the New Critics' theory of poetry as a unity of meaning within the functional metaphor has been similarly dismissed. For more than a century and a half, our most exciting theorists urged one or another variety of the claim that the poet could force his word to become privileged. Borrowed from our fallen language, that word was to be forced by the poet to become participatory, creating a union that filled gaps in the distances of time and otherness through the healing touch of human form. The plea for the poet to settle for nothing less required such a theorist to reject as unpoetic the practice of allegory in which, as in ornamental analogy, words settled for the arbitrary, differential role they normally had to accept. Through metaphorical union, words (and meanings) were to be manipulated into overrunning their bounds of property and propriety, overlapping—if not appearing to turn into—one another.

It is not difficult to view the monistic conception of metaphor as a romantic reversion to the sacramental union put forth in Christian theology. In Renaissance typology and in the Renaissance habit of verbal play borrowed from it, we can find a model for the way in which metaphor was supposed to work for the secular poet capable of creating symbols. The dissolution of distinctness into identity—in effect the destruction of the logic of number—is the very basis of the divine-human paradox of Christ and leads to the miraculous figure behind such breakthroughs as the Trinity and the transubstantiation in the Eucharist.[5] Further, through the typological *figura*, the unredeemed sequence of chronological time can be redeemed after all into the divine pattern, that eternal, spatial order which exchanges history for eschatology. With every moment existing doubly—both in the temporal order and in the timeless structure—history remains history even while it is rewritten as a divinely authored myth. Every act or person seems random, arbitrary; yet each is a necessary signifier that partakes of the single Transcendental Signified. In borrowed form, this paradoxical relation between what is in time and what is out of time is also turned into a model for poetic form. As in the special sequence of events that transforms history into teleology in metaphysics or transforms history into poetry in the proper Aristotelian tragedy, as in the manipulation of words into fully embodied metaphors by the symbol-making poet, so the rules of earthly time, which put the separateness of distance between isolated subjects, are suspended and transgressed by the divine Author as by the human author in imitation of Him. It is in this context that we perhaps better understand Coleridge's definition of the primary imagination as "a repetition in the finite mind of the eternal act of creation in the infinite I AM."[6]

Since the latter half of the nineteenth century we have been increasingly concerned about the extent to which these formulations in the realm of poetics require a metaphysic or even a theology to authenticate them. Whatever the sources of metaphor in the substantive miracles of theology, does the poetic production of a verbal identity between distinct terms and concepts or does the poem's overcoming of the disappearing sequence among verbal entities rest upon a substantive mystery that can be justified only by a literalizing faith? Or can verbal devices earn the aesthetic illusion of such identities and spatial forms—if only in the realm of appearance—in the secular precincts of a poetry without faith? The quarrel is essentially the one that was carried on against Matthew Arnold by his antagonistic follower, T. S. Eliot. In "The Study of Poetry," Arnold defined the need for poetry to serve as a substitute for religion, producing a psychological satisfaction that was the more secure and effective because it no longer rested on the "sup-

---

5. See my book, *A Window to Criticism: Shakespeare's Sonnets and Modern Poetics* (Princeton: Princeton University Press, 1964), especially parts 2 and 3, for a study of this Renaissance habit of modeling its poetic metaphors on elements borrowed from typology and Christian sacrament.

6. *Biographia Literaria*, chap. 13.

posed fact" which had failed religion and undermined its capacity to function psychologically any longer in the way that poetry, in its absence, now could. Here was the call for a poetic ungrounded in any metaphysic—indeed, one that depended on our keeping it free of untenable truth claims. If myth was to challenge the dull factuality of history with its own man-made transformations of time into human pattern, it was to remain true to its own domain of psychology and emotion and was not to pursue its challenge into the verifiable realm of "what is." One might say that the verbal power of metaphor depended upon its resistance to "existential projection," upon the shrewdness with which it avoided becoming "a literalist of the imagination."

Eliot, who was not afraid of being literally devout, rejected making poetry a substitute for religion but rather—in a Christian fashion that recalled Renaissance typology with its literalizing of metaphor—saw the secular and sacred elements of metaphysics as one. His search in *Four Quartets* for the "still point of the turning world" was also a search through language for the still point of the moving words, which would transform them into the moving Word, a projection of the Unmoved Mover. The passages about human experience and the passages about the poet's struggle with words become increasingly reflective of one another, so that the poem's theological quest and its poetic quest to subsume human temporality within the divine should become for the reader a single, simultaneous quest. The poem's meaning is its method is its medium. Yet, of course, if we come to the poem with the cool, skeptical eye of an Arnoldian modernist, we can find its apparent religious doctrine utterly subsumed within its verbal metaphors, so that the resolution of movement in a stillness which is still moving is but a brilliant aesthetic effect whose theological extensions seem momentarily persuasive only because of the power of its dramatic resolution in words. The aesthetic effect may be a breakthrough within the realm of myth and may thus affect our vision, but it need not break through as a literal alteration of our external world and our beliefs about what can or cannot transpire in it.

Eliot is perhaps our ultimate modernist poet, and his efforts to dissolve time into his spatial forms, to press his language toward a filled presence, and to fuse his thematic problems with technical ones, are efforts we look for in modernism generally. The work of these modernists (think, among the poets, of Yeats and Stevens also, for example) seems continuous with the hopes for poetry of those who, distinguishing symbol from allegory, asked for the creation of symbols. Indeed, that work, shortly to be followed by poets writing to a different prescription, turned out to be the furthest realization of those hopes. In

Reconsideration of Special Texts for Special Reasons

addition, these poets seem to have sponsored their own criticism as a fulfillment of those critical notions that we earlier traced back to those writing in the wake of Kant, the fullest realization of which was the New Criticism.

Early in the heyday of the New Criticism, Joseph Frank provided, with his doctrine of "spatial form," a major notion to characterize its practices, as well as the practice of the modernist literary works which helped inspire it and which provided an endless field on which it could sharpen its instruments. It is in Frank that the "still movement" of Eliot is pressed into a candid insistence on simultaneity, a formal play that "dissolves sequence" by undermining "the inherent consecutiveness of language."[7] In *The Waste Land* "word groups must be juxtaposed with one another and perceived simultaneously" (p. 12). But Frank sees such formal devices as also altering our philosophical attitudes toward time and space, history and myth. It is as if, in modernist works, words can annihilate time thematically by destroying their own serial nature technically. The return of the supremacy of myth over history is the thematic consequence of the poet's overcoming verbal sequence by the forms of his spatial imagination. So the aesthetic devices reshape our sense of reality by reasserting the primary role of the mythic imagination over mere facticity.

The skeptical reader may worry about how easily Frank slips from formal to thematic matters, thereby literalizing his metaphorical insight. Thus, in joining together the *Cantos*, *The Waste Land*, and *Ulysses* as works which "maintain a continual juxtaposition between aspects of the past and the present," Frank draws large conclusions about their effect on how we now apprehend time:

> By this juxtaposition of past and present . . . history becomes ahistorical. Time is no longer felt as an objective, causal progression with clearly marked-out differences between periods; now it has become a continuum in which distinctions between past and present are wiped out. . . . Past and present are apprehended spatially, locked in a timeless unity that, while it may accentuate surface differences, eliminates any feeling of sequence by the very act of juxtaposition. . . .
>
> What has occurred, at least so far as literature is concerned, may be described as the transformation of the historical imagination into

---

7. *The Widening Gyre: Crisis and Mastery in Modern Literature* (Bloomington: Indiana University Press, 1963), pp. 15, 10. The essays on "Spatial Form in Modern Literature" originally appeared in 1945. Frank does not himself refer to *Four Quartets* but confines himself to Eliot's earlier works. For more recent discussions, by Frank and others, of the claims made in the original essays, see *Critical Inquiry* 4 (1977).

myth—an imagination for which historical time does not exist, and which sees the actions and events of a particular time only as the bodying forth of eternal prototypes. (*The Widening Gyre*, pp. 59–60)

Now, this is an extreme statement and smacks of a literalistic extension of the metaphor of spatial form. One of Frank's central terms, *juxtaposition*, is seriously suspect. Having borrowed the term from Lessing (who reserved it for the spatial arts) in order to move the time art of poetry toward space, he seems to be begging the question in his use of it: as if the word itself could generate enough figurative force to persuade us of its literal applicability to modernist literature. After all, it does not seem that we can speak literally of juxtaposing passages of words that are widely separated—not unless we naïvely believe that the spatial copresence of books literally represents the copresence of discourse and our experiencing of it. So the word *juxtaposition* itself claims a reality that verbal sequence belies, as verbal sequence similarly belies any literal sense of simultaneity.

If we are talking about our response to a work and, in that response, about an illusionary impression of something for which we use the metaphorical notion of simultaneity, sponsored by something in the work that feels like juxtaposition, then we still are acknowledging the primary constitutive role of temporality in language and in experience, however strongly we entertain a momentary illusion of verbal stasis. But Frank, coming toward the end of the symbolist tradition and fixing its claims in their most uncritical and extravagant manifestation, would lose temporality altogether in the instantaneity of spatial form.[8] This version of the symbolist aesthetic, so easily adapted to the objectives of the New Criticism, seems most exposed to the skeptic's charge of evasive mystification. It is similar to the nostalgic celebration of sacramental presence in the work of the historian of religion, Mircea Eliade (mentioned favorably by Frank), who defines sacred time as time again and again redeemed, as the continuing recurrences of cut-off entities that take on the characteristics of objects in space.

Once we take the matter of juxtaposition less literally, we can accept repetition as the temporal analogue to juxtaposition and can see literary form—found in the many kinds of repetitious arrangements invented by the poet or his tradition—as that which returns time on itself, shaping temporality out of its nature as pure, unelevated sequence. In this sense we may define form (as I have elsewhere) as the imposition of

---

8. Frank's discussion takes off from Pound's definition of an image as "that which presents an intellectual and emotional complex in an instant of time." The quote appears in *The Widening Gyre*, p. 9.

Reconsideration of Special Texts for Special Reasons

spatial elements on a temporal ground without denying the figurative character of the word *spatial* and the merely illusionary escape from a temporal awareness that is never overcome.

Granting that repetition of one sort or another constitutes the basis for our finding form in the temporal arts, once we begin to question the extent to which repetition can be seen in such works as equivalent to juxtaposition in the spatial arts, then the radically temporal character of moment-by-moment succession can no longer be altogether transcended, and the entire transformation of history to myth is therefore threatened. Paul de Man, profound enemy of the symbolist aesthetic as I have outlined it, hits precisely at this sense in which repetition is never a total return, as he attacks the spatial basis of the symbol and its claim to an achieved simultaneity: "Repetition is a temporal process that assumes difference as well as resemblance. It functions as a regulative principle of rigor but asserts the impossibility of rigorous identity, etc."[9] In an earlier defense of allegory at the expense of symbol, de Man used *his* sense of repetition (which he says is Kierkegaard's) to justify the temporality of the allegorical process and to deny the feasibility of the symbolic process: "It remains necessary, if there is to be allegory, that the allegorical sign refer to another sign that precedes it. The meaning constituted by the allegorical sign can then consist only in the *repetition* (in the Kierkegaardian sense of the term) of a previous sign with which it can never coincide, since it is of the essence of this previous sign to be pure anteriority."[10]

De Man's stalwart attack upon symbol in the name of allegory is a climactic moment in the theoretical turnaround against the long and impressive development of organic poetics from the late eighteenth century through the New Criticism. After so long a period during which allegory was shunted aside as an unpoetic impostor while the symbol was held aloft in unchallenged glory, allegory began to have its good name reestablished as critics arose, beginning in the late 1950s, to push the New Criticism, and almost two centuries of organic theorizing behind it, from its position of dominance. After early signs of the

---

9. *Blindness and Insight: Essays in the Rhetoric of Contemporary Criticism* (New York: Oxford University Press, 1971), p. 108.

10. "The Rhetoric of Temporality," in *Interpretation: Theory and Practice*, ed. Charles S. Singleton (Baltimore: Johns Hopkins Press, 1969), pp. 173–209. This quotation appears on p. 190. I should acknowledge at the outset that, in de Man's more recent work, there are refinements and even changes in these claims that would have to be discussed if this were a study of his career. (I mention some of these changes in Chapter 3, above.) But in the study of the career of the relations between symbol and allegory, it is de Man's work of the late sixties and early seventies that I find central.

reversal in Edwin Honig's *Dark Conceit: The Making of Allegory*[11] and the development of it in Angus Fletcher's monumental volume, *Allegory: The Theory of a Symbolic Mode*,[12] it was in de Man's "The Rhetoric of Temporality" that the theoretical consequences of the resurrection of allegory and the casting out of the symbol marked out and grounded the theoretical revolution that had taken place. It is de Man's formulation which my presentation here of the case that has been made for the symbol, as well as of the excesses and naïveté in the making of that case, has been intended to anticipate. For, however unsympathetic his response to the symbol, his is a most important response with which one must deal before being able to salvage any part of the symbolist tradition—as I wish to do.

We have seen that, in his concept of repetition, de Man insisted on retaining a residue of temporality and of difference, so that he could prevent the term from serving a sense of simultaneity, that which could achieve an identity of several moments that together would sacrifice the unique before-ness and after-ness of their relations to one another within a succession of unrepeatable moments. With that other, simpler notion of repetition from which—as in juxtaposition—time and its differences were purged, the infinite variety of time's movements could be fused into a unity into which all would converge: an instantaneous emblem, the very essence of the romantic symbol, and of spatial form. De Man is too faithful to the need for existential authenticity, to the need for a demystified confrontation of the temporal conditions of the human predicament, to allow to literature the privilege of evading these through the romantic delusions of the symbol; so he denies the simpler sort of repetition. In the linguistic world of difference, the dream of identity is just such a delusion; in the fading-away world of time, the dream of true simultaneity ("which, in truth, is spatial in kind") is, again, such a delusion: "Whereas the symbol postulates the possibility of an identity or identification, allegory designates primarily a distance in relation to its own origin, and, renouncing the nostalgia and the desire to coincide, it establishes its language in the void of this temporal difference" ("The Rhetoric of Temporality," p. 191).

[In this quotation and elsewhere, de Man seems also to create spatial metaphors of his own ("distance," "void") for time: we might claim "distance" to be his spatial equivalent of "temporal difference," much as symbolists treat juxtaposition as a spatial equivalent of repetition. But the antisymbolist would be quick to point out that, unlike "jux-

---

11. (Evanston: Northwestern University Press, 1959).

12. (Ithaca: Cornell University Press, 1964).

taposition," which—with its sense of simultaneity—adds elements which repetition, as a temporal concept, cannot warrant, the de Man equivalent ("distance" for "temporal difference") is not misleading since it emphasizes those very attributes (void, hiatus) which characterize the temporal. So "distance" does not transfer to time for time's benefit any privileged attributes of space (such as simultaneous form) but only suggests those attributes that space, as broken up, shares with time. To put it another way, we might say that de Man is giving us only an analogy or allegory, not a metaphor or symbol, in his use of spatial language for temporal claims.]

It is the monistic pretense, the claim that in poetry sign and meaning can be made to coincide, that constantly bothers de Man about the symbolist aesthetic. And it bothers his existential sense as well as his aesthetic sense: indeed, for de Man, literature, as temporal, seems to enjoy a special mimetic advantage over the spatial arts in its relation to experience. Consequently, in the temporal extremity of language, whose signs seem to march in imitation of the temporal extremity of existence, there can be neither total repetition nor coincidence, these being other terms for simultaneity or identity, spatial concepts all. For sign and meaning to coincide, then, is for literature to evade "the fallen world of our facticity" (*Blindness and Insight*, p. 13). In effect, literature would be seeking to abrogate the terms upon which language serves as mediation; and "unmediated expression is a philosophical impossibility" (p. 9). Instead, in obeying the dualistic conditions upon which mediation rests, literature can claim no privilege and must abandon the deluded hope of coincidence: "The discrepancy between sign and meaning (*signifiant* and *signifié*) prevails in literature as in everyday language" (p. 12). Thus literature should accept allegory as being as much of a device as it can hope for, if, as discourse (*any* discourse), it is to claim authenticity in its relation to existence. The rest—any notion of a separate definition and destiny for poetry based on a dream of unity that transcends time and difference—is at worst "an act of ontological bad faith" ("The Rhetoric of Temporality," p. 194) and at best nothing but a delusion born of despair. It is tantamount to a denial of death and "the fallen world of our facticity"—and about as vain. In life and discourse, time is unredeemable, and any dream of redemption requires a mystification probably as inflated as the Christian myth, with its paradoxical extensions into metaphor, that I referred to earlier.

But it is quite evident that de Man does some privileging of his own—not of literature, but rather of the world of unredeemed time which all of us, all events, and all our writings serve as part of an egalitarian doom. The modestly dualistic role he assigns literature is supposed to be standing on bedrock existential reality, calling back the more flighty among us, from our heady imaginings, reminding us that the one truth is below and inescapable and that our metaphors are mere dreams from which reality must awaken us. In "The Rhetoric of Temporality" de Man freely uses terms or phrases like "in truth," "authentically temporal," "actual," to describe our "truly temporal predicament." But is not this metaphysical confidence in time's objective truth—the one reality from which delusions can be gauged—an extralinguistic dependence that stacks the deck in matters both philosophical and literary? Does it not also predispose us to valorize those literary works which, thematically, oppose facticity to dream, oppose the reality of death to our attempt at escaping it by means of mystification? Are we not being encouraged to valorize such works or, even worse, to interpret all works we wish to valorize as having this theme? We may ask, in other words, whether the defense of allegory on these grounds is an aesthetic claim or a thematic one, whether it is grounded in a semiotic or in an existential ontology of temporality.

After the long reign of a symbolist aesthetic grown too self-confident, de Man has performed an indispensable service in reminding us of the mystifications which that aesthetic too long assumed to be theoretical truths. He has helpfully warned against our reification of the literary object through taking the special metaphor of poetic form literally in a way that belies the serial nature of the medium and of our experiencing of it. This freezing of verbal sequences, he also reminds us, creates sacred objects whose spatial presence permits us to think we have found a way to transcend time through the unifying power of imagination; in this way we exaggerate unrealistically the human power to transform ineluctable fact. So, for de Man, this aesthetic has unfortunate, because delusive, existential or thematic consequences as well.

In warning us effectively against such mystification, however, does not de Man urge the other extreme too strongly? If the uncritical projection of spatial categories vitiates the authority of myth, does not the acceptance of the reality of temporal categories enslave us to history as facticity? My way of putting this question presupposes my answer, since in referring to time as no less categorical than space, I am not viewing spatiality exclusively as an empty metaphor constructed to evade a temporality that is viewed as unquestionably real. In recent linguistic theory, after all, the diachronic, no less than the synchronic, relates to, and can function only within, the arbitrary conventions of human creation; the temporal model is as much the linguist's construction as is the spatial model. If, as we conceive it, the temporal shares with the spatial the state of being a constructed reality, then we cannot

Reconsideration of Special Texts for Special Reasons

easily find a point of privilege to justify a claim about which serves as a metaphor for which. It can go either way, depending upon the purposes of the discourse—whatever we may claim to know about the facts of clock-time and the inevitability of death. It may be that de Man implicitly concedes as much when—as I pointed out earlier—he himself is forced to resort to spatial language to portray man's "truly temporal predicament." Terms like *distance, void*, or even *space* itself in the phrase *blank space*, remind us that even the metonymic consecutiveness of existence and of discourse (of existence *as* discourse?) may require borrowings from the spatial realm to express our metaphorical understanding of it. Indeed, the myth of temporality may be the more insidious, may woo us the more seductively from our sense that it *is* but discursive, because of our lifelong obsession with the reality of death.

I want us to earn a chance to retain some of the symbolist's ambitious hopes for what man, as fiction-making creature, can accomplish in language, without falling prey to the ontologizing impulse that symbolist theory has previously encouraged. To do so we must balance a wariness about projecting our myths onto reality with an acknowledgement that we can entertain the dream of symbolic union, provided it does not come trailing clouds of metaphysical glory. Within the aesthetic frame of a fictional verbal play, the poem can present us with a form that creates the illusion of simultaneity, though even as we attend it we remain aware of its illusionary nature. What else except such spatial relations have literary critics since Aristotle been celebrating in their celebrations of structural unity? It is only when an excess of enthusiasm leads some of them to reify these illusions that we must draw back to a more modest claim. On the other side, under the auspices of the same aesthetic occasion, the poem may well remind us of those temporal and decentering metaphors that threaten each moment to undo (or at least to "unmetaphor")[13] those spatial configurations that we conspire with the poem to create.

So I suggest that we can meet de Man's concerns while still conceding—if only provisionally—the special unifying force that the symbolists have attributed to poems. If we are conscious of the provisional nature of the aesthetic dream that the poem nurtures, we also look for the poem's own self-consciousness about its tentative spatializing powers. Its fiction, and our awareness of it, contain the twin elements of symbol and antisymbol, of words that fuse together even while, like

---

13. I borrow the term from Rosalie L. Colie, who invented it to describe the act of literalizing the image. It functions importantly throughout her book, *"My Ecchoing Song": Andrew Marvell's Poetry of Criticism* (Princeton: Princeton University Press, 1970).

words generally, they must fall apart in differentiation. Even further, the poem, together with our apprehension of it, combines its transformation of time into myth with its resignation to the countermetaphor of time as mere historicity.

The poem and its fully attending reader arc in the ambiguous position of the speaker in Keat's "Ode to a Nightingale." What is the nature of his illusion, or delusion? of the lasting or evanescent metaphorical force of the bird or its song? of the residue of these after the vision or dream passes? Are we, observing and listening, to consider the bird as a true metaphor or as the speaker's mistaken metonymy: are we, that is, to consider the bird as one with its voice and thus with all nightingales that have lived, or are we to consider the voice as only a sign of the bird and to be distinguished from it as it is distinguished from other nightingales? Or are we, somehow, to consider the bird both ways? and, if so, at different times or simultaneously?

Indeed, the bird seems to function for the enraptured speaker as a metonymic metaphor. The magic of the speaker's momentary indulgence leads him to identify the single, mortal bird with its voice and song and to make the voice and song identical with those of the distant past. All nightingales become one bird because the songs are one song, heard but unseen.[14] On the strength of this transfer Keats treats the bird itself as immortal, in contrast to his own mortality and that of the historical or mythological personages who earlier heard the same bird (voice, song). Humanity's individual lives are tied together by the bird once it has been turned into the all-unifying metonymic metaphor, so that history across the ages has been turned into the instantaneous vision of myth. Thanks to a repetition so complete that it achieves the identity of eternal recurrence (de Man's objections notwithstanding), time is redeemed.

This strange conversion of history reminds me of Keats ascribing to the Grecian urn the role of "sylvan historian" in the companion great ode. It is a historian which does not respond to the series of factual questions put to it by the speaker. As "sylvan," the "silent form" is a

---

14. I have shown elsewhere how romantic poets make use of their hearing rather than seeing the bird to allow them to move from identity of song to identity of occasion (and of bird), as they use their auditory (and blindly visionary) experience to collapse time. See *The Classic Vision: The Retreat from Extremity in Modern Literature* (Baltimore: Johns Hopkins Press, 1971), pp. 161–64. It is this swift—indeed immediate—movement ("on the viewless wings of poesy") that causes the speaker's reason ("the dull brain"), trapped in the empirical world that requires sight, to slow him down in confusion ("perplexes and retards"). As we shall see, the struggle between poetic vision and the brain never altogether lets up.

Reconsideration of Special Texts for Special Reasons